"This work is a timely reflection on our polarized political landscape and imperiled democracy. Impeccably researched, Thompson's book offers a sober assessment of our troubled times, drawing a number of intriguing parallels between our social-political situation and the thought of the Danish philosopher Søren Kierkegaard. It is full of fresh insights and perspectives that will be of great interest to readers concerned by the current trajectory of the age."

—Jon Stewart
Researcher, Institute of Philosophy, Slovak Academy of Sciences

"An unlikely but fruitful pairing; thoroughly researched, convincingly argued! Thompson, asking where God may be discerned to be potently present in our tumultuous situation, incisively critiques Trump's presidency by digging insightfully into Kierkegaard's profound probing of human existence. New light is shed on both men. Thompson's categorical structure and norming values suggest a constructive theological ethic winsomely addressing the challenge of being civil and gracious across the divide. A creative going deeper to go forward."

—Paul R. Sponheim
Emeritus Professor of Systematic Theology, Luther Seminary, St. Paul

"Resources from Meister Eckhart to March Madness inform Curt Thompson's exceptional call for individual and communal choices to overcome polarization and the disregard for truth and rule of law now endangering American democracy. He argues concretely and convincingly that Kierkegaard's distinctive analysis of his own era's moribund conformism can help us 'resurrect' democracy and thus 'trump Trump.' Thompson's sophisticated SK primer reminds us how much we can learn from the wisdom of the past."

—**Carol Schersten LaHurd**
Distinguished Affiliate Professor at the Lutheran School of Theology at Chicago

"Trump and Kierkegaard? It may sound like the set up to a joke, but Thompson's nuanced understanding of Kierkegaard leads the reader to a far more subtle understanding of Trump and 'Trump-world.' That, coupled with Thompson's Kierkegaardian appreciation of divine possibility, makes this a must-read book for all who hope to get past the lamentations and handwringing and on to the hard work of rebuilding and reconstruction in a post-Trump world."

—**Warren G. Frisina**
Hofstra University

Kierkegaard Trumping Trump

Go to curtislthompson.com
for questions to be used in an eight-session study
of *Kierkegaard Trumping Trump*.

Kierkegaard Trumping Trump

Divinity Resurrecting Democracy

CURTIS L. THOMPSON

WIPF & STOCK · Eugene, Oregon

KIERKEGAARD TRUMPING TRUMP
Divinity Resurrecting Democracy

Copyright © 2019 Curtis L. Thompson. All rights reserved. Except for brief quotations in critical publications or reviews, no part of this book may be reproduced in any manner without prior written permission from the publisher. Write: Permissions, Wipf and Stock Publishers, 199 W. 8th Ave., Suite 3, Eugene, OR 97401.

Wipf & Stock
An Imprint of Wipf and Stock Publishers
199 W. 8th Ave., Suite 3
Eugene, OR 97401

www.wipfandstock.com

PAPERBACK ISBN: 978-1-5326-8686-3
HARDCOVER ISBN: 978-1-5326-8687-0
EBOOK ISBN: 978-1-5326-8688-7

Manufactured in the U.S.A.   07/23/19

To my grandchildren—Soren Kristian Hedderick, Brekken Anders Hedderick, and Eloisa Dove Thompson—in gratitude for their inspiring vitality and fullness of life.

If you want to maintain your love, you must see to it that love, caught for freedom and life, continually remains in its element by means of the infinitude of the debt, otherwise it wastes away and dies—not sooner or later, because it dies immediately, which is precisely a sign of its perfection, that it can live only in infinitude.

—Søren Kierkegaard, *Works of Love*

Contents

Preface | ix
Acknowledgements | xiii

Introduction | 1

1 Narrativity or Story | 12

2 Interiority or Earnestness | 33

3 Normativity or Measure | 56

4 Eternality or the Moment | 82

5 Subjectivity or Freedom | 109

6 Possibility or the Future | 133

Conclusion | 159

Appendix: Sweet 16 Questions for Going Deeper in Order to Go Forward Or 16 Ways to Help Divinity Resurrect Democracy Or Kierkegaardian Top 16 List Or The Sweet 16 Inquiries to Facilitate Resurrecting Democracy Or 16 Elements of a Personal Examination of Conscience

Bibliography | 181
Index | 187

Preface

I now submit to the publisher a book on Trump that will join the ranks of many others. This submission happens at the beginning of a week in which Attorney General Barr has promised to release a fuller version of the Special Counsel Mueller Report. We have been warned that there will be many redactions, with each of the four types of redaction being given its own special color-code. The masses are hoping that, even in its heavily redacted form, the Report will disclose major results of Mueller and his team's labor. Suspicions are widespread, though, that gaining adequate access to the Report will involve a long process that will possibly not be completed until the Democrats land their candidate in the White House.

This points to the reality that as I bring my writing project to a close in mid-April of 2019, the closure is taking place very much in the middle of things, as the accounts of Trump and Trump-world continue to garner headlines as they have for close to four years now since Donald first announced his decision to enter the 2016 presidential race. Obviously, the current state of affairs on Trump's status and America's response to him are still in flux. It could be suggested that it would be better to wait until later to submit my manuscript, so that it could represent more of what will unfold in this saga that consumes so much of our attention. I readily grant that the air is full of uncertainty as far as what might be happening in the near future concerning events pertaining to Donald Trump and his status as President of the United States. However, the import of these events for the relevance of this book is not completely clear. That is because, whatever takes place at the top executive level, the deep polarization existing within our country is likely going to continue and will remain for some time as a major challenge for us to deal with. The focus of this book only secondarily concerns itself with how we deal with Donald Trump. Its primary focal concern is on how we might better relate to each other in this time of profound division of

Preface

our nation. That critical issue will be at the forefront regardless of the fate of Donald Trump. Therefore, the time is still ripe for this book to be able to have its intended effect.

The second thought that comes to mind is that this book features sparring partners who are quite an uneven match. We have here, in the battle between Kierkegaard and Trump, many might suggest, a contest between eminently unequal partners. Kierkegaard is a heavyweight thinker, one of the world's greatest thinkers some would say, and Trump, by many accounts, is a lightweight thinker, whose greatness as a world thinker exists in only one mind—his. I don't have any issue with the first part of this claim, that Kierkegaard is a great thinker, but I do take issue with dismissing and underestimating Trump's power. He possesses tremendous power, and that power resides in his capacity to utilize media to serve his purposes, to relate to people's primal instincts and passions, and to evoke fear in his followers by portraying select "others" in a negative light. If evil is determined less by the intrinsic nature of an action and more by the particular purposes that action serves, then the Donald's power is especially important because it finds its expression in actions that very often fall into the evil category as judged by the purposes they serve. Kierkegaard did not give much respect to the Hegelian category of the "world-historical," because he thought it was an abstraction whose content was often determined by chance or luck as opposed to the earnest quality of an individual life. That might be the case, but Trump has taken on world-historical dimensions as not too many individuals before him have accomplished, so he ought not be taken too lightly. Donald Trump is known by more people in the world than few before him have been. The mismatch between these two figures is not as great as one might think on first glance.

Let this brief text go out, then, to join others who have had something to say about Trump. It will also be able to assume its place among many others who have had something to say about Kierkegaard. My hope in releasing this little creation is at least threefold. First, that those more interested in Trump will come to see that the lessons Kierkegaard can teach usher us into a consideration of important issues of life that Trump bypasses, issues that can help us to deal with each other more effectively in this time when democracy is being threatened. Second, that those more interested in Kierkegaard will come to see that Trump and his world are posing a challenge to our political life that demands our attention, including turning our consideration to highlighting thoughts of the Danish Socrates to nurture individuals' ability to love the other. Third, that a little bit of space might be carved out in the discussion to make room for speaking of the presence of divinity, the loving power of creative transformation that is active in the world to lure its creatures toward greater love.

Acknowledgements

Images play their part in this book, but they contribute only to the Kierkegaard and Kierkegaard-World side of the ledger. No images have been included in the Trump and Trump-World portions of the book because they have effectively managed the media to such an extent that overexposure has been the result and no photos are called for on their behalf. The case is different when considering figures from Denmark's nineteenth century. An image of Kierkegaard's girlfriend or father, along with different images of Søren, can help to bring to life his various relationships that are discussed. The use of more than one image of Søren himself helps to highlight different aspects of who he was. The reflective Søren at his desk portrays quite a different person from the activist Søren attacking Christendom, just as the feeling-tone conveyed by the young Kierkegaard differs significantly from that created by an image approaching a caricature. All of these images, except for one, are used courtesy of The Royal Library, Copenhagen. The exception is the image of Søren's father, which appears according to an agreement with The Museum of National History at Frederiksborg Castle. The painting (on ivory), 7,5 x 5,8, "Michael Pederson Kierkegaard (1756–1838)," was done by Frederik Christian Camradt in 1794, and the photograph was taken by Kit Weiss. I thank May-Britt Raarup Bunsgaard, of Photo Sales at the Museum, for her kind assistance in procuring use of this image.

I also want to acknowledge many people who in ways large and small have contributed to this writing project. I wish to thank Paul Sponheim, my teacher, mentor, and friend who has given significant support to my work on this book as well as on other endeavors of scholarship and life. I give an affectionate hug to my son, Aaron Kristian Thompson, for the thoughtful statements he sent to me. Also, my appreciation goes out to former colleague Derek Nelson for giving helpful critical remarks and suggestions

Acknowledgements

on an early articulation of the projected content of the book. Larry Ort's close reading also caught unintended mistakes. And Margaret Johnson offered encouraging words after reading an early overview of the project. My profound gratitude goes out to those who consented to read the book and offer an endorsement of it. In addition, I appreciate the attention given to the whole or portions of the book by the following readers: Diann Kuder, Martin and Sally Roth, Judy Carlson, Joyce Visser, and Dan Larson.

Portions of these chapters were presented over five sessions to the adult education class at Holy Trinity Lutheran Church in Greenville, Pennsylvania. I acknowledge their interest in the project. Participants were: Sue Achenbach, Paul Bittler, Sue Bittler, Fran Black, Ken Black, Alicia Eppley, Dan Eppley, Jacob Eppley, Michael Eppley, Henry Heil, Ruth Heil, Bonnie Massing, Bob Massing, Nancy McLaughlin, Judi Moinet, Julie Morgan, Matt Morgan, Sean Oros, Pancey Schikwambi, Barbara Schwartz, Marge Stubert, Kathy Thompson, John Weaver, and Nicole Weaver. I thank editors Matt Wimer, Rodney Clapp, Stephanie Hough, Ian Creeger, and others at Wipf and Stock for their assistance in this project.

Finally, my most significant acknowledgement goes to my wife and partner Kathy. She proofread the whole of the manuscript with the usual care she bestows in all her endeavors. Kathy embodies and exemplifies for me and others an incredible power of loving embrace, which my freedom and life catch daily, and which keenly reminds me of the infinitude of the debt created by that love; this remembrance allows that love to maintain its freshness and vitality, just as Kierkegaard proclaims in the book's epigraph.

Introduction

We are in trying times these days and we don't want to allow ourselves to be overwhelmed by their catastrophic character. Most people in the United States who take stock of perceptions prevailing upon us in 2019 notice a rather intense mixture of countervailing—negative and positive—feelings. On the one hand, since the presidential election of 2016, many citizens of the United States have been sensing that our American democracy is increasingly in peril. Now, more than two-and-a-half years later in mid-2019, we are not yet convinced of democracy's imminent demise, but we are extremely troubled by democratic safeguards being systematically eroded and democratic institutions being persistently assaulted, resulting in the incremental dismantling and unhinging of the political structures of our American way of life. Darkness encroaches upon us and seemingly intensifies weekly. While the full-bodied night of democracy's total collapse has not yet arrived, such a prospect is on the horizon and could become a reality—but it need not do so. We definitely sense, though, that we are in a high-stakes time of transition that includes the negative feeling of democracy's daunting dusk.

On the other hand, in this critical time in America not all is doom and gloom. Signposts of hope are being manifested. Constructive responses to the crisis of our time are emerging in multiple quarters. Many women are being politicized and are running for office at all levels. Many young people are recognizing the importance of becoming engaged in the fray and finding ways to involve themselves in meaningful action. Many citizens who previously were not invested in the day's issues are now participating in groups that sponsor discussion of concerns and guide actions prompting change. Many across the country are coming to recognize that every person's vote matters and that participating in elections is democracy's means to register criticism of the way things are and to effect a transformation of the political landscape into the way it ought to be. The newly-elected Representatives in the House who reported for action in 2019 are providing a palpable intensifying of diversity and broadening of concerns within Congress. In these rather incredible signs can be seen breaking forth a grassroots awareness of the existential threat facing our nation. Many identify the makings of a widespread spiritual awakening taking place before our eyes. This radiant bursting forth of light into the darkness seems to be pointing to the advent of a new day, and some of us might even boldly identify this as one basis for discerning divinity's dawn.

Our present experience, then, includes both a more dreadful sense of democracy's daunting dusk and a more hopeful sense of there being afoot in our time the possibility of discerning divinity's dawn. The task of this little book is to sharpen the contours of these two countervailing perceptions. Donald Trump and Søren Kierkegaard will be my primary resources for this sharpening. Trump needs little introduction in our time, so discussion of him can begin without much fanfare. With Kierkegaard, the situation is different; he will not be well-known to most readers. He hails from a different time and place, so care will be taken to present him in his situation, a situation, we will learn, in which his struggles were with many of the same issues that plague us. I believe Kierkegaard is worth getting to know because he can help to acquaint us with many clues for discerning divinity's dawn in our time and for recognizing the prospects of divinity resurrecting democracy.

Before turning to further initial words about Kierkegaard, I should clarify that by the word "democracy," I am affirming the notion of a "liberal constitutional democracy," as that notion is defined by Ginsburg and Huq. Their definition disallows identifying democracy merely with the holding of competitive elections; they insist instead that two other factors must be present in order for authentic electoral competition to be sustained. Therefore, they regard a working democracy to require three core institutions: first, "free and fair elections"; second, "the liberal rights of speech and association that are necessary for the democratic process"; and, third, "the stability, predictability, and publicity of a legal regime usually captured in the term *rule of law*—a quality of special importance when it comes to the machinery of elections."[1] For them, a country can own the label "liberal constitutional democracy" only when all three of these elements are

---

1. Ginsburg and Huq, *Constitutional Democracy*, 9.

Introduction

present.² "These three elements—elections, speech and association rights, and a bureaucracy governed by the rule of law—are conceptually separate"; but "the effective operation of democracy is most likely to be characterized by their entangled and mutually supportive operation."³ In our current context, the harmoniousness of the threefold nexus is not what it needs to be.

Søren Kierkegaard (1813–1855) was a Danish philosopher, religious thinker, and theologian who produced a vast literary authorship during his rather short life. His writings responded to mid-century-Copenhagen culture, which, although effectively cultivating many people of refined taste in the capital city of about one hundred thousand, was regarded by Kierkegaard as an ethos of conformism that robbed people of their individuality. He wrote of his present age as being dominated by no less than the six leveling forces of "the public," "the press," "the crowd," "the numerical," "the professor," and "the church." Each of these in its own way contributed to the leveling of distinctions and passionate living that undermined public discourse and the institutions of Danish society. It could be said that the cultural network of Golden Age Copenhagen worked to dehumanize people, lifting up these six "ideals" that were in actuality mere abstractions that called people away from a profound participation in the rich particulars of life's relationships. Together losing themselves in the general universals represented by these abstract cultural norms, individuals of the society were relinquishing their personal responsibility to give voice to their own thoughts and perspectives.

The newly emerged notion of "the public" held up the lowest common denominator as that to which each person should aspire, and those superior folks with a flair for individual expression were criticized for not conforming to this ghostly standard. "The press," whose power at this time had increased significantly, provided the go-to viewpoint, which was to inform thinking and discussing of the day's issues and which allowed anonymous viewpoints to be cheaply presented with no responsible ownership being taken for claims made. "The crowd" was regarded as being the mass conglomerate that allowed people to flee from their individual freedom and freedom's criterion and hide amidst the collective that gave expression to the view of the majority that is to be regarded as the right view. "The numerical" held power because quantitative determination, in short-sighted fashion, functioned as supplying the evidential basis for decision-making.

2. Ginsburg and Huq, *Constitutional Democracy*, 10.
3. Ginsburg and Huq, *Constitutional Democracy*, 13–14.

"The professor" won the respect of all because he (and in that day all professors were "he") was the magistrate over reason, and solid rational positions were supported by the clear thinking and arguments of those in the academy. And, finally, "the church" in Denmark was a state Lutheran church in which membership began with one's baptism and expectations for being a Christian placed little to no demand on a person's actual religious life. In each of these cases, the so-called "ideal" had an enervating effect on the individual, putting a leveling force in place that drained people of passionate existence and demolished qualitative distinctions between the important and the unimportant, the good and the bad, the true and the untrue, the serious and the trivial, etc. The leveling impact of these six so-called ideals or norms extended into the political arena and took its toll on the structures of democracy.

A number of parallels can be seen between Kierkegaard's present age and that of our own time, which in many ways is even worse and would likely be seen as such if our powers of sensitivity and critique were as potent as Kierkegaard's were. Kierkegaard identified a legitimate critique of each of the six ideals, whereas in the case of Trump we encounter criticisms lacking in legitimation. In our world of Golden Age Trump, we have the same leveling forces at work, although they have come to be understood in many different ways by people, depending on whether one operates from outside or inside the Trump orbit. "The public" in our setting must identify the potent role played by social media in shaping people's viewpoints, but it must also include the fact that Russia continues to wage information warfare on the American public to influence our voting, and that this meddling in one of our most treasured democratic processes has been facilitated by Trump's unwillingness to legitimate this concern. "The press" in the United States is depicted by Trump as creating "fake news" to discredit the current POTUS, and this is continually criticized and countered by a delusional narcissist's prolific flow of tweets that present alternative facts and oftentimes make statements of public policy. The category of "the crowd" has become those gatherings of cherry-picked rally participants from which Trump has received the positive strokes he needs from his base to feed his omnivorous ego that never garners enough praise. "The numerical" is that arena in which Trump is able to manipulate the facts to serve his purposes, e.g., that allows him still to claim that he had the largest number of people attending his inauguration in history. In countless instances he has played fast and loose with the numbers. "The professor" in Trump's view holds no respect

INTRODUCTION

because for him knowledge, books, and theories have nothing to offer one who intuitively knows all that is required for being a fantastic leader. That's why Trump's daily national security briefing reports have been shortened dramatically and sometimes include as many images as words. Finally, instead of interpreting "the church" as Christendom in which New Testament Christianity is largely absent, as in Kierkegaard's case, this category in our time can be interpreted as "Christ, Inc." to use Catherine Keller's language.[4] Christ Inc. in Trump's world serves as the foundation for racist views of white nationalism, sexist views of male misogyny, and classist views of capitalism as severed from a concern for equality and justice, along with the degradation of public discourse that happens when such views become normalized.

Because of peculiar features of his particular time, Søren Kierkegaard gave thought to the question of how divinity's dawn might be discerned in the midst of an era in which democracy's daunting dusk seemed to be at hand, how divinity might be seen to be at work resurrecting democracy. As in dealing with most questions, he avoided giving this one a simplistic answer. In 1852 he wrote in his *Journal*: "God is not an external palpable power who bangs the table in front of me when I want to alter his will and says: No stop! No, in this sense it is almost as if God did not exist. It is left up to me."[5] For Kierkegaard, faith is an important factor in this matter. Faith opens the individual to relating to the divine: the stronger the relating, the stronger the sense of the divine reality before whom one is existing. As he writes: "To believe is not an *indifferent relation to something* which is true, but an *infinitely decisive relation to something*. The accent falls upon the relation."[6]

Kierkegaard's writings include resources that can be drawn on to respond to the question of how divinity's dawn can prevail over democracy's dusk, of how divinity can resurrect democracy. Highlighted in the book will be delineating ways in which Kierkegaard's existential response to this

---

4. Keller, *Intercarnations*, 2–3, states that Christ Inc., has a sovereign Lord who has claimed "His monopoly on religious truth," guided by an "incorporated orthodoxy of The Incarnation" that after three centuries became consolidated "under the sign of one cross, one sword, one religion," in order more effectively to carry out violence against the other, be it the other of differing Christians or non-Christians.

5. *Pap.* X5 A 13 (See Kierkegaard, *Søren Kierkegaards Papirer* in bibliography, referred to throughout as *Pap.*, followed by reference to volume, section, and number in the standard Danish edition); Kierkegaard, *Journals and Papers* 2, 1273

6. *Pap.* VI B 19:1–10; Kierkegaard, *Journals and Papers* 4, 4537.

question can help to address the crisis of our time. The book's chapters are structured around six concepts or categories that might strike the reader as appearing rather haphazardly as from out of nowhere. Actually, I chose these particular six concepts or topics because I know Kierkegaard has quite a bit to say about them, and I thought it would be interesting to investigate what place they have within Trump's orbit. Therefore, in the book's chapters I consider respectively six "places" or *topoi* where Kierkegaard might regard divinity in actuality as being potently present and discernible. In each case, we will find that Trump explicitly or implicitly considers these topics or concepts to be weak. The topics or concepts that will be considered respectively in the six chapters are: narrativity or story; interiority or earnestness; normativity or measure; eternality or the moment; subjectivity or freedom; and possibility or the future.

In each instance I consider respectively not just the take on the particular topic or concept of Trump and Kierkegaard, but of Trump and Trump-world and Kierkegaard and Kierkegaard-world. Trump-world refers to the family and political cronies of Trump along with those who uncritically embrace him, and Kierkegaard-world refers to the family of pseudonyms of Kierkegaard, to individual personalities who were very influential on him, and to those who are open to appropriating his message. I alert you in advance, with a little attempt at humor, that in doing research into these two I have discovered that there are some fairly stark differences between them. The result of this comparative exercise is a sixfold critique that points to how Kierkegaard's thoughts can possibly contribute to dealing with our problem of a society in which public discourse and institutions are being torn down. I think Kierkegaard can be of assistance in trumping Trump.

It is important to clarify that in placing the focus on "trumping Trump," I do not intend for this book to be merely a bashing or slamming of Trump. Donald J. Trump has his shortcomings and, given the position he is in as President of the United States, those shortcomings can possibly lead to some scary consequences for the nation as a whole, for our country's relationships with other countries, as well as for the individual lives of US and global citizens. So hearty critique is definitely called for, but this is not for the purpose of belittling or demeaning this one who has suddenly ascended into prominence in our midst and upset almost every applecart of traditional customs, standards, and etiquette that we had grown accustomed to in the more tranquil days of previous decades. If Donald were

Introduction

writing this book,[7] we could expect him to belittle and demean, to bash and slam the target of his opposition. But that doesn't mean that such treatment ought to be given him. He is a human being, created in the image of the divine, whose standing as a creature of the divine means that a level of dignity and respect needs to be shown him even as the spirit of criticism is unleashed fully so that an unvarnished portrait of this person's behaviors and actions, policies and principles can be painted. This endeavor to be fair and judicious applies to the treatment of Donald as well as to the treatment of Trump-world, including those who count themselves among Trump's base. The purpose of the book, then, is not to vilify but to elucidate and motivate. The deliberate intention to avoid taking the low road in this study is so that a diagnostic analysis of the situation can be undertaken, with a sense gained of how it is that the concatenation of factors that came together to bring us where we are at this point in our life as a nation—took place. Any insights gained into how we got where we are should prove helpful for advancing us to a new place.

I am operating with the view that what is needed is not to go to the left, or to go to the right, but—as others too have suggested—to go deeper. Preferring the language of trumping rather than bashing Trump is closely related to preferring the language of going deeper rather than going to the left or to the right. Some might object, saying, "You speak of going not left or right but deeper, and yet you, Thompson, clearly are not neutral but are coming at this matter from the left." The objection has a point. However, in urging us to go deeper, I'm surely not saying that I'm giving up my firmly established place on the left; I sympathize in more ways than one with the reminder of liberation theologians that, in our bodies, the heart is situated on the left. However, neither am I asking someone on the right to give up her stance. I can only offer the call from where I'm at. But a relativizing of positions, of those on the left and the right, needs to take place. To be able to move ahead, it seems that little will happen until the conversation can take place at a different level, and I suggest that different level is a deeper level. We don't go deeper to arrive at a cheap or superficial standoff in avoidance of making needed changes, we go deeper in order to make possible a creative advance that brings change. I sincerely hope these are not

---

7. Without bashing or slamming Trump, it should be stated for purposes of information and clarity that Trump does not write his own books. They have been written by ghost writers, though most likely in quite close consultation and collaboration with Donald. In attempting to refrain from bashing and slamming, the reader might find that on occasion I have sinned in this regard.

merely words that carry little meaning, for it seems that a diagnosis of how we got where we are, joined together with insights from Kierkegaard about how we can each become fuller human beings, can give us a deeper way of looking at things and an appreciation for the complexity of where we are at. The hope is that bringing the conversation to that new terrain might open up ways of connecting with "the other" that would not come about were the right-left confrontation continued in the same old way with the same old results or lack thereof.

In the following pages I will be attempting to articulate this in a way that doesn't allow going deeper to become an excuse for not going forward. Instead, I take going deeper to be a way of operating transcendentally (in the Kantian sense) by becoming the necessary condition for making possible a genuine conversation about that which is truly important. The hope is that such sharing in turn might engender a reconciliation that can lead to new efforts to work at compromise toward consensus rather than having to settle for the stalemate of absolute, dogmatically-entrenched positions. Our mantra, therefore, ought not be, "Don't go left or go right but go deeper." Rather, it needs to be, "Don't go left or go right but go deeper, *in order to go forward*," to go forward into that new situation in which new ways of relating can become a reality. That second step is central to divinity's work of resurrecting democracy. The purpose of this book will not be fully realized unless it addresses in specific ways this resurrection process or just how going deeper is to culminate in going forward.

A final introductory word is needed on my use of the word "divinity."[8] This book on Trump and Kierkegaard originated in the context of a session of the Kierkegaard, Religion, and Culture section of the national meeting of the American Academy of Religion in Denver in November 2018. The session, entitled "Where Is God? Kierkegaard and the Denigration of Public Discourse," was organized by session coordinators Marsha C. Robinson of Syracuse University and Avron Kulak of York University. They are planning to publish a book on Kierkegaard and politics and would like to incorporate papers presented at the AAR Denver meeting. My paper at that meeting was on "Fake News, Eroded Civility, and Christ Inc.: Why It Is 'as if God did not exist.'" For this current writing project, I surely do not want to take the ideas of Marcia and Avron that served to configure that session

---

8. For a little more thorough discussion of this concept of divinity or the Godhead than is able to be set forth here, see the discussion in Thompson and Cuff, *God and Nature*, 119–22.

Introduction

and employ them as the guiding thoughts for my project. Therefore, for this book I have developed a different framing structure from the one that informed that AAR session in order to avoid infringing on the thoughtful, creative labors of Marcia and Avron. An absolute avoidance of overlap is impossible, but I hope I have managed to keep any overlap to an acceptable minimum. One of the major changes in framework made to establish an independent terrain for this book is a shift of focus from "God" to "divinity," and to speak of the notion of the divine wherever possible instead of the concept of God. The question of "where is God today?" is no longer the central concern in this book.

By divinity I mean the notion of "Godhead," which has a respected place in the history of religious thinking. Within Christian thought it is the mystics especially who have invested themselves in thinking profoundly about the Godhead, and this is usually as over against the notion of "God." We could say that for them the Godhead is the mysterious pantheistic substance lying at the heart of all things and God is an historically developed conception which reveals in a more personal way the true essence of the divine. The medieval mystic Meister Eckhart (c. 1260-c. 1328) communicates his deep appreciation for the Godhead, with which he entered into union in mystical experience:

> When I stood in the Godhead's ground and the Godhead's depths and the Godhead's circle and the Godhead's source, none asked me about my will or my doing. When I flowed forth I heard all creatures speaking about God. They asked me: Brother Eckhart, when did you leave home? Then I was home, though I was outside. Why were they speaking only about God and not the Godhead? All that is within the Godhead is one and cannot be spoken of, God and Godhead are not the same. God works and creates; the Godhead works nothing; it is quiet and immovable within itself. When I return to the point I departed from, my entrance is better than my departure, for I bring all creatures with me in my reason. When I enter into the ground and deep and circle and source of the Godhead none question from where I have come, or where I have been—and none missed me. Here all becoming is laid aside.[9]

To be mentioned in this context is also Friedrich Wilhelm Joseph Schelling (1775–1854), a philosopher in the tradition of German idealism who was influenced by Eckhart. In differentiating God as Absolute (the

---

9. A quote from an Eckhart sermon cited in Thompson and Kangas, *Between Hegel and Kierkegaard*, 173.

Godhead) from God's nature (God), Schelling understands the Godhead as the very ground of God's existence which engenders a longing to give birth to God.[10]

I want to pick up on this category of longing that Schelling locates at the center of the Godhead, a thought that Eckhart too holds dear. I understand the power of the Godhead present in all things as bestowing on the human creature a longing, a yearning, a desire for ultimate reality. Divinity donates to creatures a desire for the divine. This longing or desire draws the human forward into the infinite beyond and humans give imaginative shape to what they long for as construals of the divine or God. Since each and every particular construal of God falls short of capturing the fullness of ultimate reality for which the human is longing, the process of longing and re-imagining the divine is an ongoing one. With the Godhead as the source of all such longing, it is natural for humans to long to be united with the Godhead that seems to lie beyond God. That gives meaning to Eckhart's famous line, "Therefore pray God that we may be free of God." Eckhart desires to be free of his construal of God in order to be united with the Godhead. We could say that for him, Godhead or divinity trumps God or the divine. We might not agree with that judgment. We might think that the God of revelation ought to trump the Godhead of nature and creation. However, in our disagreement over that matter, we can still acknowledge the importance of divinity or the Godhead. Eckhart's statement indicates the dissatisfaction with our construals of God and the desire to go deeper to be united with the Godhead as the source of our deepest longing. But not all construals of the divine are created equal. Some construals seem more accurately to represent that which can most fully satisfy our longing, and those most satisfying construals generally have much to say about love. For Kierkegaard, we can say, love is "the category proper" of the divine; that is to say, love is the defining, essential attribute of the divine in relation to which all other divine ascriptions or attributes need to find their meaning.[11] As divinity donates a desire for love to human creatures, those human creatures can find fulfillment of that desire in loving the divine—and since the divine is love, humans find their greatest fulfillment in loving love. Therefore, the human's deepest longing is fulfilled in loving. This desire of divinity given to human beings is the rich resource we can access by going

---

10. Schelling, *Of Human Freedom*, 31–34.

11. I am indebted to Paul Sponheim, for this formulation of love as the category proper of God. See, e.g., his *Speaking of God*, 44.

Introduction

deeper. As we do that, we become equipped for going forward. This process of appropriating love is that by which divinity can resurrect democracy. And I believe Søren Kierkegaard can guide us into that process.

1

Narrativity or Story

Trump and Trump-World

We ask initially, why might it seem as if divinity, which implants in the human the desire for the divine or God, is not readily discernable in relation to Trump and Trump-world on narrativity or story?

Trump's narrative is informed by a dark vision. That vision presents images of caravans of immigrants invading the country, of America's streets filled with MS-13 gang members, of police officers being gunned down, of Islamic radicals entering our nation, of other countries that have been ripping us off for years, and of federal regulations that have been inhibiting our economic growth. The narrative, putting forth "a right-wing, nativist, protectionist, anti-immigration populism,"[1] is a story giving expression to a politics of fear. As Trump famously responded to Bob Woodward's question, "What is power?": "Real power," he said, "is fear."[2] For Trump, real power gives rise to fear.

At a deeper level, though, Trump's story is all about Trump. He himself proudly proclaims, "There is nobody in the world who is a better

---

1. Unger, *House of Trump*, 252.
2. The details of the interview of Trump appear at the beginning of Bob Woodward's book, *Fear*, and the claim "real power is fear" is repeated numerous times throughout the book.

self-promoter than Donald Trump."[3] Bringing coherence to Trump's narrative and offering a quick explanation as to why our democracy stands in peril is a simple fact pointed out by Seth Abramson, which is "that this presidency is not an American presidency but a *Trump* presidency: a course of ill governance that is *for* Trump, *about* Trump, and inextricably tethered to the interests *of* Trump."[4]

To understand Trump's story, Craig Unger contends that it needs to include an account of his long relationship with the Russian Mafia and the assistance he received from a Russian intelligence operation to make it into the White House.[5] I too think Trump's connection to Russia is an important part of his story, and in the pages ahead, we will make some queries into that part of the story. Robert Mueller's "Report on the Russian Interference in the 2016 Presidential Election," according to Attorney General William Barr's four-page letter detailing its main findings, stated that the "investigation did not establish that members of the Trump Campaign conspired or coordinated with the Russian government in its election interference activities."[6] While the investigation did not establish such conspiracy or coordination to meet Mueller's standard, there is room for further inquiry into this issue, and in the coming months intense scrutiny into the matter will likely continue in order to shed more light on this aspect of the Trump story.

We will see that Kierkegaard utilized pseudonyms or pen names in telling his narrative. In communicating his story, Donald also has not hesitated to make use of pseudonyms, which for him are false names. In his case, though, the primary purpose in doing so has been to protect his anonymity. In the 1980s and 1990s, Trump would use different names in calling in to the media and representing himself as a spokesperson for the Trump organization. This was focused on the media outlets of New York City. Favorite pseudonyms in that setting were "John Barron" (or "John Baron") and "John Miller." It's interesting that Donald gave his favorite name of Barron to his youngest son who was born in 2006. More recently, in legal documents, especially non-disclosure agreements with various

---

3. Isikoff and Corn, *Russian Roulette*, 7.
4. Abramson, *Proof of Collusion*, 315.
5. Unger, *House of Trump*, 5.
6. Tiff Fehr et al., "Read Attorney General William Barr's Summary of the Mueller Report," *New York Times*, March 24, 2019, https://www.nytimes.com/interactive/2019/03/24/us/politics/barr-letter-mueller-report.html.

women, Trump's frequently-used name was "David Dennison." Kierkegaard's relation to pseudonyms was of quite a different nature.

Trump's favorite platform for communicating his narrative is Twitter. He prefers that direct way of delivering his story to his followers, without any censoring. He believes he's great at it. When Twitter extended the length of a tweet from 140 to 280 characters, Donald was sad, as he put it, "because I was the Ernest Hemingway of 140 characters."[7] These tweets cover a broad range of topics, but they have a coherence to them: they serve the single purpose of lifting up Donald J. Trump before the public.

In telling his story to promote himself, he finds helpful "truthful hyperbole," as he explains in his *The Art of the Deal*:

> The final key to the way I promote is bravado. I play to people's fantasies. People may not always think big themselves, but they can still get very excited by those who do. That's why a little hyperbole never hurts. People want to believe that something is the biggest and the greatest and the most spectacular.
>
> I call it truthful hyperbole. It's an innocent form of exaggeration—and a very effective form of promotion.[8]

Many rightly contend that Trump's truthful hyperbole is not always so truthful.

In fact, in Trump's telling of his narrative, that usually involves not telling the truth. Donald lies. As Seth Abramson clearly declares: "Never has a presidential campaign birthed so many lies from so many different mouths: lies of indifference, lies of carelessness, lies of callousness, lies of pique [resentment], lies of strategic advantage, lies of ignorance, lies of malicious intent, lies of ulterior motive."[9] He normalizes lying, and when the press criticizes him, he charges them with setting forth "fake news" and functioning as "the enemy of the people." In the fall of 2018, he even removed the "hard pass" press credential of CNN's chief White House correspondent Jim Acosta, accusing Acosta of being a "grandstander" and "bad for the country": this action was met with legal action by CNN, backed by CBS News and other outlets including, somewhat surprisingly, Fox News, and fortunately Acosta's journalistic privileges were restored after a federal judge ruled in his favor.

---

7. Woodward, *Fear*, 207.
8. Trump with Schwartz, *Art of the Deal*, 58.
9. Abramson, *Proof of Collusion*, 315.

Narrativity or Story

The press that Trump constantly runs down has always mattered deeply to him; daughter Ivanka witnessed growing up how her father "lit up or blew up depending on how the press depicted him."[10] For Donald, a free press is "fake news," unless it is Fox.[11] Fox News does sponsor a steady flow of what Kellyanne Conway dubbed "alternative facts" as core viewers have their prejudices ratified by "a news network that distorts, misrepresents, and oftentimes outright ignores the country's most exciting domestic news story."[12] Michael Hayden, former Director of the National Security Council and CIA, thinks we are in "uncharted waters" in our Republic, where we're not arguing "over the values to be applied to objective reality, or occasionally over what constituted objective reality," but rather over the very "existence or the relevance of objective reality itself."[13]

The narrative of Trump is tied intimately to the story of Trump's close relation to the Fox News operation. Sean Hannity, who admits he is not a journalist but rather a talk show host, Ann Coulter, and Tucker Carlson have done much to promote Trump's message. Because of that, they possess much power over him. This became blatantly apparent when Trump did an about-face on the issue of closing down the government at the end of 2018, when these media icons along with Rush Limbaugh harshly criticized him for not demanding that money for building the US-Mexico wall be included as part of the deal to keep the government open. In a healthy democracy, it is essential that the press be given the freedom to express the judgments it has arrived at after careful investigation of a situation. The viewpoints from reporters will be many and varied. Political leaders should be ready to hear those viewpoints, to take them into consideration, and to learn from them what they can. In Trump's case, he has essentially narrowed down the viewpoints to one. A White House informant in-the-know testifies that there was close communication "between Fox News and the Trump campaign," . . . and "the back-and-forth of daily communication between individuals at Fox and the Trump White House continues to this day. People joke that Trump gets his talking points by watching Fox News, and that is certainly true. But individuals at Fox News are also speaking directly to his team of advisers every single day. The channel's channels

---

10. Fox, *Born Trump*, 182.
11. Hayden, *Assault on Intelligence*, 208.
12. Frum, *Trumpocracy*, 47.
13. Hayden, *Assault on Intelligence*, 250.

are wide open."[14] Evidently, many days Trump watches 6 to 8 hours of TV, much of it Fox, although he surfs quite a bit too.[15]

Another element in the Trump story is his love of being a storyteller. In their studies of oral as opposed to literate cultures, anthropologists have identified the essential role played by the storyteller. With oral cultures, the storyteller is a reservoir of memory of a clan or tribe's myths and "history" and these two, myths and history, are often merged. When the storyteller makes an appearance, regular activities cease and full attention turns to the one whose words serve a multiple function: they speak powerfully to the imagination, they remind one and all that the community to which they belong is alive and well, they reassure the listeners that their distinctive values and principles are still at hand, they fill each participant with a sense of well-being at harmoniously sharing life with other like-minded folk, and they stir enthusiasm for continuing to give themselves to the high purpose and cause of the group.[16]

Donald Trump as storyteller is maybe his greatest strength. In fulfilling that function, he creates myths that speak to the imagination of those who share his deep but misguided desire to live unperturbed by people who are different from us, meaning those who are not white, are not citizens, are not seriously dependent financially, are not politically progressive. If Trump's storytelling possesses a strong dose of the mythical, it doesn't matter, because people are tired of hearing discourse that follows the rules of rationality and factuality. That sort of boring, constrained, and reductionistic verbiage never makes it to the level of genuine storytelling. A long rational discourse can go into details that promptly lose people's attention. Better is the brief, hard-hitting tweet. And better yet is the personal communication that becomes possible in speaking to large crowds of people. In that setting, listeners from the base set aside their normal routines and activities, giving their rapt attention to the master storyteller, whose mythical narrative makes a connection at a deep, primal level that validates a significant aspect of who they are. To his base, this contemporary storyteller becomes a folk or national hero whose bigger-than-life existence transpires

---

14. Newman, *Unhinged*, 118–19.

15. Woodward, *Fear*, 299.

16. For a terrific account of "El Hablador" or "the storyteller" from which one can learn much about the storyteller's function amidst a people of oral culture, see the novel by Peruvian author and Literature-Nobel-Prize-winner Mario Vargas Llosa, *The Storyteller*.

Narrativity or Story

on a higher plane of reality, leaving him exempt from the normal criticisms of ordinary mortals.

Trump's narrative and the dark vision informing it emerge organically from his person. They reflect his instincts, which he tends to trust. But his narrative and vision have also been bolstered by key figures in Trump-world, most specifically by his duo of white national populist Stevens, that is, former Chief Strategist of the White House Steven Bannon and Senior Policy Advisor Steven Miller. Miller "was an ideological clone of Bannon—a hardliner on immigration and trade who believed we should always maintain a confrontational posture with the press," and Bannon thought Miller had his back; but the book by Cliff Sims, Trump's former Special Assistant to the President, makes known that Miller was actually instrumental in convincing Trump to fire Bannon, who, Miller reported to Trump, "won't stop leaking to the press and undermining Jared [Kushner]."[17] These two ideologues—Bannon and Miller—helped to conceptually round out Trump's more primitive intuitive perspective.

In her ambitious and magisterial history of the United States, Jill Lepore makes a remarkably astute and perspectively keen statement on Trump's impact on our country, especially since the proximate temporal distance of the past happenings she describes fades away in the realization that these are also events in which she and we are still very much immersed. She writes: "American history became, in those years, a wound that bled, and bled again. Gains made toward realizing the promise of the Constitution were lost. Time seemed to be moving both backward and forward. Americans fought over matters of justice, rights, freedom, and America's place in the world with a bitter viciousness, and not only online. Each of the truths on which the nation was founded and for which so many people had fought were questioned. The idea of truth itself was challenged. The only agreed-upon truth appeared to be a belief in the ubiquity of deception."[18] That period of the recent past—in which "a politics of reasoned debate, of inquiry and curiosity, of evidence and fair-mindedness" seem to have been eradicated[19]—is still with us, and it calls us to account on the matter of how we are going to respond to the narrative of Trump and Trump-world.

Relevant for the reception of Trump's message has been the proliferation of news outlets, and this pluralism of media has increased the number

---

17. Sims, *Team of Vipers*, 208–9.
18. Lepore, *These Truths*, 728.
19. Lepore, *These Truths*, 728.

of viewpoints available to people. Folks have settled on their outlet of choice and this had resulted in the creating of silos of information, which leaves citizens living in information bubbles that reinforce particular grievances.[20] The major divide is between followers of Fox News and select radio show hosts on the one hand and the CNN-MSNBC option on the other. Two quite different stories are told by these sources and people tend to buy into one or the other. When Trump's narrative that plays fast and loose with the truth is combined with this complex situation with the media, it makes for some confusion. Then when we add in, first, social media, second, consumer profiling results from a firm like Cambridge Analytica,[21] and, third, the Russian disinformation campaign effectively targeting particular groups, we've got Trump's narrative finding a warm reception among one side of the divide of a polarized society.

The story behind "fake news" has to include two other figures, which carries us into Trump-world. First, it needs to extend back to Vladislav Surkov, who has been identified as "the real genius of the Putin era." He was the Kremlin's chief ideologue, the puppet master who privatized the Russian political system which was the way Putin created a new strain of authoritarianism.[22] Surkov's portfolio was very broad. He was into the Moscow art scene.[23] And he became a public relations figure, and the shape-shifting power of PR gave Surkov a new niche, now as a superstar. He joined the Kremlin as a political technologist and served for Putin in a role somewhat comparable to that played by Karl Rove in the George W. Bush administration. His task was to merge theater and public relations and to apply this merger to Putin's bureaucracy. The result is that he turned Russia into one great reality show.[24]

"Surkov's version of democracy," writes Malcolm Nance, "is crafted by a centralized control system for information and narrative manipulation through the use of mind control and influence techniques, and where certain words and images were repeated mantra-like over and over."[25] He

---

20. Albright, *Fascism*, 235.

21. The data-mining firm of Cambridge Analytica had been involved in 2014 congressional campaigns; Unger explains: "Specializing in 'psychographic' profiling, the company used online data to create sophisticated personality profiles for voters, who could then be targeted with specifically tailored messages that could encourage—or discourage—them from voting one way or another." Unger, *House of Trump*, 233.

22. Unger, *House of Trump*, 191.

23. Unger, *House of Trump*, 192.

24. Unger, *House of Trump*, 193.

25. Nance, *Plot to Destroy Democracy*, 66.

created fake reality, with fake news and alternative facts, which set out to destroy the very notion of reality. Unger explains: "By undermining the whole notion of truth, of what actually happened, Surkov was able to create a never-ending conflict about perception that helped the Putin regime's ability to control and manage Russia. The result was that the opposition was completely befuddled because the ceaseless flood of contradictory stories meant that no one knew what the enemy was up to or even who they really were, or what was really going on. Meanwhile supporters who listened to lie after lie were allowed to choose whichever fiction they preferred to believe—and to dismiss the rest as fake news."[26]

Then, later, in February of 2013, Valery Gerasimov presented a 2,000-word paper that articulated how the rules of war have changed, as nonmilitary means have become much more important than military objectives, for now the intent is to distract, divide, and demoralize the enemy. This new approach to warfare came to be called the "Gerasimov Doctrine."[27] This document set forth "a new form of conflict in which 'frontal engagements' by army battalions and fighter aircraft would become a 'thing of the past,' replaced by hackers and skilled propagandists trained to exploit existing rifts within the ranks of the adversary."[28] It seems to me that the most important collusion between Putin's Kremlin and Trump's administration has been the adopting of the Surkov-Putin playbook and applying it within our American national context, although the illegality of such borrowing of ideas is less easy to establish than is a direct form of conspiring with the enemy to intrude into our election processes, which it seems has also been part of our contemporary political situation.

An account of "fake news" needs to draw in a second figure, Alexander Dugin. "Aleksandr Dugin," writes Malcolm Nance in *The Plot to Destroy America*, "was a former professor of sociology at Moscow State University and an advocate of neo-Eurasianism, a geopolitical policy that advocates for the seizure of former Soviet Union territories. He has been referred to as 'Putin's Rasputin'[29] by Breitbart News and has become the loudest voice

---

26. Unger, *House of Trump*, 194.

27. Unger, *House of Trump*, 195, and see the note on this page and 262.

28. Isikoff and Corn, *Russian Roulette*, 44.

29. Wikipedia in this instance can adequately serve us as a useful source. It informs us that "Grigori Yefimovich Rasputin was a Russian mystic and self-proclaimed holy man who befriended the family of Tsar Nicholas II, the last monarch of Russia, and gained considerable influence in late imperial Russia." He was assassinated on December 30, 1916, in Moika Chapel, St. Petersburg, Russia.

of the Russian fringe as it reflects the global conservative themes prominent in right-wing circles in American and Europe."[30] There is mutual admiration between Putin and Dugin, which is furthered by the fact that Dugin "sees Russia as having gone through a national awakening under Putin's leadership, a Russian Spring."[31] Supposedly "inspired by the writings of Adolf Hitler and the German philosopher Martin Heidegger," Dugin is at war against the "unipolar globalization" that is functioning to unite all peoples into a singular system that destroys all particular nationalities, and helping him to fight against the "globalists" are followers from various tribes of anti-globalists and nationalists; relevant for our narrative of Trump's narrative is the fact that Dugin's "brand of radical, almost fascist conservative populism is very popular in the pro-Trump circles."[32]

Interestingly, Dugin promoted a lecture Carter Page gave in Moscow on July 7, 2016 by broadcasting it live on Tsargrad, a TV station he founded; in his talk Page surprised his audience by "praising Putin as stronger and more reliable than Obama," and Dugin in turn praised Page for his support of Trump as "'an alternative for the U.S.'"[33] Dugin endorsed Donald Trump for president in 2016 and depicted him as "'a common man of the time and thus a challenge to the 'global elite.'"[34] Steve Bannon's ideologies owe much to Duginism: Dugin "glorifies the lost Tsarist Russian empire, just as Bannon glorifies the racist, genocidal Jacksonian America of the 19th century," . . . and Bannon likens "himself to Dugin in the belief that American democracy" is "doomed, and that the world should be led by autocrats and dictators in alignment with nationalist beliefs."[35] Despite having been fired by Donald, "Bannon still believes that Trump is the natural leader of the worldwide populist, anti-globalist movement."[36] Bannon is currently raising money and visiting strategic spots around Europe to stir the fight of nationalist movements against globalism, which he is convinced can be won. On last word, Bannon was refurbishing a deserted monastery built in 1204 CE in the mountains southeast of Rome. Evidently, the 800-room monastery is intended to serve as "a gladiator school for culture warriors"

30. Nance, *Plot to Destroy Democracy*, 67.
31. Nance, *Plot to Destroy Democracy*.
32. Nance, *Plot to Destroy Democracy*, 67–68.
33. Isikoff and Corn, *Russian Roulette*, 159–60.
34. Nance, *Plot to Destroy Democracy*, 68.
35. Nance, *Plot to Destroy Democracy*, 74–75.
36. Nance, *Plot to Destroy Democracy*, 75.

in order to save the Western world "by restoring Judeo-Christian values to the heart of the political conversation."[37]

A final word on Trump's narrativity can come from a very able critic of his. Seth Abramson has engaged in an exceedingly thorough investigation of Trump and Trump-world and has gathered a mountain of evidence in support of the claim that collusion of many sorts has taken place between Trump and the Kremlin. He thinks that a "theory of the case" for this claim needs to be developed, that is, required is "a narrative that connects all other narratives" concerning all this evidence. Such a narrative can then work in concert with that presently available evidence.[38] Abramson holds that there is only one theory of the case that makes sense of the evidence, and that is: "that Donald Trump and a core group of ten to twenty aides, associates, and allies conspire with a hostile foreign power to sell that power control over America's foreign policy in exchange for financial reward and—eventually—covert election assistance."[39] Abramson is convinced that this theory of the case manages to "explain decades of suspicious behavior by Donald Trump, his family, and his closest associates, behavior that suggests that these bad actors expected and received a massive financial reward for taking policy positions friendly to the Kremlin and adverse to the interests of the United States."[40] The effective method of this storyteller gives us a grand narrative that makes considerable sense of Trump's narrative. The fact that initial reports about Mueller's findings run counter to this view should not divert us from continuing to entertain the feasibility of Abramson's theory of the case, for there are still many lines of inquiry and dimensions of ongoing investigation into these matters that might well establish the veracity of Abramson's putative narrative. His book, *Proof of Collusion*, he announces, "aims to provide a careful, comprehensive, and compelling presentation of the evidence supporting the only theory of the case that answers the question of what's happening in America right now and how we can stop it."[41] Those of us serious about gaining a full sense of Trump's narrativity and

---

37. Nicholas Farrell, "Steve Bannon's Gladiator School: A view From Within," February 7, 2019, *Chronicles: A Magazine of American Culture*, https://www.chroniclesmagazine.org/2019/March/44/3/magazine/article/10846082/.

38. Abramson, *Proof of Collusion*, 9.

39. Abramson, *Proof of Collusion*, 10.

40. Abramson, *Proof of Collusion*, 10.

41. Abramson, *Proof of Collusion*, 11.

story will want to look to benefit from this author's method of allowing evidential material and narrative to mutually enrich one another.

Kierkegaard and Kierkegaard-World

Correspondingly, how is it that divinity, which implants in the human the desire for the divine or God, might be potently present in actuality and discernible according to Kierkegaard and Kierkegaard-world on narrativity or story?

Søren Kierkegaard prides himself on being able to exercise his skill in dialectic or in logical thinking. He can hold his own with the best of the world's thinkers. However, he utilizes his thinking in order to make the case for human beings to take seriously their own existence. He thinks it is too easy for people to use thinking, which generally deals in abstractions, as a way to pull people away from their personal living and into a fantasy world of thought that distracts from the primary task at hand. Therefore, in discussing Kierkegaard's contributions, an effort will be made to keep it real and not allow the discussion to turn into a series of abstractions. To keep it personal, some attention will be given to those people in Kierkegaard-world who played a key role in Søren's life.

Figure 1: Søren Kierkegaard (1813–1855)

Narrativity or Story

One particular individual who entered into the life of Kierkegaard ended up having a formative place in both Søren's existing and his thinking. That person was Regine Olsen (1822–1904). She was fifteen when he first met her as a university student nine years her elder. That difference in age would not be a major focal issue when Søren would later call off their engagement. Other factors, some of which we do not know, were more important for that decision. Accounts of the Regine-Søren relationship are many,[42] because it discloses much about Kierkegaard. Journal entries of Kierkegaard abound and communicate all the dynamics of passion and thought at work within him as he struggled to arrive at a resolution on this matter. A few words from Alastair Hannay's fine biography convey a general sense of why Kierkegaard returned the ring Regine had given him, an act symbolizing the breaking of their engagement: "The engagement had lasted thirteen months. He said later that the day after he had proposed he knew it was a mistake. It wasn't that he didn't care for her, on the contrary he was totally captivated and once said it would have been impossible to live without her had he not been so sure that his own 'melancholy and sadness' were bound to get in the way. Not, however, *just* because it would be unrealistic to suppose that he could get rid of them. In fact, in his complicated state he saw them as a blessing in disguise."[43] Hannay goes on to explain that far from merely being a justification for fleeing from Regine, Kierkegaard's "melancholy and sadness now seemed inextricably bound up with what was most 'him'": "Rather than leave himself behind, he was determined that something good should come of it, that is, of him . . . Helplessly pinned down under the weight of melancholy and sadness, it was in these that he had to find anything infinite in his life, not in the yea-saying, world-affirming experience of love."[44]

---

42. See, for example, Hannay, *Kierkegaard*, Garff, *Søren Kierkegaard*, and Backhouse, *Kierkegaard*.

43. Hannay, *Kierkegaard*, 154.

44. Hannay, *Kierkegaard*, 154.

Figure 2: Regine Olsen (1822–1904)

Reading between the lines, Hannay gains the sense that Regine more admired Søren than loved him, and that Søren "had not so much loved her in any erotic sense as been touched by the child in her."[45] Reflections inscribed years later, in 1849, testify to Kierkegaard's love for Regine, albeit not in an erotic sense of love: "I cannot quite place her impact on me in a purely erotic sense. It is true that the fact that she yielded almost adoringly to me, pleaded with me to love her, had so touched me, that I would have risked anything for her. But the fact that I always wanted to hide from myself the degree to which she touched me is also evidence of the extent to which I did love her, though this really has nothing to do with the erotic."[46] Kierkegaard thought that marriage is all about disclosing oneself fully to the other. With his life of melancholy and sadness—but also secrets of various sorts, a complex vocation that could not easily be communicated, complicated twists and turns in his personal history—there was much to be disclosed, maybe too much, both for him to share and for Regine to receive.

Kierkegaard was a product of his time. Part of that time was gender stereotypes. There is no question that because of his assumptions about the capacity of women and the place of women in society, he underestimated

---

45. Hannay, *Kierkegaard*, 154.

46. *Pap.* X2 A 68 and X5 A 149, the latter reference in Hannay, *Papers and Journals*, p. 414, and cited in Hannay, *Kierkegaard*, 155.

Narrativity or Story

what Regine would have brought to the relationship and the degree to which she could have participated in a relationship of full reciprocity and mutuality. History has given us primarily Søren's side of the story; Regine's side, until recently, had been confined to a few scattered remarks. That situation changed with the publication of Joakim Garff's book on Regine.[47] Garff was giving a lecture on Kierkegaard in a rural area of Denmark and afterward was approached by the granddaughter of Regine's older sister; the granddaughter offered to share with Garff over one hundred letters exchanged between her grandmother and Regine.[48] About six years after the breakup with Søren, Regine married Johan Frederick (Fritz) Schlegel—none other than the person who had served as Regine's tutor after he received his law degree in 1838—who became a government official and received an assignment to be governor of the Danish West Indian Islands, located 4,000 miles from Denmark. The letters between the sisters were exchanged over a period of many decades while Regine was in this setting playing the role of the colony's first lady.[49]

In his book, Garff succeeds in presenting Regine from many different vantage points and in showing her, not as lacking an interior register of being, but "instead as the woman of flesh and blood, and opinion and desires, that she really was."[50] We know that the relationship was of paramount importance to Kierkegaard until his death. Here we learn that Regine, too, continued to hold a place in her life for Søren throughout her days. Søren and Regine, as Garff says, "seemed enigmatically bound to each other," and for years after the breakup they would "find pretexts and opportunities to meet as often as possible, preferably so as to make it look as if they were meeting quite by chance," never to speak to each other, for the encounters were silent, but to be in one another's presence.[51]

Both were avid walkers, so as they anticipated the route of the other, "chance" meetings could take place, and sometimes this would mean meeting once or twice a day each day for over the course of a full month. The accidental meetings were, in fact, completely non-accidental. The two did not speak in these encounters, and this went on for fourteen years; but then an event demanded words to be uttered:

47. Garff, *Kierkegaard's Muse*.
48. Garff, *Kierkegaard's Muse*, xii.
49. Garff, *Kierkegaard's Muse*, xiii.
50. Garff, *Kierkegaard's Muse*, xiv.
51. Garff, *Kierkegaard's Muse*, 1.

On Saturday the 17th of March 1855, fourteen years of silence are broken. Departmental Chief Johan Frederik Schlegel has been appointed governor of the West Indies for a five-year term. On the very day of their departure Regine in all haste leaves her apartment in Nybrogade and ventures out into town in the hope of meeting her old love. And . . . it is not long before her eyes fasten on the familiar figure with the broad-brimmed hat. As she passes him by, she says under her breath: "God bless you—may all go well with you!"

For just an instant that Saturday meeting in a random Copenhagen street turned everything upside down. Regine's blessing succeeded in rendering speechless a man never otherwise at a loss for the right words and made him stand still in a more or less symbolic posture, hat in hand . . . What went through the masterthinker theologian's mind in that moment of blessing, no one knows. Perhaps, just for once, there was no thought in his mind at all, simply acceptance of this blessing from the woman in his life.[52]

Søren Kierkegaard died a few months after this exchange.

A couple of months after his death, Regine and Fritz received a letter from Peter Christian Kierkegaard, Søren's brother, informing them that Søren had died and had left a last will and testament. These documents indicated that his former fiancée, Mrs. Regine Schlegel—since to his mind "an engagement was and is just as binding as a *marriage*"—was to inherit all that he left behind and that the same woman, Mrs. Regine Schlegel, was the person to whom his entire authorship is dedicated.[53] Initially, Regine apparently was also the one and only "single individual" to whom he addressed his writings, although the reference would eventually come to be expanded to include any reader ready to appropriate his message.[54] The response to Peter, written by Fritz because of the day's brutally restrictive patriarchal context, was that Regine declined to accept any of Søren's small estate, but she requested to retain any letters and several small items found among the property of the deceased, which formerly belonged to her.[55] Garff concludes that over the years, "Regine seems to have had no difficulty in being simultaneously Schlegel's wife and Kierkegaard's fiancée." Near the end of her life, when Julius Clausen, a librarian cataloging the nearly 7,000

---

52. Garff, *Kierkegaard's Muse*, 9–10.
53. Garff, *Kierkegaard's Muse*, 51–52.
54. Garff, *Kierkegaard's Muse*, 7.
55. Garff, *Kierkegaard's Muse*, 53.

books from Fritz's collection that were to be sold at an upcoming auction, held meetings with Regine, she was not reticent to speak of Søren; however, in her pronouncements, the "rather small, white-haired old lady with the friendliest of expressions" seemed to follow a pattern: "It always began with Schlegel, whose excellent qualities she praised in high-toned fashion, but it ended with—Kierkegaard."[56]

Kierkegaard's relationship with Regine was finally judged to be unworkable because of a rival, which was Kierkegaard's authorship. Søren Kierkegaard successfully defended his dissertation on *The Concept of Irony* in 1841, and this earned him the Master of Arts degree in the area of philosophy that was equivalent to the PhD in other fields at the University of Copenhagen.[57] With degree in hand, Kierkegaard was free formally to begin his life as an author. His authorship, though, would not assume a normal form, for his understanding of his life's work was interlaced with religious and theological commitments that complicated matters significantly. When Kierkegaard reflected closely upon his authorship in 1848, one point he emphasizes is that from the beginning he planned on two concurrent series of publications: one consisting of aesthetic, pseudonymous writings and another consisting of writings that were more devotional in tone and ethical-religious in content. He tells us about his personal story in "The Point of View for My Work as an Author," which he completed in November, 1848. However, he did not publish that piece because he was worried that in doing so people might get the wrong idea, that is, they might get the sense that he was an extraordinary person, which he did not want to present himself as being. So he decided the piece should not be published until after his passing, which it was by his brother Peter in 1859, four years after his death.[58]

The posthumous publication, we learn from the subtitle, is a "Direct Communication." Kierkegaard distinguished between direct and indirect communication, where the former is a more objective way of communicating information with little attention given to how the recipient receives or appropriates the information, and the latter, conversely, is a mode of communicating in which the stress is placed not on the content or "what" of the information so much as on the subjective matter of "how" it is received

---

56. Garff, *Kierkegaard's Muse*, 286–87. Garff here quotes from Kirmmse, *Encounters with Kierkegaard*, 52.

57. Kierkegaard, *Concept of Irony*, xii.

58. Kierkegaard, *Point of View for My Work*.

and appropriated by the recipient, with great care shown to honoring the recipient's freedom. The pseudonymous series of writings offered with Kierkegaard's "left hand" employed more indirect communication, and these therefore were not signed by Kierkegaard, whereas the signed series of writings offered with the author's right hand employed a more direct style of communication. When indirect communication is being used, clarity on the author's intention can be lost; that is why Kierkegaard was convinced that he needed to communicate directly just what his intentions were in relation to his authorship. He wanted his readers to know that all of his writings were marked by a continuity because of being coherently united under a coalescing idea, namely, "the idea of religiousness in reflection."[59] Or as he states at the outset of *The Point of View for My Work as an Author*: "The content, then, of this little book is: what I in truth am as an author, that I am and was a religious author, that my whole authorship pertains to Christianity, to the issue: becoming a Christian."[60] But in his discussion of the issue Kierkegaard opens the door to greater ambiguity having been present than his narrative actually indicates.

Kierkegaard might have known full well from the beginning that his double-series authorship was informed throughout by a religiously guided purpose, or it could be that he only gradually became fully conscious of that purpose over time; but either way, by 1848 Kierkegaard was convinced that Governance or the providential God had been continually at work within his authorship from the very start. A statement in which Kierkegaard seems to be doing his best to honestly account for this tension is the following:

> If I were now to state as categorically definitively as possible Governance's part in the whole work as an author, I know of no expression more descriptive or more decisive than this: It is Governance that has brought me up, and the upbringing is reflected in the writing process. To that extent, then, what was developed earlier, that all the esthetic writing is a deception, proves to be in one sense not entirely true, since this expression concedes a little too much along the line of consciousness. Yet it is not entirely untrue, because I have been conscious during the upbringing, and from the beginning. The process is this: a poetic and philosophic nature is set aside in order to become a Christian. But the unusual thing is that the movement begins concurrently and therefore is a conscious process; one gets to see how it happens; the other does

---

59. *Pap.* X6 B 4:3; Kierkegaard, *Journals and Papers* 6, 6770.
60. Kierkegaard, *Point of View for My Work*, 23.

not commence after a separation of some years from the first. Thus the esthetic writing is surely a deception, yet in another sense a necessary emptying. The religious is decisively present already from the first moment, has decisive predominance, but for a little while waits patiently so that the poet is allowed to talk himself out, yet watching with Argus eyes lest the poet trick it and it all becomes a poet.[61]

Divinity or the Godhead in the form of divine Providence or Governance, Kierkegaard is convinced, has been at work behind his writing process. Søren was maybe pretty invested in the aesthetic while engaged in his aesthetic writings, even if he was slowly being nudged to a stance that was at once becoming more critical of the aesthetic and more open to the Christian. A faint awareness of this progression or upbuilding taking place within him was more the case at the beginning than was a full-blown conscious awareness of the deceptiveness of the aesthetic.

A complex understanding of the relation between his aesthetic and religious writings is present in Kierkegaard's own mind. Helpful insights into this matter come from Carl Hughes's demonstration that the great Danish author's project is a rhetorical one, meaning that his writings "present staging after staging in order to catch readers up in desire," to "solicit an ever more passionate relationship to God," to embrace the theme of longing for the infinite.[62] Hughes rightly contends that for Kierkegaard the dialectical tension between aesthetic and religious concerns runs throughout his authorship. In other words, it is not a matter of aesthetic concerns operating in the aesthetic writings and religious concerns in the religious writings; rather, both concerns are tensively present in both series of writings, for that dialectical tension heightens the rhetorical effect and more effectively brings the reader into the performative action of entering passionately into relation to what I am understanding as divinity nurturing us into the divine.[63] Hughes also underscores Kierkegaard's viewpoint that the religious nature of his writings cannot be objectively demonstrated in advance but "can be perceived only by those who allow themselves to be affected by them"; this emphasis on self-involvement leads to a form of theology that is less interested in seeking to formulate "static doctrinal truths" and more interested in seeking to express "whispers and shadows"

---

61. Kierkegaard, *Point of View for My Work*, 77.
62. Hughes, *Kierkegaard and the Staging of Desire*, 14–15.
63. Hughes, *Kierkegaard and the Staging of Desire*, 17–20.

that move performers to fan the flame of divinity's desire."[64] Putting it into my language, this style of theology allows the participants to be enfolded by divinity as they, full of holy desire and longing, rejuvenate their questing for the infinite and refine their images or construals of the divine.

A crucial ingredient in Søren's telling of his narrative is pen names. Kierkegaard's use of many pseudonyms—such as Johannes de Silentio, Constantine Constantius, Vigilius Haufniensis, Johannes Climacus, Anti-Climacus, to name just a few—strikes us as a bit strange because this practice is not very common in our time. The case was just the opposite in his time. In Kierkegaard's era of Golden Age Denmark and Copenhagen, pseudonym usage was commonplace. Kierkegaard himself took his pseudonyms very seriously. Thus in his personally signed five-page postscript to his pseudonymous *Concluding Unscientific Postscript*, he declares that "in the pseudonymous books there is not a single word by me"; so "therefore, if it should occur to anyone to want to quote a particular passage from the books, it is my wish, my prayer, that he will do me the kindness of citing the respective pseudonymous author's name, not mine."[65] Postmodern scholars have insisted upon taking Kierkegaard at his word, while other eminent scholars such as Jon Stewart argue that pseudonyms were used in the small, close-knit intellectual community of Copenhagen simply as "a common precaution . . . to avoid embarrassment or unnecessary offense," so that it would be a mistake to read too much into them."[66] Here I will be respectful toward the pseudonyms within limits. In reflecting on the relation of pseudonyms to his authorship, the author took care to determine their place, if any, in that focused writing. Kierkegaard makes the case that he necessarily had to use pseudonyms in the aesthetic works because he was a religious person writing as though he were not, so the pen names were required instead of sending them out under his own name as though they represented his views.[67] In like manner, he could not think of publishing his writing on his work as an author under a pseudonym because the whole point of that writing is to communicate his personal narrative about his labors as an author so that it must be a signed writing.

We have already seen evidence of Kierkegaard's interest in and commitment to walking. Kierkegaard, like Aristotle who taught philosophy

64. Hughes, *Kierkegaard and the Staging of Desire*, 20, 14, 16.
65. Kierkegaard, *Concluding Unscientific Postscript*, 1:626–27.
66. Jon Stewart, *Kierkegaard's Relations*, 42.
67. Kierkegaard, *Point of View for My Work*, 86, note.

while walking, was a peripatetic philosopher in the modern era, notorious for regularly making his way down Copenhagen's Strøget, which is still Europe's longest pedestrian street, engaging in long conversations with one person after another that he met. That was why he once said, "I regard the whole of Copenhagen as one great social gathering." In an 1847 letter to his sister-in-law, Sophie Henriette Glahn Kierkegaard, whom he called Jette, wife of Kierkegaard's brother Peter Christian Kierkegaard, eventually to become bishop of Aalborg, Kierkegaard offered counsel on the curative function of walking:

> Above all, do not lose your desire to walk: every day I walk myself into a state of well-being and walk away from every illness; I have walked myself into my best thoughts, and I know of no thought so burdensome that one cannot walk away from it. Even if one were to walk for one's health and it were constantly one station ahead—I would still say: Walk! Besides, it is also apparent that in walking one constantly gets as close to well-being as possible, even if one does not quite reach it—but by sitting still, and the more one sits still, the closer one comes to feeling ill. Health and salvation can be found only in motion . . . Thus, if one just keeps on walking, everything will be all right.[68]

Another snippet from a long 1848 Letter to Janus Lauritz Andreas Kolderup-Rosenvinge, a frequent walking partner, communicates more about Søren and walking: "My view of life is like that of the parson: 'life is a path.' That is why I go walking. As long as I am able to go walking, I fear nothing, not even death. For as long as I am able to go walking I can walk away from everything. When I am unable to go walking, I fear everything, especially life, for when I am unable to go walking, nothing goes well for me."[69] His walks were intrinsically important to him as can be seen from these two quotes. However, they were also dear to him because they provided the opportunity to encounter people and to engage in conversation with them. These conversations fed his imagination and gave him content for creating viewpoints different from his own, which were developed by him and attributed to pseudonyms.

In comparison with Trump's narrative, Kierkegaard's is informed by a more upbeat vision. That vision presents different images and voices and

---

68. Kierkegaard, *Letters and Documents*, Letter 150, from S. Kierkegaard to Henriette Kierkegaard, 214–15.

69. Kierkegaard, *Letters and Documents*, Letter 184, from S. Kierkegaard to J.L.A. Kolderup-Rosenvinge, 255.

viewpoints of how human beings can operate in existence, in the living out of their lives. The narrative of this authorship is addressed most generally to "that single individual," which we have seen had its original reference in Regina but was later cast more inclusively to include a broader field of recipients. In the Christian address "He Was Believed in the World," Kierkegaard writes about telling a story that poses a question to conscience, so that the person addressed has to answer it for her- or himself.[70] The storyteller and the addressee realize that the discourse of the story is not all about the teller; in fact, just the opposite, the questioner comes to disappear as the addressee becomes aware that this question in the deepest sense is all about the relationship this one has with him- or herself, and this is precisely the question of conscience.[71] This question establishes itself so firmly in the person's inner being and gives her no rest until she answers it for herself before the divine.[72]

Kierkegaard's narrativity is not turned in upon itself as Trump's is; it is rather exocentric. It reaches out not to solicit praise of oneself but to challenge individuals to recognize that they possess the capacity for giving shape to their lives. Kierkegaard's authorship, consisting as it does of pseudonymous and signed writings, of indirect and direct communication, constitutes a complex narrative through which divinity can become manifested when and where that single individual is confronted by truth and enters more deeply into existence as stirred by faith.

---

70. Kierkegaard, *Christian Discourses*, 235.
71. Kierkegaard, *Christian Discourses*, 235–36.
72. Kierkegaard, *Christian Discourses*, 235.

2

Interiority or Earnestness

Trump and Trump-World

Second, why might it seem as if divinity, which implants in the human the desire for the divine or God, is not readily discernable in relation to Trump and Trump-world on interiority or earnestness?

Interiority and earnestness point to the ability to take life seriously. One's earnestness sometimes becomes apparent in the case of students by how they engage in their studies. Steve Bannon gave advice to Army Lieutenant General H. R. McMaster prior to his two-hour meeting with Trump at Mar-a-Lago, and it reveals a bit about Trump's earnestness. Bannon told him: "Don't lecture Trump. He doesn't like professors. He doesn't like intellectuals. Trump was a guy who 'never went to class. Never got the syllabus. Never took a note. Never went to lecture. The night before the final, he comes in at midnight from the fraternity house, puts on a cup of coffee, takes your notes, memorizes as much as he can, walks in at 8 in the morning and gets a C. And that's good enough. He's going to be a billionaire.'"[1]

In the case of Trump, we can also consider his earnestness in relation to the church or Christ, Inc. Do we find much earnestness in Donald's relating to the corporate church of Trump-world? For starters, it can be stated that a number of years ago, Trump did give a positive response to the question "Do you believe in God?" His answer was: "Yes. There has to be a

1. Woodward, *Fear*, 86–87.

reason we are here. What are we doing? You know there is an expression: 'Life is what you do while you're waiting to die.' ... There has to be a reason that we're going through this. There has to be a reason for everything. I do believe in God. I think there just has to be something that's far greater than us."[2] If that statement actually represents Donald's view, there seems to be at least a modicum of earnestness being expressed in it.

More recently, though, it's telling that when the question of God and Christianity comes up for Trump, he is quick to make a reference to a very earnest disciple at first hand, one who is very close to him, in fact, he's second in command within the Trump-world corporation. At a National Prayer Week gathering, Trump drew luster to himself from his cozy association with this real, genuine believer, Mike Pence. And Donald is very earnest about just how earnest Mike is in his Christian faith and commitment. In Christ, Incorporated, corporate connections count for something, as Trump miraculously receives pixie dust of earnestness from the wealth of interior earnestness possessed by the saintly Pence. Being a believer at secondhand rather than a believer at firsthand is a better fit for Donald's way of life.

It's somewhat ironic that an important place for Donald Trump is the Chapel in Marble Collegiate Church on Fifth Avenue in New York City. Growing up, his family had prayed there, his marriage to Ivana took place there, he and Marla Maples flirted in the pews of that chapel during their affair and were eventually married there, and Donald's father Fred's funeral was held there with Mayor Rudy Guiliani eulogizing him.[3]

It should not go unnoticed that the pastor of Marble Collegiate Church for much of the time that Donald and his family attended there was none other than the Rev. Norman Vincent Peale, who was one of America's most famous pastors. Trump's first wedding ceremony was conducted by Peale, and his second wedding ceremony to Ms. Maples was officiated by the Rev. Arthur Caliandro, Peale's successor.[4] In the 1950s the Trumps worshiped at First Presbyterian Church in Jamaica, Queens; Donald was confirmed there when he turned 13. Then in the 1960s the family was attracted to Marble College Church, as *New York Times* reporter James Barron explains: "The

2. O'Brien, *TrumpNation*, 209.

3. Fox, *Born Trump*, 86, 105, 148, 159.

4. James Barron, "Overlooked Influences on Donald Trump: A Famous Minister and His Church," *New York Times*, September 5, 2016, https://www.nytimes.com/2016/09/06/nyregion/donald-trump-marble-collegiate-church-norman-vincent-peale.html. I am indebted to Derek Nelson for pointing out this article to me.

Interiority or Earnestness

lure was Dr. Peale, a household name since the publication of the 1952 best seller that transformed 'the power of positive thinking' into a national catchphrase. Today he is remembered for preaching optimism and personal fulfillment, asserting that it was possible to achieve spiritual and material success in life. He himself became a wealthy man who lived on Fifth Avenue opposite the Metropolitan Museum of Art."[5] A cousin of Donald's, the family historian, reports that Donald was very taken by Peale, as was his father. In an interview Donald described Dr. Peale as "a great preacher and a great public speaker" but didn't mention anything about religious beliefs he might have emphasized. Donald indicated that when Peale had concluded a sermon, he felt like he was still hungry to hear more.[6]

Marble Collegiate Church's current senior minister, Dr. Michael B. Brown, when asked about the possible superficiality of Peale's brand of Christianity, "suggested that there were really two Norman Vincent Peales—'Peale the motivator and Peale the pastor'"—and that Dr. Peale's ministry at Marble is often misunderstood because "a lot of the public thinks Peale the pastor was saying the same stuff as Peale the motivator . . . In the motivational speaking world," Dr. Brown added, "he would say, 'You can if you think you can.' In the pulpit, he would quote Philippians 4 and say, 'I can do all things through Christ who strengthens me.'"[7] Barron notes that the presence of Dr. Peale made Marble church "a favorite of business leaders, and he helped influence the way Mr. Trump takes on the world."[8] Norman Vincent Peale was all about the notion of success, so there might be some connection between that teaching and Donald's confession that "everything he does is about winning," about winning and not losing.

Donald, as we are learning, is eager to be recognized and praised, so he likely did not mind his admiration for Dr. Peale being reciprocated, as Barron indicates it was: "In 1983, Dr. Peale sent Mr. Trump a note—shared by the Trump campaign—congratulating him on the opening of Trump Tower. Dr. Peale recalled predicting that 'you were going to be America's greatest builder. You have already arrived at that status,' Dr. Peale wrote, 'and believe me, as your friend, I am very proud of you.'"[9] Later, Dr. Caliandro attempted to get Trump to contribute to a new roof for the church.

---

5. Barron, "Overlooked Influences."
6. Barron, "Overlooked Influences."
7. Barron, "Overlooked Influences."
8. Barron, "Overlooked Influences."
9. Barron, "Overlooked Influences."

Caliandro's son described the situation: "My father is walking down the aisle in the middle of the sanctuary," Paul Caliandro said. "Donald Trump is telling him things to finish the work, do this and this and this. He asks for his financial support, and Donald Trump says: 'I just gave it to you. I saved you $100,000.'"[10]

Emily Jane Fox reports that "Trump didn't mind going to church; . . . But he liked to do his worship in churches that knew they had to worship him a bit, too, in exchange for his presence on Sundays."[11] He didn't want to go to Marla's hillbilly church, as he would tell her, "'If I'm going, I want to go to a church where somebody knows me.'"[12]

Solemn religious holidays can sometimes bring moments of earnestness within people. Some Christians at Christmas time might reflect on celebrating peace on earth and goodwill to all. David Frum informs us: "At 4:46 a.m. on Christmas morning, 2016, Trump tweeted his holiday greeting: a photograph of himself standing in front of a decorated Christmas tree, his fist raised in a gesture of militancy and dominance."[13] For Trump, no occasion is so special that it ought not be co-opted for self-promotional purposes.

In her book *Unhinged*, Omarosa Manigault Newman, a former White House staff assistant, writes of her conversation with Trump when he had to select a Bible for the swearing in portion of his inauguration. He asked her what she thought of him being sworn in on *The Art of the Deal*: he indicated, "*The Art of the Deal* is a bestseller! It's the greatest business book of all time. It's how I'm going to make great deals for the country. Just think how many copies I'd sell—maybe a commemorative inauguration copy!'"[14] She told him the idea was a little too crazy and counseled him not to repeat it to anybody else.[15]

Trump takes himself seriously enough to be self-absorbed, but interiority and earnestness do not seem to be his forte. Republican strategist and extremely witty writer Rick Wilson writes: "Famous nonreader Donald Trump, scanner of headlines, ignorer of summaries, writer of nothing longer than a tweet, has by many accounts never read much of anything

---

10. Barron, "Overlooked Influences."
11. Fox, *Born Trump*, 315.
12. Fox, *Born Trump*.
13. Frum, *Trumpocracy*, 201.
14. Newman, *Unhinged*, 195.
15. Newman, *Unhinged*, 196.

INTERIORITY OR EARNESTNESS

and appears to have absolutely no interior intellectual life."[16] Elsewhere he opines that "Donald Trump has the attention span of a gnat on meth . . . This is a man with a notoriously shallow intellect, and a marked inability to stick to a consistent line of thinking."[17] As journalist Andrew Marantz wrote of Trump in *The New Yorker*, "'Reading documents a lot' is high on the list of activities it's nearly impossible to imagine Trump doing, along with foraging . . . and introspection."[18]

And yet on Trump's unwillingness to engage in reading, there seems to be at least one exception, according to his first wife. David Cay Johnston, in his book *It's Even Worse Than You Think*, writes that Ivana Trump "put into the public record in 1990 that Trump read now and then from a book of Hitler's speeches, which he kept in a cabinet next to their bed."[19] It was determined that "the book was *My New Order*, Hitler's collected speeches," and Johnston adds: "Anyone seeking power and wanting to know how to manipulate people, especially in crowds, would do well to study Hitler's addresses."[20]

It's intriguing and somewhat surprising to learn the degree to which religion's interiority and earnestness have influenced both Vladimir Putin and the Russian Mafia of Trump-world. This influence has had significant impact on Orthodox communities of faith, both within Christianity and Judaism. In assessing these matters, it is very difficult to ascertain the degree to which religious earnestness present within Vladimir's interiority has shaped his actions, for with most of his moves political purposes appear to have also exerted their affect.

First, as regards the religion of Christian Orthodoxy, Putin has become personally involved in it, to one extent or another. Isikoff and Corn report that one monk in particular has gained entrance into Putin's life. Their secret source was a Russian official who has shared information on happenings within Putin's court. They write: "The source claimed that Putin was increasingly being influenced by a telegenic, ultranationalist Orthodox Russian monk, Father Tikhon Shevkunov, whose principal message was that Putin had a divine mission to save Russia from its demise and to

---

16. Wilson, *Everything Trump Touches Dies*, 228.

17. Wilson, *Everything Trump Touches Dies*, 89.

18. Marantz, "How Fox and Friends Rewrites Trump's Reality," *New Yorker*, January 15, 2018, cited in Wilson, *Everything Trump Touches Dies*, 200.

19. Johnston, *It's Even Worse*, 237.

20. Johnston, *It's Even Worse*, 237–38.

defend Christian values against the liberal, secular West. This monk had become a regular at Putin's side, even accompanying him on foreign trips. There had been rumors swirling around the Kremlin that the xenophobic Father Tikhon had become Putin's confessor and, having ushered him into Orthodox faith, was his *dukhovnik*, or godfather. The Russian official depicted the monk as a modern-day Rasputin."[21] The monk has been put into action whenever the moderates seem to be making progress on foreign policy matters in order to offer support to Putin.

President Putin has taken actions that appeal to the conservative Orthodox Church. In June, 2013, he signed a Russian federal law passed by the Russian Duma (the legislative body in the ruling assembly of Russia), to protect children from being exposed to information concerning homosexuality, or more specifically, homonormativity, or materials that present homosexuality as being a norm in society, because such materials go against traditional family values.[22] In March, 2014, Putin gave a speech justifying Russia's military take-over of Ukraine's Crimea, the grabbing of the Black Sea port of Sevastopol, and "Crimea's formal annexation into the Russian Federation—the first seizure of land from another nation in Europe since the end of World War II"; in articulating the justification: "He declared that Crimea represented 'our shared history and pride.' He invoked the spirit of Prince Vladimir the Great, who in the year 988 had been baptized in Khersones, the ancient name for Crimea, giving birth to Christian Russia. 'After a long, hard and exhaustive journey at sea, Crimea and Sevastopol are returning to their home harbor, to the native shores, to the home port, to Russia!' Putin proclaimed."[23] Russian Orthodoxy here joins forces with Russian nationalism and listeners respond with "thunderous applause." In 2016, Vladimir unveiled a giant statue of his namesake, Vladimir the Great, near the Kremlin, honoring him "as one of the founders of the Russian state."[24]

Religion in Russia and Ukraine cannot separate itself from the political-military battle going on between these two countries. After Ukraine gained its political independence from Moscow in 1991, explains *New York*

21. Isikoff and Corn, *Russian Roulette*, 51.
22. Isikoff and Corn, *Russian Roulette*, 9.
23. Isikoff and Corn, *Russian Roulette*, 50.
24. Andrew Higgins, "As Ukraine and Russia Battle Over Orthodoxy, Schism Looms," *New York Times*, December 31, 2018, https://www.nytimes.com/2018/12/31/world/europe/ukraine-russia-orthodox-church-schism.html.

Times reporter Andrew Higgins, "rival churches [with orientations shaped either by Russian or Ukrainian traditions] were often left using the same places of worship on alternate Sundays or different parts of the same building": since the revolution of 2014, the tension between Russia and Ukraine over Orthodoxy has exacerbated, and now, with the movement to form a new, breakaway Orthodox Church of Ukraine having succeeded, the issue of "which group controls which property . . . risks turning into a free-for-all as the new church seeks to assert its authority, aided by the Ukrainian security service and politicians."[25] As the church in Ukraine has broken free from the church in Russia—the process of which began officially in December 2018, with the head of the new autonomous Ukrainian church being chosen—the movement has slowly progressed in shifting allegiance away from the Moscow patriarch. Neil MacFarquhar reports that so many have wanted to sever ties to the Russian Orthodox Church because "the Kremlin has been "using the church as an instrument of its old imperial control": "This has been especially true under President Vladimir V. Putin of Russia, who has maneuvered diligently in recent years to revive the idea that Moscow should be the capital for all Eastern Orthodox Christians, in effect making the Russian church an extension of his efforts to restore the country's superpower status. Mr. Putin bolstered the church both to sell Russia as a bastion of 'traditional values,' and to paint his Kremlin as heir to the holy traditions of the czarist empire."[26]

Critical to gaining autonomy for the Ukrainian church is being granted "autocephaly," a term in the church for "independence." The authority for granting this status resides in the ecumenical patriarch Bartholomew I, the spiritual leader of the Eastern Orthodox Church located in Istanbul, Turkey. According to journalist Carlotta Gall, on January 6, 2019, the eve of the Orthodox Christmas, the new Ukrainian church was granted legitimacy": for that occasion, the newly elected leader, "Metropolitan Epiphanius, traveled to Istanbul to receive an official charter from the Constantinople patriarchate, a longtime rival power center to Moscow."[27] The four-hour ceremony formalized "a split with the Russian church to which it had been

25. Higgins, "Ukraine and Russia Battle."

26. Neil MacFarquhar, "Russia-Ukraine Tensions Set Up the Biggest Christian Schism Since 1054," *New York Times*, October 7, 2018, https://www.nytimes.com/2018/10/07/world/europe/ukraine-russia-orthodox-church.html.

27. Carlotta Gall, "Ukrainian Orthodox Christians Formally Break From Russia," *New York Times*, January 6, 2019, https://www.nytimes.com/2019/01/06/world/europe/orthodox-church-ukraine-russia.html. See also Higgins, "Ukraine and Russia Battle."

tied for more than four centuries, . . . cleaving millions of Ukrainians from the Russian Orthodox Church."[28] For President Petro O. Poroshenko of Ukraine "the occasion was an affirmation of independence from Russian influence in his embattled country," a "guarantee of spiritual freedom," and "the key to social harmony."[29] Patriarch Bartholomew exhorted the new leader of the Ukrainian Orthodox Church "not to exclude any believers from his church, including those loyal to Moscow, and urged him to build bridges and unite the people."[30]

Putin's Moscow had been attempting to prevent this from happening. In an article from October 15, 2018, MacFarquhar indicated that: "The Russian Orthodox Church on Monday moved to sever all ties with the Constantinople Patriarchate, the Orthodox mother church, to protest its moves toward creating an independent church in Ukraine": "The decision taken by the hierarchy of the Russian church barred all its adherents from taking part in rituals like communion, baptism and marriage at any church worldwide controlled by the Patriarchate."[31] Putin, "having promoted himself for years as a defender of Russia's reach as an Orthodox power, also has a keen political interest and desperately wants to keep Ukraine under the wing of the Moscow patriarch."[32] He is doing what he can to bring the Russian Orthodox Church with its traditional values and in all its fullness within the orbit of the old Russian empire. The dominion of the Russian Church has given credibility to Putin's imperial project of portraying "his government as a reincarnation of the old czarist empire," helping to buttress his claim that Russians, regardless of political boundaries, are "still one people, one church and one culture," all belonging to the "Russian world."[33]

The Russian Orthodox Church currently counts about 150 million adherents in its fold, but about one-third of those are in Ukraine; this official split between the two countries decreases the power and prestige of the Moscow-based church. The religious schism between Russians and Ukrainians also points to the possibility of a larger schism within Orthodoxy. In

---

28. Gall, "Ukrainian Orthodox Christians Break."
29. Gall, "Ukrainian Orthodox Christians Break."
30. Gall, "Ukrainian Orthodox Christians Break."
31. Neil MacFarquhar, "Russia Takes Further Step Toward Major Schism in Orthodox Church," *New York Times*, October 15, 2018, https://www.nytimes.com/2018/10/15/world/europe/russia-orthodox-church.html.
32. Higgins, "Ukraine and Russia Battle."
33. MacFarquhar, "Russia-Ukraine Tensions."

1054, Christianity experienced the Great Schism, between the West and the East, as the Eastern Orthodox churches established their center in Constantinople (now Istanbul, Turkey) in parting ways from the Catholic churches of the West centered in Rome. Currently, there are about 300 million within the Eastern Orthodox Church, so one-half of those are in the Russian Orthodox Church. Putin has given the Russian Church strong financial support, has called Moscow "the protector of all Orthodox Christians," "has pushed to make Moscow the capital for all Eastern Orthodox Christians," and agrees with Russian church leaders "that Bartholomew, who is based in Istanbul, has no right to remove the Ukrainian Orthodox Church from under the wing of the Moscow patriarchate without its consent."[34] The Ukrainian church was under Moscow's authority since 1686, when it abandoned allegiance to Constantinople after receiving pressure from Russia.[35] The mother church in Istanbul is down to about 3,000 parishioners in Turkey, which is a predominately Muslim country, so Moscow's political and ecclesial leaders believe "its large number of adherents gives it the right to lead."[36] Now, though, its numerical clout has been diminished by one-third with the Ukrainian loss. In a recent development, Russian ships attacked and seized three Ukraine naval vessels in November, 2018, and twenty-four Ukrainian sailors are still in Russian custody. The United States has offered no words of rebuke against Russia. Since Russia's occupation and annexation of Crimea and invasion of Ukraine, tensions between the neighboring countries have remained high. Despite this most recent victory for Ukrainian Christians, the intimately entangled wars of politics and religion between Russia and Ukraine are not likely to subside soon.

Second, as regards the religion of Jewish Orthodoxy, Putin again has reached out to become involved in their community. Craig Unger underscores how "extraordinarily unusual" this outreach is, given "the long and bitter history of anti-Semitism in Russia": "Even though the 1917 revolution theoretically ended official tsarist policies that persecuted Jews, Stalin instituted anti-Semitic policies that sent tens of thousands of Jews into the gulags and, in the long run, gave birth to the Russian Mafia. But anti-Semitism endured even after the demise of the Soviet Union, and the rise of the Russian Mafia and the new oligarchs, many of whom were Jewish, provided fodder for anti-Semites. As a result, the Russian Mafia was sometimes

---

34. MacFarquhar, "Russia-Ukraine Tensions."

35. Gall, "Ukrainian Orthodox Christians Break."

36. MacFarquhar, "Russia-Ukraine Tensions."

referred to as the Jewish Mafia or the Kosher Nostra."[37] While Putin's rather remarkable open friendliness to Jews is exemplary, it is also the case that he needed to control the key players in his regime, including his oligarchs, and many of them were Jewish, and about one-fourth of the richest 200 people in Russia were Jewish.[38]

Until Putin's rule, the Russian Jewish Congress had been the major Jewish organization in Russia, and its leader, Vladimir Gusinky, besides showing little respect for Putin or Russian oligarchs and gaining the respect of Israel, for a time was acknowledged as the number-one Jew in Russia because of his effectiveness in bringing together leaders of various Jewish groups.[39] In order to gain more influence within the Jewish community, Putin in 1999 recruited two oligarchs who were good friends to create "a new religious community called the Federation of Jewish Communities of Russia" with the purpose being to unite "various Orthodox Jewish communities in Russia through an Orthodox Hasidic sect known as Chabad."[40] Heading up the Federation was "Rabbi Berel Lazar, a leader in the Hasidic movement called Chabad-Lubavitch."[41] Lazar's "parents immigrated to the United States from Europe and became Chabad followers. Lazar was born in Italy, where his parents were sent on a mission by the Lubavitcher Rebbe [a rabbi, especially in the Hasidic sect]. Like them, he also became a Chabad emissary, arriving in the Soviet Union in 1987. Afterward he returned to the United States for a brief period, married and then returned to Moscow to act as the rabbi of the Chabad community there."[42]

Unger informs us further about this Hasidic group: "Founded in the late eighteenth century, the tiny, Brooklyn-based Chabad Lubavitcher movement is a fundamentalist Hasidic sect centered on the teaching of the late Rabbi Menachem Schneerson, who is sometimes called a messiah—*moshiach*—a savior and liberator of the Jewish people. It is antiabortion, views homosexuality as a perversion, and often aligns itself politically with other fundamentalistic groups on the right."[43] One of this group's biggest

---

37. Unger, *House of Trump*, 115.
38. Unger, *House of Trump*, 115.
39. Unger, *House of Trump*, 115–16.
40. Unger, *House of Trump*, 115.
41. Unger, *House of Trump*, 116.
42. Yossi Melman, "No Love Lost," *Haaretz*, December 8, 2005, htts://www.haaretz.com/1.1.4885476.
43. Unger, *House of Trump*, 116.

donors is Charles Kushner, the American real-estate developer and father of Jared Kushner and father-in-law of Ivanka Trump.[44] Rabbi Lazor, the leader of this group, was given Russian citizenship in May of 2000, and he has gained recognition as Putin's rabbi.[45] This reorganization of Jewish Orthodox religion in Russia might have brought some positive elements to the faith, but it surely provided Putin with a restructuring of Jewish "organizations that were loyal to him" and "with a unique way of consolidating power among the oligarchs."[46] Yossi Melan points out that an important "reason for the close ties between the Putin government and FEOR [Federation of Jewish Communities in Russia] lies in the promises made by Leviev [Lev Leviev, the billionaire "King of Diamonds," who is monetarily the largest supporter of Chabad] and Lazor that they would make their connections available to Putin and assist the Kremlin to open doors in the corridors of power in Washington."[47] Those promises have led to direct networks of association between Putin and Donald Trump. Three days before the presidential election of November 2016, "Ivanka and Jared Kushner made a pilgrimage to the grave of the Chabad rebbe Menachem Mendel Schneerson in the old cemetery in Queens, New York . . . Jared and Ivanka reportedly made a special prayer for Ivanka's father there, at the grave of a man whose adherents believed he had not really died, that he was the messiah, a man who had been the leader of a movement that somehow led directly to Vladimir Putin."[48] We encounter the presence of earnestness at work here, but it cannot be discerned that the religious concern is primary and the political secondary.

As concerns Putin, who has both a Russian Orthodox Christian monk as his confessor and a personal Hasidic rabbi, it must be said that he has shown considerable interest in and given support to these two Orthodox religions in Russia. However, Malcolm Nance, for one, is skeptical about the degree of genuine earnestness to be found in Putin. On the one hand, he acknowledges the image: "Putin knew the powerful draw of God in the post-Soviet world. He portrays himself as a man of God quite publicly, often praying in front of television cameras. He put the church on a pedestal"; on the other hand, Nance senses that it's just for the sake of appearances: "it's a

44. Unger, *House of Trump*, 116.
45. Unger, *House of Trump*, 116–17.
46. Unger, *House of Trump*, 117, 159.
47. Melman, "No Love Lost."
48. Unger, *House of Trump*, 260.

portrayal crafted for his own political purposes. Like all autocratic leaders and skilled propagandists, he also likes to produce a constant stream of masculine, macho imagery that portrays him as a virile leader who hunts whales, wrestles with bears, rides motorcycles with biker gangs, scuba dives to rescue antiquities, and plays with tigers . . . usually shirtless."[49] I think Kierkegaard would counsel us to be cautious on judging others and to give the benefit of the doubt where we can. But there does seem to be something short of an authentic "purity of heart" operating in Putin's engagement with religion.

Kierkegaard and Kierkegaard-World

Correspondingly, how is it that divinity or God might be potently present in actuality and discernible according to Kierkegaard and Kierkegaard-world on interiority or earnestness?

Kierkegaard completed writing his major work, *Concluding Unscientific Postscript to Philosophical Fragments*, at the end of 1845 and it was published in February of 1846. His writing career had begun with the publication of *Either/Or* (by the pseudonym Victor Eremita) in 1843, followed by *Fear and Trembling* (by Johannes de Silentio) in 1843, *Repetition* (by Constantin Constantius) in 1843, *The Concept of Anxiety* (by Vigilius Haufniensis) in 1844, *Prefaces* (by Nicolaus Notabene) in 1844, *Philosophical Fragments* (by Johannes Climacus) in 1844, and *Stages on Life's Way* (published by Hilarius Bookbinder and written by William Afham, the Judge, and Frater Taciturnus) in 1845. Beside these pseudonymous writings there were concurrently published the more devotional discourses. Over the course of three years, this was an amazingly productive output. One recalls that in 1844 Kierkegaard had engaged the services of philologist and linguist Israel Levin, both as a copyist and as one who took dictation; Levin was astonished by Kierkegaard's voluminous consumption of extremely strong coffee poured into a cup overflowing with sugar.[50] Between the secretarial assistance and the energy gained from the coffee-sugar surge, Kierkegaard was well-fortified for functioning with fruitful efficacy, but still the level of productivity was exceptional. With the *Postscript*, though, Kierkegaard thought (erroneously) that he would be terminating his work as an author, at least as concerned his pseudonymous writing (thus the

---

49. Nance, *Plot to Destroy Democracy*, 47.
50. Kirmmse, *Encounters with Kierkegaard*, 208.

"Concluding" Unscientific Postscript); and he anticipated taking a pastoral position in a Lutheran congregation (which also did not happen).[51] In the *Postscript* a critique of speculative, scientific philosophy is offered while setting forth a way of thinking that concentrates on the art of existing, which has no need of the professor but only concentrates on the learner (thus the Concluding "Unscientific" Postscript).[52] This work followed up on a theme raised in *Philosophical Fragments*, and Kierkegaard ironically presents *Postscript*, a big book that is five times longer than *Fragments*, as a little P.S. or addendum (thus the Concluding Unscientific "Postscript").[53]

Figure 3: Søren Kierkegaard (1813–1855)

Kierkegaard has Johannes Climacus pen the *Postscript*, but near the end of the book there are a few of passages that strike the discerning reader as possessing an autobiographical quality. If the plan at that time was for this book to bring Kierkegaard's life as an author to an end, it could be that he is here yielding to a deep desire, which he has thus far held at bay, to give public expression to this issue in his formal writing. The issue was his complicated relationship with his father—Michael Pedersen Kierkegaard (1756–1838)—although here, of course, the discussion is conducted at the general level of father and son. Kierkegaard, through Johannes, writes: "If it happened that a father, even the most loving and solicitous father, at the

---

51. Kierkegaard, *Concluding Unscientific Postscript*, 2:xi.
52. Kierkegaard, *Concluding Unscientific Postscript*, 2:ix.
53. Kierkegaard, *Concluding Unscientific Postscript*, 2:ix.

very moment he wanted to do the best for his child, did the worst, did the worst that may have disturbed the child's entire life—should the son, if he remembers the circumstances, therefore drown his piety in the oblivion of indifference or change it into wrath?"[54] The author, then, in deliberating on this question, concludes that, since the father was acting for the purpose of doing the best for the son and not intending him harm, the son will continue to love the father, and, even though he has been made unhappy and becomes despondent over what has happened to him, he will strive not to succumb to despair. In the next paragraph the author makes a parallel case for maintaining an understanding attitude toward and appreciation of Christianity when it has had a similar impact on one's life by bringing unhappiness into one's existence.

Presented is a view that is suspicious of religion foisting its expectations of interiority and earnestness prematurely onto a child instead of waiting until the appropriate age:

> As little as Christianity came into the world in the childhood of humankind rather than in the fullness of time, just as little is Christianity in its decisive form suitable for every age. There are times in life that demand something that Christianity seemingly wants to omit altogether, something that to a person at a certain age appears to be the absolute, although in later life the same person sees its vanity. Christianity cannot be poured into a child, because it always holds true that every human grasps only what he has use for, and the child has no decisive use for Christianity. As Christianity's entrance into the world indicates by what preceded it, the law is continually this: No one begins with being Christian; each one becomes that in the fullness of time—if one becomes that. A strict Christian upbringing in Christianity's decisive categories is a very venturesome undertaking, because Christianity makes men whose strength is in their weakness; but if a child is cowed into Christianity in its totally earnest form, it ordinarily makes a very unhappy youth. The rare exception is a stroke of luck.[55]

There is concern here for exercising sensitivity in how Christianity passes itself on to the next generation. But there is also a concern to express the hurt and pain that has been experienced in this area by the author. Here, the language of abuse in this regard is extended even to words

---

54. Kierkegaard, *Concluding Unscientific Postscript*, 1:589–90.

55. Kierkegaard, *Concluding Unscientific Postscript*, 1:590–91. I have made minor changes to the Hong translation.

communicating the experience of being raped: "If a child is not allowed, as it ought to be, to play innocently with the most holy, if in its existence it is rigorously coerced into decisively Christian qualifications, such a child will suffer a great deal . . . Be it ever so well intentioned, it is rape to coerce the child's existence into the decisive Christian categories, but it is immense obtuseness to say that childhood (literally understood) is the time for really deciding to become a Christian."[56] Is this imaginative writing from the perspective of a pseudonym? I think the language is too powerful to be taken in that way. It appears that Søren himself has undergone and sustained trauma in his early years from the "teachings" he received from his father. Maybe to make sure that this communication of pain has not been left personally unresolved in his life, Kierkegaard ends his *Postscript* with words of gratitude to Governance or the providential activity of divinity in his life and a sentence referring to his father: "After properly having asked for pardon and forgiveness if it appears inappropriate that I speak in this way, although he himself would perhaps find omission of it inappropriate, I want to call to mind, in recollecting gratitude, my deceased father, the man to whom I owe most of all, also with regard to my work."[57] Søren is still able to love the one who brought him much unhappiness.

Figure 4: Michael Pedersen Kierkegaard (1756–1838)

56. Kierkegaard, *Concluding Unscientific Postscript*, 1:601.
57. Kierkegaard, *Concluding Unscientific Postscript*, 1:629.

Like Regine Olsen, Michael Kierkegaard is a major figure in Kierkegaard-world. Stephen Backhouse informs us that Søren Kierkegaard was born into a home of eight other people: "mother Anne (aged forty-five), father Michael (fifty-six), sisters Maren (sixteen), Nicoline (thirteen), and Petrea (eleven) and brothers Søren Michael (seven), Niels Andreas (five), Peter Christian (four)."[58] Over the next twenty-two years six family members died, leaving just father Michael and sons Peter and Søren in the big house at Number 2 Nytorv ("New Square" or "New Market") facing a public square plaza in the center of Copenhagen. Søren's father was convinced that these deaths in the family came at the hand of God's wrath as punishment for misdeeds on his part. The primary indiscretion happened when Michael was a young boy tending sheep in the country, suffering from hunger and exhaustion in freezing cold weather, he cursed God.[59] At the age of twelve, Michael was sent to Copenhagen to work with his uncle who was a wool merchant. He industriously tended to his work, and after years of advancing himself in the clothing business and carefully investing his money, the hosier had become a wealthy businessman. He married a woman who died after two years of marriage, and then he married Anne Lund who had been the maid in the household. At the time of the wedding, Anne was five months pregnant, and this was a second indiscretion seen by the father as meriting vengeance. Michael mean-spiritedly directed Anne to sign a non-disclosure agreement much like the one Donald J. requires in his marriages, which included a pledge to pay an annual salary and housekeeping budget but excluded any inheritance status, although he eventually dropped that contract and treated her with appropriate respect.[60] Anne, who was likely illiterate, would give birth to seven children, five of whom died before they reached the age of thirty-four. She and Michael had a good marriage that lasted thirty-eight years. Interestingly, in all of his thousands of pages of writings, Søren did not once mention his mother. By the age of forty-one, Michael decided to place "his prosperous business in the hands of trustees and live in retirement."[61]

Respected Copenhagen merchant Kierkegaard, though not having received a formal education, was interested in philosophical and theological questions, and he devoted himself to learning what he could about the

---

58. Backhouse, *Kierkegaard*, 43.
59. Garff, *Søren Kierkegaard*, 136–38.
60. Hannay, *Kierkegaard*, 35.
61. Hannay, *Kierkegaard*, 35.

INTERIORITY OR EARNESTNESS

intellectual viewpoints of the day. Son Peter—who was himself a prize student, earned a doctorate in theology in Germany, lectured at the University of Copenhagen, served as a pastor and bishop in the Danish Lutheran Church, and was the "elder brother" that Søren resented being compared to—said about his father, "The most gifted person I have met."[62] Michael loved to engage his sons in debate, and with Søren especially he frequently went on walks of the imagination where they would reconstruct in their minds everything they saw as they made their way down the streets of Copenhagen. These imaginative exercises in creating virtual-reality experiences likely nurtured Søren's capacity for imaginatively creating points of view and personalities of his many pseudonyms. But the guilt-ridden Michael also was into religion. Growing up in a peasant setting, he had participated in a Christian community that stressed religious piety and emotion. Therefore, in the city he was drawn to the Congregation of Moravian Brothers, the *Herrnhuters*, whose message spoke to the feelings in a way directly opposed to that of most of the more liberal and rationalist Lutheran churches.[63] The Kierkegaard family participated in both of these communities on Sundays, attending the Lutheran church service in the morning and the Moravian Brothers gathering in the evening. Jakob Peter Mynster (1775–1854) would eventually become the pastor at the Church of Our Lady in Copenhagen, which the Kierkegaards attended, and Michael came to appreciate him and would converse with him in their home on fine points of theological doctrine, which Søren would sometimes overhear and internalize as a youngster. Michael Kierkegaard died in 1838, leaving Peter and Søren to split a considerable inheritance. The death of his father seems to have motivated Søren to complete his degree in theology, which he had been reluctant to do possibly out of protest against his father.

---

62. Garff, *Søren Kierkegaard*, 14.
63. Hannay, *Kierkegaard*, 37.

Figure 5: Jakob Peter Mynster (1775–1854)

Mynster, actually, is another very significant figure in Kierkegaard-world. He eventually earned a Doctor of Theology degree, participated fully in the intellectual debates of the day, and taught seminary students in the area of psychology. Hannay writes: "The influence of Mynster, perhaps Denmark's most impressive cultural figure at the time, went back to Kierkegaard's childhood and is linked with his relationship to his father."[64] In fact, in his journals, Kierkegaard has more entries centering on Mynster than any other person. Mynster confirmed Søren in 1828 and Michael strongly encouraged Søren to read Mynster's sermons, which he did.

During the early years of his ministry, Mynster had struggled with what he perceived as a gap between what he was preaching and what he was able to believe. In this situation of feeling like being a hypocrite, he experienced a religious breakthrough that was the occasion for his embracing the Christian faith in a fuller way and arriving at a theological position that accorded premier place to the notions of the unconditional nature of conscience, the truthfulness of the Gospel narratives, and the Christ as the living redeemer of human beings in their individuality, including the individual who was Peter

---

64. Hannay, *Kierkegaard*, 8.

Jakob Mynster.[65] Mynster's theology also affirmed divinity or the Godhead as planting within the human a longing, a desire, an urge, or a drive that manifests itself in fear [in the sense of deep respect] and love for the divine; and as the human with its reason and conscience comes to gain knowledge of the divine, the will affirms what is known and the reality of faith emerges.[66] Furthermore, the presuppositions of Mynster's anthropological theology emphasized the "harmony and continuity between revelation and consciousness (reason and conscience)": "The drive is implanted in the human being by God and is therefore the primary expression of the revelation. The drive is a striving in the soul for rest, an urge towards peace . . . Reason and revelation have the same origin in God and therefore cannot lead to different ends. The same thing can be said about conscience [*samvittighed*], which Mynster defines as 'co-knowing [*samviden*] with God.' Reason and conscience jointly form a consciousness about what the revelation says and a knowledge of the duty to yield before it."[67]

While Kierkegaard will come to oppose Mynster because he regards him as advocating a cultural form of Christianity that does not maintain the ideals and rigor of New Testament Christianity, it should be noted that Mynster's emphasis on the presence of the immanent God within the human is shared by Kierkegaard and appears throughout much of Kierkegaard's authorship, in both his signed and pseudonymous writings. Over the years, Kierkegaard would stop in and have discussions with Mynster in his office when he was serving as bishop and the two would present the other with their newly published writings. However, gradually, from Kierkegaard's pespective, Mynster came to stand for all that was bad about the Christian religion as it was being manifested in Lutheran Denmark. Mynster had embraced in an uncritical manner the cultural ways of the modern world and allowed them to eviscerate Christianity of its essential features and leave in its place a Christendom whose cultural religion, while still sharing some external aspects with genuine Christianity, had lost its passion, vitality, and inward earnestness. From Søren's standpoint, this confusing form of religion did the disservice of giving people the impression that they were participating appropriately in their religion, when in actuality they were falling far short of being a Christian disciple in the true sense of the word.

65. Plum, *Jakob Peter Mynster*, 132.
66. Mynster, *Meddelelser om mit Levnet*, 152–54.
67. Tolstrup, "Jakob Peter Mynster," 269.

Trump's Church of Christ, Inc. was present in a different form in Kierkegaard's context. He referred to it as Christendom. It permits a faith that can be lived in the external trappings without interiority, a faith that does not amount to more than habitually going through the prescribed motions without being passionately engaged. Kierkegaard bombastically proclaimed in *An Open Letter*, "I am a hater of 'habitual Christianity.'"[68] Externals can be distracting. Kierkegaard's pseudonym Johannes Climacus states, "the misfortune of the age is to have forgotten what inwardness is."[69] Kierkegaard agrees with Trump that one ought to focus on oneself, but the key for doing that appropriately is inwardness, which his *Postscript's* pseudonym identifies as "The transparency of thought in existence."[70] Penetrating inward and concentrating the mind on earnestness, Kierkegaard thought, is the way to discover important truths.[71] Kierkegaard's pseudonym writes in *The Concept of Anxiety* that interiority or inwardness is basically earnestness,[72] so he surely would agree that inwardness can lead to earnestness. Thus, he wrote in the Christian address mentioned above in chapter 1, "It is the nature of faith to want above all to prevent the error that one can acquire or have faith at second hand."[73] There's no pixie dust in Kierkegaard's Christianity; there's grace that is given, although that grace is to be *used* by the earnest one to empower freedom.[74] And Johannes Climacus in the *Postscript* declares: "There is no stronger expression for inwardness than—to have faith," and faith is holding "fast in the passion of inwardness"—the absurd, which "is that the eternal truth has come into existence in time."[75] Such inwardly earnest faith brings movement and change. Genuine Christianity wants to change everything, whereas Christendom leaves everything the same, yet assumes the label of "Christian."[76]

68. Kierkegaard, *Corsair Affair*, 59.
69. Kierkegaard, *Concluding Unscientific Postscript*, 1:264.
70. Kierkegaard, *Concluding Unscientific Postscript*, 1:255.
71. Kierkegaard, *Either/Or*, 1:174.
72. Kierkegaard, *Concept of Anxiety*, 146.
73. Kierkegaard, *Christian Discourses*, 238.
74. On the use of grace, see Kierkegaard's comment in the Editor's Preface to Kierkegaard, *Practice in Christianity*, 7: "The requirement should be heard . . . so that I might learn not only to resort to *grace*, but to resort to it in relation to the use of *grace*."
75. Kierkegaard, *Concluding Unscientific Postscript*, 1:210.
76. Kierkegaard, *Moment and Late Writings*, 185.

Interiority or Earnestness

Essential in becoming earnest is to do so in relation to the object of earnestness, which is oneself. The inward conception of who one really is—that's earnestness.[77] To think about oneself is not vanity, Kierkegaard warns us in *For Self-Examination*, "when it is a matter of letting God's Word have power over oneself."[78] For "earnestness is precisely this kind of honest distrust of oneself, to treat oneself as a suspicious character," which happens when I promise myself and God that I will not forget to include God in my awareness of my experience.[79] Such earnestness of the inner life is passionate striving in existence by which, as Climacus claims in the *Postscript*, a person rubs the wonderful lamp of freedom and the divine or "God comes into existence for her or him."

A closely-related notion to earnestness needs to be mentioned, even if the attention we can give it is not commensurate with its importance. That is the notion of jest. Just about every discussion Kierkegaard conducts on earnestness eventually gets around to a consideration of jest as a key concept that goes hand-in-hand with earnestness. In a journal entry from 1843, Kierkegaard writes: "Only that which is upbuilding truly united jest and earnestness."[80] In response to the question, Why is jest needed? We are informed, "No one has ever been earnest who has not learned from earnestness that one can also appear too earnest."[81] Jest helps remind the serious person of earnestness that absolutizing oneself as the earnestly serious actualizer of existence can make one insufferable. That is to say, the person who strives to become the most earnest or serious person in the world is most likely the last person with whom most of us would want to spend much time. Earnestness requires jest to humanize it. To jest in the midst of laziness is a poor form of jest or no jest at all, writes the Danish earnest one, but to go with little sleep and to put forth a maximum of energy, so that one is totally spent, and then to recognize that all one's serious, rigorous, dutiful labors in earnestness are merely a jest; that is true jest and true earnestness.[82] Kierkegaard reminds his reader that the Christ, the Word, the prototype, does not want the earnestness to become too deadly, and so he directs our attention to a diversion, the lilies of the field and the birds of the

---

77. Kierkegaard, *Three Discourses on Imagined Occasions*, 58.
78. Kierkegaard, *For Self-Examination*, 36.
79. Kierkegaard, *For Self-Examination*, 44.
80. *Pap.* IV A 80 n.d., 1843; Kierkegaard, *Journals and Papers* 4, 4924.
81. Kierkegaard, *Works of Love*, 340.
82. Kierkegaard, *Concluding Unscientific Postscript*, 1:471–72.

air. Here the earnestness is toned down, almost to a jest, and the one saying it is "so gentle, so divinely gentle."[83] Thus, earnestness is a compound or a composition, in that true earnestness is the unity of jest and earnestness, and in the ancient world Socrates has best shown this.[84] These two need to be held in a dialectical reciprocity, Johannes Climacus maintains.[85] To try to make the case that life's seriousness and earnestness fills up every second, so there is no time for jest, is a bad sign; for "in the midst of life's earnestness there really is and ought to be time to jest."[86] Earnestness that forgets the place of jest in life and in one's self-understanding, becomes unbearable and will be of little assistance in helping to solve the national crisis of our time. We might wish, with Kierkegaard, that "the age were more earnest in its earnestness,"[87] but we don't want to lose our sense of humor about our current condition, for jest or humor is one of the most powerful resources we have for contributing to a solution to the problem.

Interiority or earnestness is a pathway that Kierkegaard believes needs to be traveled in order to become an individual. For him that trip into earnestness leads as well to an encounter with divinity together with a construing of the divine or that ultimate reality which is most important in life. Such inwardness is the recipe for going deeper. This journey-toward-individuality that is taken into inwardness establishes a strong, centered personality that possesses the desire and capacity to operate as an independent figure in relation to the established customs, patterns, principles, and laws of one's socio-political world. Here can be seen the political relevance of inwardness. Going deeper leads to going forward. A genuinely free and independent individual, full of passionate existence and dialectical reflection, does not need to unreflectively capitulate to the crowd or uncritically accept society's deliverance of what is right and wrong, good and bad, proper and improper. Inwardness nurtures emancipation that does not curry favor with the establishment or kowtow to or act in an excessively subservient manner in relation to external authorities. In this regard, there is political relevance present in Kierkegaard's writings and viewpoints, admittedly more latent than explicit, but which can be mined. In this little book that sort of major excavation project cannot be carried out. We will

---

83. Kierkegaard, *For Self-Examination*, 179–80.
84. Kierkegaard, *Stages on Life's Way*, 365–66.
85. Kierkegaard, *Concluding Unscientific Postscript*, 1:71.
86. Kierkegaard, *Eighteen Upbuilding Discourses*, 253.
87. Kierkegaard, *Concept of Irony*, 247.

Interiority or Earnestness

just manage to do a little spade work on the surface of this mother lode,[88] but others have carried out impressive work on this task of identifying a socio-political ideology critique within Kierkegaard's writings.[89]

---

88. Not to be confused with one of Mike Pence's favorite terms—"lodestar" [guiding star].

89. See the writings of Westphal, *Critique of Reason and Society*, Dooley, *Politics of Exodus*, and Backhouse, *Kierkegaard's Critique of Christian Nationalism*.

3

Normativity or Measure

Trump and Trump-World

Third, why might it seem as if divinity, which implants in the human the desire for the divine or God, is not readily discernable in relation to Trump and Trump-world on normativity or measure?

Here we can say that divinity or God doesn't seem to be too close-at-hand. Donald came by his outlaw or outside-the-law behavior rather naturally. His sister, Maryanne, who became a federal judge, says, flatly, about his demeanor as a youngster, "He was a brat."[1] Even today, Trump has not lost his edge in this regard. One consistent feature of Trump's presidency has been his efforts to destroy traditional norms and principles. It's not as though Trump has no standards, but they are largely self-referential. He sees "praise on Fox News, public applause, and laurels given in his presence" as being "his measures of success."[2] Scholars have noticed his interest in other leaders. Stephen Holmes, Professor at New York University School of Law, points out how Trump "seems hell-bent on emulating East Central European attacks on democracy's core norms and institutions."[3] And the sad reality is, the more Trump breaks the rules, the more his base loves him,

---

1. O'Brien, *TrumpNation*, 49.
2. Nance, *Plot to Destroy Democracy*, 31.
3. Holmes, "How Democracies Perish," 406.

as exemplified in his frequently repeated claim that he could go out onto Fifth Avenue and shoot someone, and he'd still be loved.[4]

Distinguished American diplomat Madeleine Albright sees Trump as being "the first anti-democratic president in modern U.S. history," writing: "he flaunts his disdain for democratic institutions, the ideals of equality and social justice, civil discourse, civic virtues, and America itself"; she views him as having become caught up in a herd mentality currently popular in international affairs and "today the herd is heading in a Fascist direction," with which Trump is very comfortable because that's where his dictatorial instincts lead him.[5]

Ginsburg and Huq distinguish two pathways leading away from liberal constitutional democracy, a fast road and a slow one, which they designate respectively as "democratic collapse" and "democratic erosion"; they see the greater risk in our time as being the slow route, "the gradual degradation of democracy."[6] A fast collapse is usually associated with the rise of an authoritarian form of government, while a slow erosion is more ambiguous as the authoritarianism gains strength more deliberately as it co-mingles with vestiges of a democratic operation.[7] Faris, too, warns that we had best remember the real possibility of "'democratic backsliding'—the process of democratic systems gradually becoming less inclusive and democratic rather than disappearing in the gunpowder explosions of a coup."[8] Professor of Law David Strauss of the University of Chicago Law School, likewise, identifies our situation as an emergency to be sure, but he thinks this attack on liberal democratic norms should be characterized as a "slow-motion emergency."[9] This is the same "slow-moving coup" that contemporary prophet Bill Maher has been persistently warning us about since early in Trump's presidency on his HBO political talk show "Real Time" telecasts.

Many of us were very surprised at the result of the presidential election in 2016. In the wake of that shock, a professor of law tweeted an image of three paragraphs from a book published in 1998 by philosophy professor

---

4. Unger, *House of Trump*, 229.
5. Albright, *Fascism*, 246.
6. Ginsburg and Huq, *Constitutional Democracy*, 3.
7. Ginsburg and Huq, *Constitutional Democracy*, 39.
8. Faris, *Time to Fight Dirty*, 25.
9. Strauss, "Law and the Slow-Motion Emergency," 367.

Richard Rorty of the University of Virginia.[10] The book was entitled *Achieving Our Country: Leftist Thought in Twentieth-Century America*. Striking about the paragraphs, very slightly condensed from the original, was how they seemed to anticipate quite accurately what was to happen twenty years later. The tweet was retweeted thousands of times. Here are the three paragraphs.

> [M]embers of labor unions, and unorganized unskilled workers, still sooner or later realize that their government is not even trying to prevent wages from sinking or to prevent jobs from being exported. Around the same time, they will realize that suburban white-collar workers—desperately afraid of being downsized—are not going to let themselves be taxed to provide social benefits for anyone else.
>
> At that point, something will crack. The nonsuburban electorate will decide that the system has failed and start looking around for a strongman to vote for—someone willing to assure them that, once he is elected, the smug bureaucrats, tricky lawyers, overpaid bond salesmen, and postmodernist professors will no longer be calling the shots . . .
>
> One thing that is very likely to happen is that the gains made in the past 40 years by black and brown Americans, and by homosexuals, will be wiped out. Jocular contempt for women will come back into fashion.—All the resentment which badly educated Americans feel about having their manners dictated to them by college graduates will find an outlet.[11]

The words ring true to us, maybe even more so now than two years ago. Rural voters especially, realizing how the American system has failed them, did respond positively to a "strongman," or at least someone who assured them that he was the only one who could save the situation, because he would take on the establishment and drain the swamp. Global economic forces have given access to more people to participate in the capitalistic game, even while the big winners in that game are the few at the top of the corporate world of investment and finance, those few in what the article's author identifies as "the cosmopolitan upper class" who generally have

---

10. For an account and analysis of this event, see the article by Jennifer Senior, "Richard Rorty's 1998 Book Suggested Election 2016 Was Coming," *New York Times*, November 21, 2016, https://www.nytimes.com/2016/11/21/books/richard-rortys-1998-book-suggested-election-2016-was-coming.html. I am indebted to Derek Nelson for drawing my attention to this reference.

11. Rorty, *Achieving Our Country*, 89–90.

little concern about the plight of workers. Furthermore, suburban office workers, many of whose income pattern is close to flatline, are not quick to support measures beneficial to those with less when it means lowering their already meager take-home pay. Rorty's book argues that the left, especially in the academic world, abandoned the issue of economic justice in embracing identity politics that concentrates on the interests and perspectives of particular social groups such as women, ethnic minorities, sexual minorities, etc., and centers politics around the particular concerns of a social group. Rorty's criticism is not that the emergence of identity politics was misplaced but that that legitimate concern was picked up without continuing the other legitimate concern for social justice. The diminishment of that second concern for social justice, together with the commitment to political correctness that became linked to identity politics, has created a void in which populist politicians, such as Donald Trump, have been able to find a receptive audience. As to "whether it was white working-class despair, a racist backlash or terror about the pace of cultural change," author Jennifer Senior wisely concludes that "it seems reasonable to think that all three played a part."[12]

Donald Trump seems to thrive on breaking norms. It should be recognized, however, that the erosion of norms that is so rampant today did not begin with Trump. The key figure who initiated a whole new way of doing business in Congress was Newt Gingrich, the Republican US Representative from Georgia's 6th congressional district, who transformed American politics by slowly convincing his party that to gain power a ruthless politics of warfare was needed. As McCay Coppins wrote about him: "Few figures in modern history have done more than Gingrich to lay the groundwork for Trump's rise. During his two decades in Congress, he pioneered a style of partisan combat—replete with name-calling, conspiracy theories, and strategic obstructionism—that poisoned America's political culture and plunged Washington into permanent devolution—an effort to strip American politics of the civilizing traits it had developed over time and return to its most primal essence."[13] As early as the late 1970s, Gingrich was urging young Republicans to stop being nice and to become nasty, to learn to raise hell, to realize that politics is a cutthroat war for power that calls for less

12. Senior, "Rorty's 1998 book."
13. McCay Coppins, "Newt Gingrich Says You're Welcome," *Atlantic*, November, 2018, https://www.theatlantic.com/magazine/archive/2018/11/newt-gingrich-says-youre-welcome/570832/.

legislating and more dominating of TV news by engaging in outrageous antics and giving the press confrontations, which they like. The new approach had to be revolutionary, with the revolution destroying congressional traditions. As Coppins explains: "Gingrich had a plan. The way he saw it, Republicans would never be able to take back the House as long as they kept compromising with the Democrats out of some high-minded civic desire to keep congressional business humming along. His strategy was to blow up the bipartisan coalitions that were essential to legislating, and then seize on the resulting dysfunction to wage a populist crusade against the institution of Congress itself."[14] Gingrich took it upon himself to train the fresh members of the House in his radical ways, and he slowly won over much of his party, so that in 1995 he was elected Speaker of the House, a position he held for four years. The radical ideology this leader introduced, together with "aversion to comprise, and willingness to obstruct legislation, helped speed the end of the body's traditional 'folkways,'" so that "a new wave of polarization" was poised to impact congressional functioning right up until Trump.[15] Coppins informs us that "the most enduring aspects of Gingrich's speakership would be his tactical innovations": "Determined to keep Republicans in power, Gingrich reoriented the congressional schedule around filling campaign war chests, shortening the official work week to three days so that members had time to dial for dollars. From 1994 to 1998, Republicans raised an unprecedented $1 billion, and ushered in a new era of money in politics."[16] These changes put into place structural dynamics that deepened partisanship.

Of course, Democrats have made their own contributions to this toxic super-partisan manner of relating by which the basic presumption is that the other party members are to be demonized, according to the classic "we-they" mindset: they cannot be trusted, we can only expect the worst from them, and they are not worthy of receiving any goodwill effort on our part. Not all members of each party succumbed to such a deleterious viewpoint, but large enough numbers on both sides have contributed their efforts to make compromise non-existent apart from the most exceptional situations. With that poisonous attitude coming to dominate, especially and most persistently and systematically in the GOP—be it in the form of the Tea Party movement, the disciplined progress-impeding activities of Senate

---

14. Coppins, "Newt Gingrich Says."
15. Levitsky and Ziblatt, *How Democracies Die*, 149.
16. Coppins, "Newt Gingrich Says."

Republican leader Mitch McConnell who has been labeled America's number one obstructionist and has established his legacy as one of the worst obstructionists in congressional history, the theft of the Merrick Garland Supreme Court seat, and the House Freedom Caucus—it should be no surprise that the functioning of Congress has been effectively sabotaged by those "willing to exploit the constitutional order's reliance on informal understandings between political actors—and the absence of those understandings from the Constitution."[17]

Following the 2018 midterm election when Republicans in many states lost power, this toxic posture was put into practice in an attempt to pass legislation limiting the power of newly elected Democratic officeholders. This was the case in Wisconsin, North Carolina, Michigan, and Ohio where unprecedented efforts were successfully taken to undermine incoming Democratic leaders by passing various laws, for example, to limit actions to oversee state voter laws making it more difficult for Americans to vote or to curtail the power of the governor while expanding the powers of the state legislature that remains in Republican control. For instance, "in response to [Democrat] Roy Cooper's narrow win in North Carolina, the Republican legislature attempted to redefine the governor's powers by removing the authority to appoint trustees of the state university, eliminating four-fifths of the office's staff, extending the term of the Republican director of the state elections board, and requiring cabinet appointments to be approved by the state Senate."[18] These approved measures have weakened the democratic process by establishing policies favoring Republicans in future elections. They happened in four key states that Trump won in 2016 and could make a crucial difference in his re-election aspirations in 2020. On a more positive note, there seems to be a growing awareness of and backlash against such political attempts to manipulate the system, especially in the area of voter rights suppression as evidenced by the 2018 midterm election, with seven states passing ballot initiatives making it easier to cast a ballot and harder for partisan legislatures to gerrymander their districts and entrench power. As Sophia Lin Lakin, a staff attorney at the American Civil Liberties Union Voting Rights Project said, "That's really turning

---

17. Faris, *Time to Fight Dirty*, xxii.

18. Ginsburg and Huq, *Constitutional Democracy*, 241. And see Richard Fauset, "North Carolina Governor Signs Law Limiting Successor's Power," *New York Times*, December 16, 2016.

democracy on its head. Voters should be choosing their elected officials, not the other way around."[19]

The words populism or populist are readily used to characterize the views of Donald Trump. Clarifying the meaning of these terms might be helpful. These terms tend to have a negative meaning for us. Madeleine Albright reminds us, though, that "there is nothing inherently biased or intolerant about being a populist," if we accept Merriam-Webster's definition of a populist "as 'a believer in the rights, wisdom, or virtues of the common people.'"[20] Negative connotations attach themselves to these words because they usually point to a division of groups that sets one against the other. We see this in the definition given by historian Michael Kazin, who writes: Populism "is 'a language whose speakers conceive of ordinary people as a noble assemblage not bounded narrowly by class; view their elite opponents as self-serving and undemocratic; and seek to mobilize the former against the latter.'"[21] John Judis contends that a distinctive type of populism developed in the United States in the nineteenth century and then later made its way to Europe; this populist type has embraced the democratic competition for power rather than subverting it, and ever since the Great Recession of the 1920s it has surged.[22] Judis sees this form of populism not as an ideology but as "a political logic—a way of thinking about politics," and it can be defined in terms of right, left, or center, which enables him to regard both Bernie Sanders and Donald Trump as populists of this type.[23]

With politicians of very different stripes being included under the same populist banner, Janis finds it useful to distinguish between leftwing and rightwing populists. He writes: "Leftwing populists champion the people against an elite or an establishment. Theirs is a vertical politics of the bottom and middle arrayed against the top. Rightwing populists champion the people against an elite that they accuse of coddling a third group, which can consist, for instance, of immigrants, Islamists, or African American

---

19. Clark Mindock, "Republicans rush to curb voter rights following trouncing in midterm elections—with major implications for 2020," *Independent*, November 10, 2018, https://www.independent.co.uk/news/world/americas/us-politics/voting-rights-us-elections-midterms-republicans-2020-wisconsin-michigan-north-carolina-ohio-trump-a8673396.html.

20. Albright, *Fascism*, 226.

21. Kazin's definition is from his *The Populist Persuasion*, 1, as quoted in Judis, *Populist Explosion*, 14.

22. Judis, *Populist Explosion*, 14.

23. Judis, *The Populist Explosion*, 14.

militants. Leftwing populism is dyadic, Rightwing populism is triadic. It looks upward, but also down upon an out group."[24]

This distinction applies appropriately to Sanders and Trump. Sanders's populism was dyadic and Trump's is triadic. Judis thinks that rightwing populism in its American and Western versions is "different from an authoritarian conservatism that aims to subvert democracy."[25] Judis published his book in 2016, but I doubt that he would uphold that claim in 2019 as regards Donald Trump's populism; one of the reasons for my book is to ring the alarm concerning Trump's attempts to destroy democracy's principles, norms, and traditions in case anybody has not yet heard that alarm. Of course, Trump, in true populist form, has presented to his people the prevailing political norms "as being at odds with their own hopes, fears and concerns," so that in buying into "a politics that pits the people against an intransigent elite," his base is able to view themselves as becoming "catalysts for political change."[26] Therefore, it is not difficult agreeing with Judis that "Trump supporters fit the profile of middle American populism": for his coalition, constructed as it is around personality rather than substance, Trump became "the voice of middle American radicalism and more broadly of the white Americans who felt left behind by globalization and the shift to a post-industrial economy."[27] It is hoped that Trump's brand of populism continues to live up to one other characteristic of populism, and that is that populists tend to prefer a "personally loyal" staff to a "professionally competent" one, so with their incompetent staff they are ill-equipped for developing an effective strategy for survival.[28]

One of the extremist-related "buzz words" that people encountered in 2016 is "alt-right." The term "alt-right" originated with extremists but increasingly has found its way into the mainstream media. Alt-right is short for "alternative right." This vague term actually encompasses a range of people on the extreme right who reject mainstream conservatism in favor of forms of conservatism that embrace implicit or explicit racism or white supremacy.

Populism of the right-wing variety often has close ties to the alt-right, which, since Donald Trump has endorsed some of their ideas in tweets

24. Judis, *The Populist Explosion*, 15.
25. Judis, *The Populist Explosion*, 15.
26. Judis, *The Populist Explosion*, 16–17.
27. Judis, *The Populist Explosion*, 63, 75–76.
28. Holmes, "How Democracies Perish," 422–23.

and statements, has moved within the media from the extreme right to a more mainstream status. Mike Wendling sees this movement as being "in some ways unlike any other force of modern times": "The alt-right is an incredibly loose set of ideologies held together by what they oppose: feminism, Islam, the Black Lives Matter movement, political correctness, a fuzzy idea they call 'globalism,' and establishment politics of both the left and the right."[29] Its conservatism is usually not of a traditional variety but does generally include latent or manifest racist views or outright claims of white supremacy. In fact, "race is the movement's top obsession," beating out such topics as "gender, anti-feminism, free speech, Western civilization and video gaming"; this is in keeping with "the profoundly anti-egalitarian" character of the movement and its delight in "winning arguments, pointing out logical inconsistencies, and verbally bludgeoning their opponents into submission, which they routinely do online."[30] It is difficult to determine how many are involved in the alt-right because there are no formal organizations with members to be counted. With no metrics available to judge what their impact might be, the tendency is to underestimate their effect; but it should be noted that there are many in positions of power in politics and other areas who are sympathetic to ideas encountered in alt-right materials, even if they would not consider themselves part of the movement.[31] One demographic observation frequently cited about the alt-right that appears to represent sound reasoning is that "its ranks are mostly made up of men," as evidenced by men having "been the overwhelming presence at the handful of protest rallies" held by the movement and that "the movement's few high-profile women appear to be the exceptions that prove the rule."[32] While its message varies, there is agreement on whom the movement is countering. The form of the establishment the movement opposes is that "of academia, the Washington 'swamp,' and influential media leftists, rather than the corporate world and free-market politicians"; and one alt-righter has described the movement as "basically political punk rock: loud, abrasive, hostile, white, back to basics, and fun."[33]

Wendling divides the alt-right movement into two wide-ranging groups: "the so-called 'alt-light' and a harder core. The former group might

29. Wendling, *Alt-Right*, 3.
30. Wendling, *Alt-Right*, 4.
31. Wendling, *Alt-Right*, 5.
32. Wendling, *Alt-Right*, 149.
33. Wendling, *Alt-Right*, 9.

disagree with some of the movement's broader ideas, reject anti-Semitism, begrudgingly admit feminism may have once had a point, and dismiss the influence of extremists . . . The hard core, meanwhile, includes people who are devoted to the idea of ethno-nationalism, and encompasses bloggers and activists who claim to embrace peace, along with real, unironic, and sometimes violent neo-Nazis."[34] Fluidity marks the division between these two groups that have plenty of disagreements with one another while each contributes to the whole: "The alt-light plays down the extremists; the hard core uses the relatively more attractive and 'moderate' wing to draw people further toward its side. The latter group includes an element—small but significant—prepared to use violence to achieve the movement's ends."[35] The first group or the alt-light segment provides the movement's more "acceptable faces," such as Richard Spencer, who has been arguably its most visible leader. With the arrival of Donald Trump on the scene, Spencer was ready "to spin his twenty-first-century version of white nationalism—and a new nationalist ethno-state world order—into something fashionable, edgy and cool."[36] Spencer and his alt-right supporters were elated at Trump's victory because they anticipated it being "a cleansing revolution," the beginning of the end "for globalism, liberalism, political correctness and multicultural democracy."[37] Graeme Wood sees the success of Spencer's white identity politics as related to people's general disenchantment with the complexity and abstractions of government, as he writes: "Government has grown so complicated and abstract that people have come to doubt its abstractions altogether, and swap them for the comforting, visceral truths of power and identity."[38]

Steve Bannon's sponsorship of the alt-right, both as executive editor of Breitbart News, whose site became its primary platform, and as a chief advisor to Donald Trump, whose tweets reinforced some of its ideas, played an important role in its ascendency within the nation, especially among males thirty-nine or younger. Malcolm Nance highlights how Bannon "understood that a large part of America believed immigration, gender equality,

34. Wendling, *Alt-Right*, 11–12.

35. Wendling, *Alt-Right*, 12.

36. Wendling, *Alt-Right*, 1. One can learn much about Richard Spencer and the Alt-Right by reading the fascinating article by Graeme Wood, "His Kampf," *Atlantic*, June, 2017, https://www.theatlantic.com/magazine/archive/2017/06/his-kampf/524505/. Wood was a high-school classmate of Spencer.

37. Wood, "His Kampf."

38. Wood, "His Kampf."

diversity, political correctness, feminism, secularism, trade agreements, and Islam were the greatest threats to the American way of life. He hoped to harness a new power with gamers through Breitbart News. Regarding the gamers, Bannon said, 'These guys, these rootless white males, had monster power.'"[39] The other Steven, White House Senior Policy Advisor Steven Miller, whom Spencer counts as a "follower," had close associations with Spencer while the two were studying at Duke University; Miller disassociates himself from the white nationalist leader, even though nobody in Trump's close, inner circle has influenced Miller more than Spencer on white nationalist xenophobia or fear (leading to hatred) of those who are different and the resulting hardline policies on immigration issues.

In this context another word should be mentioned. That is the word "nationalist." Both before and after his election as president, Donald Trump has shown signs of being a nationalist. His slogan "Make America Great Again" is nationalist. For quite a while, Trump hesitated to use the term "nationalist," likely because of its association with white nationalists and Germany's fascist National Socialists or Nazism, which together with other fascist nationalist movements instigated World Wars I and II. In addition, the America First Committee, formed in September 1940, in anticipation of the US entering into World War II, was our country's premier nationalist, non-interventionist movement opposing entry into the war. Aviator Charles Lindberg, the committee's spokesperson, according to *USA Today's* editorial board, "supported eugenics [or the scientific method of improving the human race by controlled breeding to increase desired human characteristics] and made frequent trips to Hitler's Germany."[40] Trump's nationalism became an issue before the midterm elections in late October of 2018 when he claimed the term in speeches and in interviews.

In our contemporary American context, nationalism is usually joined with another word—"white." When asked about that association, Trump said, rather amazingly, that he had never heard of "white nationalism"; NPR's Ron Evling explains: "White nationalism is generally regarded as the attitude that only Caucasians should be considered part of the American nation, that the racial and even ethnic roots of the Colonial settlers and 19th-century immigrants define the proper meaning of the nation.

39. Nance, *Plot to Destroy America*, 74.

40. The Editorial Board, "Donald Trump's 'America First' nationalism betrays American values, *USA TODAY*, November 25, 2018, https://www.usatoday.com/story/opinion/2018/11/25/donald-trump-america-first-nationalism-betrays-american-values-editorials-debates/2024321002/.

That idea has long been part of the American mix, personified by the Ku Klux Klan and American Nazis but also embraced by other groups both organized and unorganized."[41] Trump's proud claim, "I am a nationalist," "was cheered by former Ku Klux Klan leader David Duke, who tweeted that Trump was really referring to white nationalism."[42] It's no surprise that in November, 2018, when French President Emmanuel Macron warned Trump about the perils of the nationalist label, Donald flaunted his use of the term and suggested that Macron should do the same in relation to the nation of France.[43] Trump's extreme anti-globalist, pro-America views receive criticism because the isolationism accompanying them cuts us off from the allies with whom our associations have proven so valuable in many ways. Such counterpoints made by critics, of course, only adds to Donald's luster for his supporters.

We have seen plenty of Donald the Bully at work over the past three or four years, and we're reminded of George Orwell's suggestion from long ago that the best one-word description of a fascist is "bully."[44] One reporter who traveled with Trump on his campaign remarked to David Frum that "He's the meanest man I've ever met."[45] John Judis also views Trump's nastiness, intemperance, and bigotry as distracting from his anti-establishment message: "Trump was highly personal in his attacks on rivals and bigoted in his characterizations of nationalities and religions and demeaning in his attitude toward women"; and "Trump repeatedly displayed the thin skin of a businessman who treasured his celebrity. At his rallies, he cheered supporters who beat up protestors. And he tried to turn his supporters against the press. Trump's actions reflected a bilious disposition, a meanness borne out of bare-knuckle real estate and casino squabble."[46] It seems that the bully nature is not simply a learned style necessarily adopted from having to perform in competitive settings; it appears to have a deeper source than that.

---

41. Ron Evling, "What Is A Nationalist in The Age Of Trump?" *National Public Radio*, October 24, 2018, https://www.npr.org/2018/10/24/660042653/what-is-a-nationalist-in-the-age-of-trump.

42. Anne Gearan, "Trump Refuses to Acknowledge the Fraught History of Nationalism," *Washington Post*, November 13, 2018, https://www.washingtonpost.com/politics/trump-refuses-to-acknowledge-the-fraught-history-of-nationalism/2018/11/13/35fd0694-e76a-11e8-a939-9469f1166f9d story.html.

43. Gearan, "Trump Refuses Fraught Nationalism."

44. Albright, *Fascism*, 209.

45. Frum, *Trumpocracy*, 72.

46. Judis, *Populist Explosion*, 73–74.

Trump takes great delight in the form of power embodied in strongmen; it seems that's an important ideal functioning for him. He has forced "others around him to lower their standards and abandon their ideals before turning against them when their usefulness ends,"[47] and he has "ripped the conscience out of half of the political spectrum and left a moral void where American conservatism used to be."[48] "The last thing a candidate who respected liberal-democratic norms would say about his partisan opponent is 'lock her up.'"[49] Even more revolting is the palpable glee with which the crowd—his rally participants—shouts out that phrase. His trashing of ethical norms has contributed to further exacerbating the disconnect of many Americans "from ideals that have long inspired and united us."[50]

Normativity in a democracy is present in the rule of law, and there are written and unwritten forms of lawful rules. Noah Feldman, Professor of Law at Harvard Law School, explains that the features of the constitutional tradition that provide protection against a democratic reversal tend not to be "grounded in the fundamental structures of the Constitution as written": rather, "it's the unwritten constitution of the contemporary US—a set of ideas and practices that encompasses political economy, institutional independence, and non-state/nongovernmental institutions—that eases" his mind.[51] The strength of the American political system rests on principles such as freedom and equality, but these principles cannot acquire their legitimate place within the system apart from additional procedural principles that enable them to gain legitimacy. Especially the procedural norms of mutual toleration and institutional forbearance are essential. These unwritten norms, crucial shared codes of conduct, are "the soft guardrails of American democracy, helping it avoid the kind of partisan fight to the death that has destroyed democracies elsewhere in the world,"[52] for these norms "tell politicians how to behave, beyond the bounds of law, to make our institutions function"; therefore, these procedural values need to be respected, because "without them, our democracy would not work."[53]

---

47. Hayden, *Assault on Intelligence*, 215, and see the reference on 277.
48. Frum, *Trumpocracy*, 208,
49. Holmes, "How Democracies Perish, 390–91.
50. Albright, *Fascism*, 241.
51. Feldman, "On 'It Can't Happen Here,'" 173.
52. Levitsky and Ziblatt, *How Democracies Die*, 9.
53. Levitsky and Ziblatt, *How Democracies Die*, 213.

Normativity or Measure

"American exceptionalism" is a phrase that has often been used to distinguish the United States from all other nations as being unique in a positive sense with respect to its strong democracy and degree of personal freedom. Some have even thought that because of its glistening political characteristics the United States is impervious or impregnable to assaults that might assail it. The phrase actually emerged in the 1930s in the sphere of American Communism to "explain the apparent immunity of the United States to proletarian revolutions."[54] Ginsburg and Huq warn that it is "a mistake to think that America is exceptional in the sense of standing aside from the current riptide of democratic backsliding."[55] America's exceptionalism, they claim, resides in the fact that our Constitution has been functioning continuously since 1787, which is unparalleled and thus exceptional; but the noble quality of being old also carries with it the troublesome characteristic of not necessarily reflecting the learning and insights of subsequent years and decades: in other words, the US Constitution "calcifies the mistaken assumptions and prejudices of a long-dead generation ... It is the dearth of new learning in the Constitution's text that makes" the threat of forces currently attacking democracy in our country and other countries both more potent and more urgent to address.[56] This problem of needing to bring the Constitution up-to-date so that its meaning can relate effectively to our new time takes place through interpretation of the highest court, and this becomes very complex and difficult when the Supreme Court is dominated by a rigid originalist judicial view committed to strictly maintaining the original intent of those who drafted the Constitution.

Lawlessness plus greed make for a situation in which a kleptocracy can flourish. Trump "is one by one disabling the federal government's inhibitions against corruption."[57] Corruption amidst White House officials has been rampant. Sadly, as David Frum passionately and remorsefully interprets our situation, "the government of the United States seems to have made common cause with the planet's crooks and dictators against its own ideals—and the spirit of thuggery and dictatorship has entered into the very core of the American state and solemn symbolic oval center of its law and liberty."[58] The Manhattan real estate developer occupying that oval

---

54. Ginsburg and Huq, *Constitutional Democracy*, 4.
55. Ginsburg and Huq, *Constitutional Democracy*, 5.
56. Ginsburg and Huq, *Constitutional Democracy*, 5.
57. Frum, *Trumpocracy*, 65.
58. Levitsky and Ziblatt, *How Democracies Die*, 168.

center, along with those he has enlisted to execute his orders and empower his whims, have operated out of greedy selfishness and thoughtless partisanship, all the while claiming "the symbols of the republic as they subvert its institutions."[59] Peter Schweizer, author of a number of books on political corruption, maintains: "If we are to remain an effective constitutional republic, we must face and win the war on corruption at home."[60] With the results of the midterm election of November 2018 and a new look to the House of Representatives, there is hope that some progress can now maybe be made on this matter.

Kierkegaard and Kierkegaard-World

Correspondingly, how is it that divinity or God might be potently present in actuality and discernible according to Kierkegaard and Kierkegaard-world on normativity or measure?

In addressing the topic of normativity and measure we are considering the place structure plays within life and existence. Such thinkers as the philosopher Plato and the philosophical theologian Paul Tillich held the polar relation between form and dynamics to be an essential feature of reality. Normativity and measure speak to the "form"-side of that relation. In all six topics of our investigation we find great differences between Trump and Kierkegaard, but in delving into this topic we encounter the greatest difference. Commentators speak of Trump operating as an eight-year-old child, meaning that Donald's level of maturity is not very advanced along the scale of personal development. In telling a federal employee to undertake an action that involved breaking the law and then he would pardon him, Trump allowed us to learn much about his overall regard for normativity and measure. His general lawlessness and disrespect for our nation's rule of law are indicators that Trump's disdain for the formal or structural side of the form-dynamics relation, at least in the most significant areas of life, sets him on the other side of a huge chasm from his Danish counterpart. This makes it very difficult in this chapter to identify points of connection between Donald and Søren. For Kierkegaard, the many structures in life are always having their impact. In fact, he speaks of "stages on life's way," and each of these stages is characterized by a particular form or structure providing normativity or measure for the peculiar level of existing taking

59. Levitsky and Ziblatt, *How Democracies Die*, 168.
60. Schweizer, *Secret Empires*, 221.

place within that stage. We don't have full access to a person's interiority or heart, but from outward appearances it seems that Donald Trump has been developmentally challenged when examining his life from a distance through the lens of Kierkegaard's stages.

In his authorship, Kierkegaard differentiates among various stages of existence. The three major stages are the aesthetic, the ethical, and the religious. Donald Trump manifests many characteristics of the aesthetic. Kierkegaard also discusses two border territories situated between these stages: between the aesthetic and the ethical is the boundary area of irony, and between the ethical and religious is the boundary terrain of humor. The *Concluding Unscientific Postscript* most thoroughly examines these stages and border territories and how they relate to one another.

Figure 6: Søren Kierkegaard (1813-1855)

Maybe the most important distinction is between the aesthetic stage of life and the ethical stage. Kierkegaard views these two as establishing a basic either/or in life and he gives a full treatment of these two stages of existing in his *Either/Or*. This distinction is so significant because it demarcates the transition to developing and gaining an actual self. Within the arena of the aesthetic, one is caught up in the immediacy of the moment. One has not yet gained a centered self because one is lost in the deliverances of pleasure or pain that the external world is bringing one's way. In this stage one exists at the mercy of what the next moment delivers. One is embedded fully in the flow of time; one has not acquired autonomy in relation to temporality, for there is not yet an established self that stands in independence over against what is coming one's way in life. There might well be some engagement in reflection, with some thinking about various and sundry possibilities, but this reflection is merely playful and not purposeful. This purposelessness is precisely the problem of the one who exists in the aesthetic stage: this one has not employed the freedom, which is available as an awaiting potentiality, to choose a purpose, a goal, an aim for one's existence. To do that—to use one's freedom to choose a purpose—is to advance to the ethical stage. In making that decision, one gains a self that gives one a relative independence from the world and from time; for the self now is gifted with a continuity of being that transcends each particular moment in its immediacy as a result of the gathering of self that happens in committing oneself to a purpose that is bigger than the moment that it then transcends.

In the ethical stage the self is able to perdure over time, and it is "able to respond" or become "responsible" in relation to the ideal that has come before it with its choice of a particular purpose. That is, if one makes a serious life choice to become a high school teacher of biology, there are ideals and norms that suddenly come into play in one's life, and as these are respected and heeded, they will help to guide the would-be-teacher on her path to becoming a teacher. The particular ethical choices that individuals make are many and varied, but each set of choices in its own way ends up functioning to place the universal ideal of becoming a human being before the individual; and as that individual lives out her or his life in relation to that ideal, she or he progresses toward fuller humanity. No longer is the human being, now as an ethical person with a unique individuality, at the mercy of the pain or pleasure that might be brought by the external world, for personal identity is no longer mired in the moment but is invested in the long haul because of the commitment to a goal that extends from the past into the future. There's a willingness to face the pain of sleeping less in order to excel as a student to earn the degree in biology and actualize the goal of becoming a teacher. An actual self has taken shape and it is intimately tied up with the ideal self that it is committed to seeing come ever more fully into reality over time. There will be setbacks from time to time, but the actual self as ethical is secure that it knows who it is and what it is up to. To have progressed from the aesthetic "self" [or not-yet self] to the ethical self feels good, for it is as though it is now more in sync with reality than when it was seemingly lost in the purposeless existence of the aesthetic mode.

The ethical person also leaves behind the fatalistic viewpoint of the aesthete who assumes the world's external happenings transpire according to the fate of the stars over and above the undertakings of human freedom and action; adopted now is a genuine sense that one's destiny unfolds in relation to how human freedom and action are exercised. We can now understand why, in *Either/Or*, volume 2, we read concerning the aesthetic and the ethical stages: "the esthetic in a person is that by which she spontaneously and immediately is what she is; the ethical is that by which she becomes what she becomes."[61]

While in the aesthetic stage, it is possible to gain relation to the realm of possibilities and to receive a sense for the infinite. To do this is to adopt the big perspective that is the doorway to moving beyond the finite realm of the momentary. This is the experience of irony. Irony conveys to the aesthete the capacity to embrace a new relation to possibilities, to ideals, and to a new form of purposeful existence. But just because one has experienced irony and been exposed to the opportunity for a new life that can come about by choosing to become ethical, does not mean that that choice will be made. The lure of the comfortable mode of existing in the aesthetic stage might continue to win out, as the chance to move to the ethical stage is denied, and irony turns cynical rather than being allowed to mediate advancement to a new stage.

Once one is in the ethical stage, it is possible to move to the next highest stage that is the religious. The border territory facilitating that progression is humor. As with irony, humor brings a broadening of the perspective of the previous stage. As with irony, that more comprehensive viewpoint carries with it a leveling. However, while irony's leveling occurs by way of abstract humanity (abstract in that the ironist keeps it at bay in not adopting it as an ethical ideal), humor's leveling occurs by way of the abstract relationship with God (abstract in that the humorist keeps it at bay in not entering into the relationship).[62] Humor enables the person in the ethical stage to see that the continual ethical striving to become all that one can be, while surely very important, maybe ought not operate as the most important or ultimate matter in life. Humor provides the infinite perspective that relativizes one's ethical exertions by allowing one to step back and recognize that the labors of self-actualization are not all there is to life. Humor opens eyes to see how the human pretentiousness and pride of self-creation

---

61. Kierkegaard, *Either/Or*, 2:178.
62. Kierkegaard, *Concluding Unscientific Postscript*, 1:448n.

can distort and disfigure the dignified desire to become a full human being. With this personal insight that humor is able to deliver, one can understand why Kierkegaard's Johannes Climacus identifies humor as "the incognito of the religious." As with irony, of course, one can become a humorist and gain access to an abstract intellectual comprehension of that next stage of the religious without personally deciding to move into that stage. Making that movement happens by becoming a religious person and committing oneself no longer merely to the ethical ideal but committing oneself, on the one hand, to the religious reality of divinity or the Godhead, as we have been describing the power of creative transformation at work throughout nature or creation, or, on the other hand, to a representation or construal of the divine as manifested in one of the world's religions. Kierkegaard presents the pseudonym Johannes Climacus as such a humorist who has not chosen to exist in the religious stage that he articulates very insightfully.

In the *Postscript*, Johannes distinguishes between Religiousness A and Religiousness B. The first form of religion, Religiousness A, is a religion of immanence, which is so called because its operations occur within the arena of human inwardness. In the context of our discussion, it is the sort of religion that takes shape as a person acknowledges the source of one's deepest desires as centered in divinity or the Godhead residing within one's being. It is the religion that can be accounted for by a full delineation of the multifarious dynamics of a person's relation with divinity or the Godhead as the power of creative transformation that is actively present in one's existence, implanting a desire for the infinite, calling one into a purposeful existence that takes seriously ideals and the normative structure of life, stirring one to love the "power of one's power" [that is, the power of divinity that empowers one's own power] by loving others and oneself. This immanent form of religion of Religiousness A is the form Kierkegaard concentrates on in most—actually about 90 percent—of his authorship.

Johannes Climacus does not suggest that, as an individual moves from one stage of existence to another, the previous stage is left completely behind. The ethical person can still appreciate life's aesthetic dimension. In the movement to the next stage, though, there is a relativizing of the previous stage, as one comes to realize that it is not worthy of one's ultimate allegiance and commitment. There is, however, a progression or an advance in moving to the next stage. That is because the next stage is higher, in the sense that existing in that next stage requires greater passion or pathos than did existing in the previous stage. Passion is the measure of existence (although we will see that, along with passion or emotion, dialectic or reason also is given its place within the human's normative structure). Johannes analyzes Religiousness A from the vantage point of pathos or passion. He devotes about 170 pages to a treatment of three different types or sub-stages of Religiousness A, which he identifies as the initial, the essential, and the decisive expressions of existential pathos. At the risk of a bit of overkill, I will offer a word on each of these sub-stages.

The *initial* expression of existential pathos identifies what it takes to move from the ethical stage into the religious. Required for the transition is: ultimate concern. In Kierkegaard's articulation of it, a person needs to adopt an "absolute orientation (respect) toward the absolute τέλος [goal] expressed through action in the transformation of existence."[63] This is basically insisting that being a participant in religion requires an absolute or unconditional commitment to divinity or to divinity as manifested in the divine, putting no other realities before that ultimate reality. This commitment is to influence one's actions, but the focus is on the action of interiority rather than externality. Occupying oneself properly with the absolute inwardly cannot be accomplished by tending fastidiously to prescribed external actions in a monastic cubbyhole. This is not to say that actions in the world are unimportant, far from it. The task is to relate oneself absolutely to the absolute goal or end and to relate oneself relatively to relative goals or ends. To do one of these or the other is not easy, but it is really difficult to do both of these simultaneously, and that's the task: I am to be committed absolutely to divinity or the divine as my highest or ultimate calling and at the same time to be committed relatively to my secondary or penultimate callings in the world such as family participant, professor, citizen, arts supporter, sports fan, etc. We can see that the ideal or norm involved in Religiousness A's initial expression of existential pathos is more complex and difficult than that of the ethical stage of existence.

The next sub-stage of Religiousness A concentrates on the *essential* expression of existential pathos or passion. If one takes seriously the religious task of relating absolutely to the divine and relatively to worldly endeavors, then one is engaged in a continuous effort of struggling to manage one's life appropriately and this is an ongoing strenuous activity. Kierkegaard's Johannes concludes that the best word to sum up this ongoing strenuous activity is "suffering." The essential expression of existential passion is suffering. The arduous activity required for being in a relationship with the

---

63. Kierkegaard, *Concluding Unscientific Postscript*, 1:387.

divine is an interior action. Therefore, we need to quickly clarify that this suffering is not to be confused with the content assigned to this word by critics of religion who charge it with being masochistic or deriving pleasure from being subjected to physical pain or domination. Neither is this suffering in the sense of physical pain and hardship visited upon someone by external happenings that bring poverty, injury, loss, etc. Rather, this is the suffering involved in the interior activity of continually attempting to undo oneself from engagement in life's immediacy to no avail; this effort at self-transformation via dying to immediacy fails and the result is suffering, or what Johannes designates as self-annihilation or the process of recognizing one's nothingness before the divine. From one perspective, this suffering is negative, but from another it is positive. For through this suffering, the religious person begins to breathe: the inwardness of active passion against one's entanglements in less-than-ultimate concerns is suffering, but this suffering enables the self to gain the appropriate relation to itself which is knowing itself as continually struggling yet failing and therefore as being nothing before the divine. That at once dark-but-bright moment is the essence of Religiousness A. Religion's greatest effort is required, but the sign that one has made the greatest effort is that through it one becomes aware of one's nothingness.[64] The self does not win its transformation, but in and through its suffering it undergoes a transformation. To this position we might ask, does it not undercut human capability? The response would be that there are two difficulties: the first difficulty is to understand that the self is capable of nothing; the second difficulty is to understand that the self *with the divine* is capable of all kinds of things.[65]

The task of existence is to live life forward. Yet, Johannes points out, the investigation seems to be going backward rather than forward. This is because the analysis is going deeper. That backward-movement continues with the *decisive* expression of existential pathos. The essential expression of existential pathos in suffering introduced a distance into the task of the initial expression of existential passion which was relating oneself absolutely to the absolute and relatively to the relative. The distance came in not being able to accomplish the task. In this third and deepest expression of religious passion, the distance is extended even further since now the self comes to recognize its guilt. Guilt-consciousness reaches its height when the self realizes that it is not simply quantitatively guilty, with an indiscretion here

---

64. Kierkegaard, *Concluding Unscientific Postscript*, 1:463–64.
65. Kierkegaard, *Concluding Unscientific Postscript*, 1:486.

and a misdeed there. When one is living one's life before the divine, one becomes aware that a single fault is enough to make one totally, qualitatively, guilty. This is why guilt is the decisive expression of existential passion. In realizing one's status as completely guilty before the divine, one experiences passion of the highest sort within Religiousness A. With this realization, the self has traveled backward and deeply into itself, and this appears as a retrogression or deterioration, but, actually, it is an advance. Johannes writes that "guilt is the most concrete expression of existence," "guilt is the expression for the strongest self-assertion of existence," "the essential consciousness of guilt is the greatest possible immersion in existence;[66] acknowledging guilt is owning one's concrete self and one's need, and therefore it is the highest passion because it indicates a readiness to open oneself to the divine. This represents an advancing forward. Here, though, religion remains that of Religiousness A, since guilt-consciousness still lies essentially within immanence. Within Religiousness A's immanence, the divine or construal of God emerges into ever greater clarity; however, the divine in this stage also is never able to get out from under the shadow of divinity or the Godhead. That changes with Religiousness B, which brings a break from immanence.

The religiousness dealt with up to this point has not yet been specifically Christian. And Johannes clearly states: "Religiousness A must first be present in the individual before there can be any consideration of becoming aware of the dialectical [Religiousness] B."[67] In moving into the Christian stage of religion, a focus on the dialectical or rational, specifically on the paradoxically dialectical, is added to the focus on pathos or passion; as these two are joined together, a new, higher pathos results. The stage of Religiousness B or Christian religion is paradoxical religion because it centers on the paradox expressed in the figure of Jesus as the Christ. A paradox is constituted by two contradictory truths that are both affirmed as being true. Religiousness A featured a dialectic of inward deepening; Religiousness B features a dialectic of paradoxical confrontation in which the customary ways of immanence must humbly yield their incessant striving after the task at hand and acknowledge a transcendent message from outside the self that will bring about a new birth. This message, centered on the Christ, claims that the eternal, which is the opposite of the temporal, has entered into time in the historical figure of Jesus. Rationally, dialectically, this paradox, is an affront, for it cannot be comprehended by the understanding.

---

66. Kierkegaard, *Concluding Unscientific Postscript*, 1:528, 531.
67. Kierkegaard, *Concluding Unscientific Postscript*, 1:556.

But the message asks not that the paradoxical Christ be understood but affirmed in faith. This calls for a new mode of operating for the self: required is "thought-passion" not to understand the paradox "but to understand what it means to break in this way with the understanding and thinking and immanence, in order then to lose the last foothold of immanence, . . . and to exist, situated at the edge of existence, by virtue of the absurd [or that against which one believes]."[68] Religiousness B, then, has reason or the dialectical in second place, in deference to the passion of faith. And we can add, it has divinity too in second place, in deference to the God incarnate in Christ. In this break from immanence, the existing person loses continuity with herself, becomes someone else, in fact, becomes a new creation.[69]

There are numerous ways to tackle the task of interpreting Kierkegaard, and many scholars have found his theory of the stages of existence as a convenient way to do that. Carl Hughes has given this approach an interesting twist by considering these stages not only as forms or structures of existence but as a reference to the theater. He reads Kierkegaard's writings as creating various "stagings" of desire and as employing rhetoric that can be described as "theatrical."[70] He explains that in regarding Kierkegaard's work as theatrical, he is "using the term to evoke the multiplicity of voices, characters, and scenes in his texts—the features that make their meaning impossible to reduce to a set of propositions"; in addition, since effective theater manages to evoke a desire to imitate or represent that which is good and valuable, he argues that Kierkegaard "set out to elicit eros—a spiritual desire"[71] that, I might add, includes a longing to love the other, to love Christ, to love God, and to love love. Huhges makes the case that Kierkegaard does not pit eros-love over against agape-love, but views these two as mutually compatible. I find the interpretation of Kierkegaard offered by Hughes as congenial; it complements nicely the emphasis I have been underscoring on the desire or longing implanted in the human by divinity. A given stage of existence together with its particular constitutive elements of staging facilitate the playing out of a distinctive performance in which desire is given a peculiar form. When the various stages and stagings are considered together, comparisons of the stages become possible and the development of desire is able to be discerned. Measures and criteria at

---

68. Kierkegaard, *Concluding Unscientific Postscript*, 1:569.
69. Kierkegaard, *Concluding Unscientific Postscript*, 1:576.
70. Hughes, *Kierkegaard and the Staging of Desire*, 6.
71. Hughes, *Kierkegaard and the Staging of Desire*, 11.

Normativity or Measure

work in the performance can be ascertained. In that development is seen the education of desire that bears witness to the normative structure of human nature.

A measure can designate, on the one hand, a measuring device or a criterion; on the other hand, it can indicate a goal or a final end, in which case it's synonymous with a purpose or an aim.[72] Kierkegaard is fully aware that the problem with the measure is that the measure with which one measures can be lowered so far that it leads to a dehumanization. That's the issue at the heart of his "attack upon Christendom." He judges his society as being filled with so-called Christians who "are not human beings but are dehumanized to being the public"; and they can have their "religion in an entirely passionless way."[73]

Kierkegaard believes that human beings need to be in a process of becoming if they are going to develop appropriately into full human beings. This becoming or development transpires within the structure of humanity that includes a normative element that needs to be heeded. Kierkegaard's pseudonym Anti-Climacus discusses this normative measure most thoroughly in *The Sickness unto Death*. We learn that the measuring device or criterion of the self can change; and with these changes, the self changes as well. That's because the measure or "criterion of the self is always that directly before which it is a self."[74] "So everything is qualitatively that by which it is measured, and that which is its qualitative criterion" is also the goal of its ethical striving.[75]

Initially the measure is the human; for at that point "the self is within the category of the human self, or the self whose criterion is the human."[76] But then the divine comes into the picture. At that point, Kierkegaard's Anti-Climacus writes, "this self takes on a new quality and qualification by being a self directly before God. This self is no longer the merely human self but is what I, hoping not to be misinterpreted, would call the theological self, the self directly before God. And what infinite reality [*Realitet*] the self

---

72. A useful comment on "measure" is offered in Kierkegaard, *Prefaces*, Supplement: 191n41: "The Danish word *Maal* is ambiguous. On the one hand, it designates a measure, a measuring device, a criterion. On the other hand, it designates a goal, a final end. The latter meaning is synonymous with *Formaal* [purpose] and *Hensigt* [aim]."
73. Kierkegaard, *Moment and Late Writings*, 207–10.
74. Kierkegaard, *Sickness unto Death*, 79.
75. Kierkegaard, *Sickness unto Death*, 79.
76. Kierkegaard, *Sickness unto Death*, 79.

gains by being conscious of existing before God, by becoming a human self whose criterion is God!"[77]

However, Kierkegaard's pseudonym clarifies that this "God is not some externality in the sense that a policeman is."[78] Again, the relational dynamic is key: "the greater the conception of God, the more self there is; the more self, the greater the conception of God."[79] Once the self is existing before the divine, the self is intensified or potentiated in proportion to the quality of its criterion, which means, in the case of the self before the divine, infinite intensification or potentiation; the self that is conscious of existing before the divine becomes "the infinite self," who is also aware of sinning before God or the divine.[80] However, there is one way the infinite self never comes to be like the infinite divine reality: "in forgiving sins."[81] So this self needs to realize that in some areas, it stands in need of divine assistance and of "becoming a nothing in the hand of the 'Helper' for whom all things are possible."[82] Or as Johannes Climacus expresses this religious nihilism in the *Postscript*, religiously, the faithful one is aware every moment of being nothing and being capable of nothing before God or the divine, while at the same time being charged with expressing this existentially.[83]

Sickness articulates a further intensification or potentiation of the self. This comes with the knowledge of Christ, which delivers "a self directly before Christ."[84] We might call this further intensification or potentiation of the self the "Christic self," the self existing before the Christ. Here again, the principle applies: "the greater the conception of Christ, the more self."[85] George Pattison helpfully contends that this further, Christic, potentiation "stimulates the highest development of consciousness and, whereas the category of 'before God' corresponds to thinking of oneself as nothing (i.e. understanding oneself in sinful separation from God) the category of 'before Christ' corresponds to forgiveness, and to self-acceptance."[86] The

---

77. Kierkegaard, *Sickness unto Death*, 79.
78. Kierkegaard, *Sickness unto Death*, 80.
79. Kierkegaard, *Sickness unto Death*, 80.
80. Kierkegaard, *Sickness unto Death*, 80.
81. Kierkegaard, *Sickness unto Death*, 122.
82. Kierkegaard, *Sickness unto Death*, 71.
83. Kierkegaard, *Concluding Unscientific Postscript*, 1:461–62.
84. Kierkegaard, *Sickness unto Death*, 113.
85. Kierkegaard, *Sickness unto Death*, 113–14.
86. Pattison, *Kierkegaard's Upbuilding Discourses*, 204.

self in its nothingness therefore receives affirmation that potentiates its somethingness.

Anti-Climacus explicates an interesting definition of faith: "in relating itself to itself and in willing to be itself, the self rests transparently in the power that established it."[87] The various forms of despair described in *Sickness* can be understood in relation to that definition of faith. When the self has not yet become a self or is lost in the immediacy of aesthetic existence, it suffers the unconscious despair of not being conscious of having a self. When it becomes a self in entering into ethical existence, it can experience either the despair (in weakness) of not willing to be oneself or the despair (in defiance) of willing to be oneself. A new life becomes possible when the advance to the religious is made. In that move, faith is at hand, which brings an awareness of sin or the intensification of despair as one now lives before the divine or God; but faith also brings the resource of a power, the power of divinity or the Godhead now construed as the divine in which the self can now rest transparently. Faith means "that the self in being itself and in willing to be itself rests transparently in God."[88]

These reflections on normativity or measure are at the heart of the corrective Kierkegaard offers in relation to Christendom, and I believe the potentiation of self it calls for is no less relevant for applying to our world of Trump.

---

87. Kierkegaard, *Sickness unto Death*, 14.
88. Kierkegaard, *Sickness unto Death*, 82.

4

Eternality or the Moment

Trump and Trump-World

Fourth, why might it seem as if divinity, which implants in the human the desire for the divine or God, is not readily discernable in relation to Trump and Trump-world on eternality or the moment?

It's safe to say that Trump is the master of the momentary. One tweet is sent to the public, and oftentimes, it's not many moments before another one has taken its place. And when an event takes place that is widely perceived as being a pretty negative moment for Trump, one can expect before long to see the appearance of some sort of distraction that is outlandish enough to draw attention away from the previous bad news. He is very consciously deliberate about this general strategy: "One thing I've learned about the press," he states in *The Art of the Deal*, "is that they're always hungry for a good story, and the more sensational the better . . . The point is that if you are a little different, or a little outrageous, or if you do things that are bold or controversial, the press is going to write about you."[1] A most egregious instance of this is the longest shutdown of the American government in history imposed by Trump's insistent demand that a governmental re-opening package necessarily include an appropriation of over five billion dollars for constructing a wall on the southern border, a form of security that most experts agree is not a good investment of money. The

---

1. Trump with Schwartz, *Art of the Deal*, 56.

record-setting shutdown began in December of 2018 and extended well into 2019. With investigations of Trump and Trump-world intensifying and the increased pressure heating up the temperature, a diversion of topics was needed in the news; therefore, Donald made sure to get the attention shifted away from the scrutinizing of him by keeping alive the story about the shutdown. It might have brought a little relief for him, but at what price? It seems he was untroubled by the devastating effect it had on the lives of federal employees who did not receive their paychecks and on the national security, which he ironically claimed was the reason for the shutdown. Trump's shrewdness in manipulating the media in this way is remarkable, but as master of the moment he has also become its slave.

Conquering the momentary takes its toll on the quality of his rhetoric. "Trumpism exists in the shallow end of the rhetorical pool," writes Wilson in *Everything Trump Touches Dies*.[2] Wilson doesn't accord much credibility to those who "follow a man whose central rhetorical tendency is to berate his opponent with middle-school nicknames."[3] Martha Nussbaum has recently reminded us of Aristotle's insight that "fear responds to rhetoric."[4] That's why Trump gravitates to "apocalyptic, conspiratorial rhetoric": his is a "negative vision, a mental landscape of threats, horrors, imagined enemies, Fox news bogeymen, and other members of his nightmare closet."[5] It's interesting how this rhetoric resonates at a deep level with his followers and affords him the opportunity to engage in his favorite activity of revenge. Trump and Trump-world rhetoric has not learned from the wise words of Shirin Ebodi, Iranian activist who won the Nobel Prize for Peace in 2003 for her efforts to promote democracy and human rights, especially for women and children. She says: "Cruelty to humans begins with cruelty to words."[6]

Another area where Trump's succumbing to the momentary has had devastating consequences is the environment. A summary of damages brought to the environment and to the place of science in governmental decision-making by the Trump Administration could fill this whole book. Here we can only highlight more recent outrageous actions.[7] Aggressive

2. Wilson, *Everything Trump Touches Dies*, 91.
3. Wilson, *Everything Trump Touches Dies*, 92.
4. Nussbaum, *Monarchy of Fear*, 55.
5. Wilson, *Everything Trump Touches Dies*, 88.
6. Cited in Hayden, *Assault on Intelligence*, 222.
7. See Michael Greshko et al., "A running list of how President Trump is changing

efforts at deregulation have led to the revocation of many policies from the Obama era that were intended to curtail climate change and to restrict environmental pollution. In January 2019, according to the *National Geographic's* running list, EPA criminal enforcements hit a 30-year low (likely due to the steep reduction in enforcement staff), an executive order called for sharp logging increases on public lands, and Acting EPA Administrator Andrew Wheeler, former coal lobbyist, was nominated to be the permanent EPA administrator. Wheeler, who follows Scott Pruitt who resigned from the position after intense media scrutiny and numerous ethics scandals, has largely continued the rollback policies of Pruitt. Sarah Gibbens identifies fifteen ways that Trump's administration has changed environmental policies, and her list suggests just how sweeping and devastating these changes are for our air, water, wildlife, public lands, and security and enforcement.[8] The negative effects of these policy changes will be with us for decades, even if we can reverse them after bringing a change in presidential leadership with the 2020 election. Worshiping the momentary to win a short-term monetary gain robs the future of its resources and security.

If one's ultimate reality is one's divinity, then, by all appearances, for Donald Trump we would have to say that divinity is located in money or material wealth. The Bible warns that you cannot serve both God and mammon, but that's assuming they are not one and the same. Rick Wilson again evokes a chuckle with his comment stating: "I'm not entirely sure which doctrinal strain of Christianity . . . Trump represents, but I believe it emerges from the First Church of Greed, Manhattan Synod. Trump's only faith is in himself, and his only God is Mammon. His obsession with money and the trappings of wealth don't exactly scream out that this is a guy who will pass through the eye of a needle, but perhaps I'm just not up on my Prosperity Gospel."[9]

Trump has taken seriously his concern for "upbuilding," but in a different sense from that of Kierkegaard's. Trump's second wife, Marla, was irked by the fact "that Donald cared more about work than his children, and spent far more time concerned with building 'the prettiest buildings all around the world' than nurturing his family within his own home. 'His

---

environmental policy," *National Geographic*, January 17, 2019, https://news.nationalgeographic.com/2017/03/how-trump-is-changing-science-environment/.

8. Sarah Gibbens, "15 ways the Trump administration has changed environmental policies," *National Geographic*, February, 1, 2019, https://www.nationalgeographic.com/environment/2019/02/15-ways-trump-administration-impacted-environment/.

9. Wilson, *Everything Trump Touches Dies*, 61.

main priority is moneymaking and that's where we differ tremendously' she said, continuing with: 'I don't think that's a good life to bring a child up in. I think basic values are much more important. That's something money can't buy.'"[10] Major differences, indeed, so the fact that they divorced is no wonder. Donald has given himself more to building up buildings than being concerned about helping to build up others.

Bob Woodward provides various examples of Trump's allegiance to the almighty dollar. He reports that when asked to sign a sensitive order relating to Libya, President Trump defiantly proclaimed that he wasn't going to sign it: "The United States should be getting oil. The generals aren't sufficiently focused on getting or making money. They don't understand what our objectives should be and they have the United States engaged in all the wrong ways."[11]

Trump was obsessed "with the United States paying for the defense of others in Asia, the Middle East and NATO."[12] Trump's protests all centered around money: "But we're losing so much money in trade with South Korea, China and others."[13] "'Other countries . . . who've agreed to do security things for us only do it because they're taking so much of our money . . . We're spending massive amounts for very rich countries who aren't burden sharing . . . I think we could be so rich, . . . if we weren't stupid. We're being played [as] suckers.'"[14]

In discussing our relation with South Korea as an ally, Trump couldn't understand its value. All he could see was that we spend billions of dollars in that setting and have 28,000 troops there. Trump marched out of the meeting after commanding that we need to bring all the troops home. Rex Tillerson was upset over the way Trump berated the generals in the meeting. He also thought "the president was speaking as if the U.S. military was a mercenary force for hire. If a country wouldn't pay us to be there, then we didn't want to be there. As if there were no American interests in forging and keeping a peaceful world order, as if the American organizing principle was money."[15] For Donald, his self-understanding is intimately linked to

---

10. Fox, *Born Trump*, 323.
11. Woodward, *Fear*, 230.
12. Woodward, *Fear*, 305.
13. Woodward, *Fear*, 306.
14. Woodward, *Fear*, 306–7.
15. Woodward, *Fear*, 224.

his understanding of power and money, and this precludes him from being able to appreciate the larger picture.

Two other figures in Trump-world who are also apparently preoccupied with the unremitting pursuit of money and power are Ivanka and Jared Kushner. In fact, Timothy L. O'Brien explained in an interview that he gave the couple the single, powerful nickname "Javanka," because he thinks "of it as shorthand for the joint—and relatively unchecked—power they wield in the Trump White House given their proximity to the president and the financial and familial ties that they share with him."[16] Vicky Ward, who refers to the couple as "America's prince and princess," describes them as well-mannered, self-controlled, and greatly concerned about appearance, but with "a toxic mix of arrogance and ignorance" beneath the polish.[17] When each assumed strategic positions within Trump's inner circle in the White House, many were hopeful they would be able to moderate some of Trump's extreme actions. It seems that their track record on that front has not been great. That's maybe because other concerns, such as furthering respectively Ivanka's brand and Jared's Kushner Empire, are more important for them. That's maybe also why General John Kelly, Trump's former Chief of Staff, remarked in a private conversation that "Jared and Ivanka are just playing at government," which most people find offensive.[18]

Ward notes that Ivanka has designs on becoming "the most powerful woman in the world": "Not long after her father plopped down behind his desk in the Oval Office, she had started her unofficial campaign to become the first Selfie President."[19] Jared, on the other hand, who has major issues with transparency that has gotten him repeatedly into trouble, has managed to dodge many "lethal bullets": "investigations asking about his meetings with Russians, which he omitted from his security clearance forms; misuse of a personal email account; criminal questions about the firing of James Comey, in which he played a critical role; ethics questions about his limited divestiture; ethics questions about loans to Kushner Companies; questions about Kushner Companies' alleged misuse of the EB-5 visa program. His secretive bromance with the crown prince of Saudi Arabia,"

---

16. Benjamin Freed, "Javanka is the Perfect Celebrity Nickname for Our Strange Era," *Washingtonian*, March 7, 2017, https://www.washingtonian.com/2017/03/07/regarding-javanka-the-celebrity-couple-name-of-our-strange-era/.

17. Ward, *Kushner, Inc.*, 55, 57.

18. Ward, *Kushner, Inc.*, 180.

19. Ward, *Kushner, Inc.*, 236–37.

who the CIA concluded "had ordered the brutal murder of journalist Jamal Khashoggi."[20] Ward believes that, in spite of difficulties to be faced, "the future looks bright for Javanka."[21]

We see that the theme of money is big for Trump and Trump-world, and it is also big for discerning the actual nature of the relationship between Trump and his campaign and Russia. While Special Counsel Mueller chose not to "follow the money" in investigating Russia's interference in the 2016 election, much can and will be learned as congressional investigations take seriously this admonition. It can be instructive, therefore, to do a comparison of the place of money in the lives of two people—Putin and Trump. In chapter 2 we already counted Vladimir Putin as one of the most important people in Trump-world, and we can here add that Donald Trump is one of the most important people in Putin-world; furthermore, it is fascinating how their journeys on the road to gaining greater and greater power and money share similar features and then are joined as these two come to be rather intimately interrelated. Our wise guides for carrying out a comparative analysis of these two money-seekers are two quality scholars. The first is Craig Unger, whose book *House of Trump, House of Putin: The Untold Story of Donald Trump and the Russian Mafia* presents a compelling, well-researched and well-documented account of these two and their relationship. The second, on the Putin side, is Russian studies expert Karen Dawisha, whose book, *Putin's Kleptocracy: Who Owns Russia?* offers much insight as well.

Vladimir Putin was born in 1952 into a family of modest means but with some ties to governmental officials: his paternal grandfather had been a cook for both Lenin and Stalin in Moscow, and this, along with reading spy stories, evidently provided Vladimir with enough knowledge about how things worked in Russia for him early on to want to join the KGB and become a Soviet spy.[22] He picked up judo and learned much from numerous coaches, including coming to view the sport as a philosophy that taught respect for one's elders and opponents.[23] One of his coaches was a mobster, a key figure in a St. Petersburg (formerly Leningrad) criminal gang known

20. Ward, *Kushner, Inc.*, 237.
21. Ward, *Kushner, Inc.*, 238.
22. Unger, *House of Trump*, 67 and A. C. Grimes, "How Vladimir Putin went from poor kid to president, *Grunge*, September 25, 2017, updated, October, 22, 2018, https://www.grunge.com/87531/vladimir-putin-went-poor-kid-president/.
23. Grimes, "How Putin Rose to President" and Unger, *House of Trump*, 68.

for its heroin smuggling; Putin, while still in his mid-teens, encountered at his judo workouts "a world that was a precursor to the kleptocracy he later created."[24] Unger claims that it was at the Trud athletic club "where Putin met the men to whom he has been forever loyal," and this club "was to Putin as Manhattan's boardrooms and back rooms were to Trump: the place where they met the men who built them and gave them power."[25]

Putin joined the KGB in 1975 after earning his law degree, went to spy school in Moscow in 1984 after a number of dreary assignments in Leningrad, and in Moscow "became a great proponent of the use of 'active measures,' including disinformation, both within Russia and abroad, by disseminating conflicting accounts of events to create the impression that there are no reliable facts."[26] Dawisha informs us that during the final days of the Soviet Union, control over a vast amount of foreign money dropped into the hands of KGB agents with access to these accounts; and when national assets became available for sale inside the country, that money was used by those controlling it to invest in purchases: "By the early 1990s KGB veterans who knew the details of these accounts needed like-minded officials in key positions who could help control who would get to invest in Russia and who would not. For this they found willing allies among the KGB and Party veterans who flooded into the new cooperative movement," and among them was the "junior KGB official Vladimir Putin."[27] This positioned Putin for being able to begin to create an elaborate kleptocratic tribute system in which, eventually, all participants in it would be obliged to recognize his authority, with loyalty being rewarded, and disloyalty being punished.[28] In March 1991, after Soviet republics split off from the USSR, "600 companies run by 'retired' KGB officers, often as joint ventures in the Baltics or Israel," were launched; these companies "were to function as real companies, as major corporations, to make money, to finance operations against the West, to launder money, and to gain intelligence that could be used against the West."[29]

After the fall of the Wall, Putin had returned to Leningrad, worked with the KGB, and took an administrative post at Leningrad State University

24. Unger, *House of Trump*, 68.
25. Unger, *House of Trump*, 69.
26. Unger, *House of Trump*, 70.
27. Dawisha, *Putin's Kleptocracy*, 16.
28. Dawisha, *Putin's Kleptocracy*, 36.
29. Unger, *House of Trump*, 71.

Eternality or the Moment

(where he had earned his law degree) as a cover for his KGB work.[30] One of his former law professors became mayor of Leningrad (the second-largest city in Russia) and needed to appoint as an assistant a KGB officer who was not well-known, and he selected the low-profile Putin as his deputy mayor and chair of the External Affairs Committee with "the mandate of encouraging, regulating, and licensing foreign investment in huge formerly state-owned enterprises."[31] Charged with overseeing how goods were put into stores, "Putin had acquired the power to determine who could become wealthy" and in his new position—according to a commission chair investigating missing food imports—he "'made a killing by signing export licenses, despite lacking the authority to do so, for various companies'" and "'he doled out more than $120 million in goods to highly suspect people—and the city received nothing in return.'"[32] During his five years as deputy mayor, Putin made between 60 to 70 trips to Finland, where in Turku he evidently nurtured close ties to organized crime.[33]

In this "Wild West" setting, Mafia gangs stepped in to provide "protection" to various players in the system; these "criminals needed export licenses, tax exemptions, below-market-rate loans, business visas, and freedom from prosecution and their crimes," and all this could be obtained from Putin and his corrupt subordinates.[34] In this context Putin controlled the movement of money internationally, and he established closer ties with Mafia leaders, to whom he handed over control of companies in exchange for help in regulating "the airport, the seaport, rail stations, and various other choke points through which flowed 20 percent of all Russian imports and exports."[35]

By 1994, with the Russian economy in difficulty, a plan was adopted for Russian banks to lend "the government money in exchange for temporary stakes in the state-owned companies that were to be auctioned off": however, no genuine auctions took place, as the banks organizing the auctions ended up winning them, "usually at only a fraction over the

---

30. Unger, *House of Trump*, 72.
31. Unger, *House of Trump*, 72–74.
32. Unger, *House of Trump*, 74.
33. Dawisha, *Putin's Kleptocracy*, 105. Dawisha notes that Putin chose to travel abroad when he had something important to communicate, because anywhere inside Russia there was always the fear of being bugged. Dawisha, *Putin's Kleptocracy*, 105.
34. Unger, *House of Trump*, 74.
35. Unger, *House of Trump*, 74–75.

minimum bid."[36] As a result, the huge companies went to those rich investors who would become richer. This is how, according to Professor Marshall Goldman, Mikhail Khodorkovsky became the richest of the oligarchs, by obtaining "a 78 percent share of ownership in Yukos [the oil and gas giant] worth about $5 billion, for a mere $310 million, and how Boris Berezovsky got Sibneft, another oil giant, worth $3 billion, for about $100 million."[37] Utility companies and others were disseminated in this way, and "natural resources such as oil, iron, and steel, and aluminum; high-tech arms; airline industries; diamond mines; and most of Russia's banking system went for next to nothing"; in total, 150 state-owned Russian companies were privatized for just $12 billion, and this gave birth to Putin's kleptocracy, which would be "an era of unimaginable corruption and greed."[38]

With corruption now permeating the system of "a Mafia state run by a kleptocrat who ruled over a web of crooked patronage networks," the money soon began to flow and friends did well, becoming billionaires, as did those who remained loyal to him over time.[39] In the 1990s, criminal activity in Russia was rampant, and Putin managed to get things done in St. Petersburg because his practical approach to the criminal world found him making illegal activity legal and using the global mafia because "it could move money, it could hide money, and in any case, some of that money would come back to St. Petersburg for investment."[40] Putin's scandalous tenure as deputy mayor was investigated for many of his corrupt activities, but they were essentially whitewashed; Vladimir had become a person of enormous wealth.[41] Putin, who had contacts in Moscow, was ready in this time of continuing political volatility for a move to center stage; that happened when in 1996, with St. Petersburg's mayor losing his reelection bid and Vladimir thereby losing his deputy position, he was invited to Moscow to be a deputy to Boris Yeltsin's chief of staff.[42]

---

36. Unger, *House of Trump*, 75.

37. Marshall I. Goldman, "Putin and the Oligarchs," *New York Times*, November 23, 2004, http://courses.wcupa.edu/rbove/eco342/040compecon/Soviet/Russia/041123olig.txt.

38. Unger, *House of Trump*, 76.

39. Unger, *House of Trump*, 76–77.

40. Dawisha, *Putin's Kleptocracy*, 157–58.

41. Unger, *House of Trump*, 77–78.

42. Unger, *House of Trump*, 95.

Once in Moscow, Putin soon gained a job overseeing hundreds of properties, was then promoted to deputy chief of staff in the presidential administration, and before long was given authority to investigate abuses in government spending: as lead investigator, he attacked his enemies and whitewashed and protected potential allies, taking "disciplinary action against hundreds of officials."[43] Putin was "a highly disciplined model of discretion," with his written reports being "a model of clarity"; thus, he was chosen over many to lead "a complete overhaul of the Russian security apparatus."[44] Dawisha summarizes Putin's new opportunity in heading up the FSB (formerly called the KGB): "Putin used his time at the FSB to completely restructure the agency and bring in his cohort of KGB classmates from Petersburg, ... who would help support his ascendency, while at the same time promoting their own. Specifically two key agencies within the FSB were eliminated by Putin ... These were the agencies charged with investigation of high-level economic crimes, such as those surrounding the oligarchs [and Putin and his associates] ... These two directorates were replaced with six new ones, filled with Putin loyalists from Petersburg"; and during this time Putin worked "actively with the long-time veterans" to ensure that he maintained "the support of the former senior KGB leadership."[45]

Putin secured his power and by 1999 had been appointed acting prime minister of Russia. Then, a series of large explosions left people in Moscow and the surrounding area full of fear; Putin appeared on national television to soothe and console them by convincing them that he would deal with these foreign terrorists, and a national hero was born.[46] But then, after "terrorists" were caught on video bringing explosives into another large building to bomb it, journalists determined the perpetrators were actually an elite team from the FSB; over three hundred Russians had been killed in the various bombings, and this was all an inside "operation that enabled Putin to consolidate power."[47] Fortunately for Putin, few Russians were cognizant of what really happened, so the newly appointed prime minister "won popularity overnight."[48] Perceived as utilizing "a strong hand

43. Unger, *House of Trump*, 96.
44. Unger, *House of Trump*, 96–97.
45. Dawisha, *Putin's Kleptocracy*, 183–84.
46. Unger, *House of Trump*, 102–3.
47. Unger, *House of Trump*, 103.
48. Unger, *House of Trump*, 103.

in handling crises," Putin strategically and happily filled the people's "longing for an energetic and steadfast leader"; thus, in his "Millennial Address" of December 1999, "Putin called for the country to rally around a unified state to prevent Russia from becoming a 'third tier country. Everything now depends entirely on our own ability to recognize the level of danger, to unify and rally ourselves and get ourselves ready for prolonged and difficult labor.'"[49] Two days later, Putin would be appointed acting president by Boris Yeltsin after he resigned.

Now the most powerful person in Russia, Putin moved ahead to enable "the Russian Mafia to participate in multibillion-dollar trade deals that appeared, on the surface, to be entirely legitimate."[50] The scam involved creating hidden intermediary companies, with lack of clarity on their owners and their roles, to facilitate the redirecting of funds in "the lucrative Ukraine energy trade": gas "transferred by Moscow to Ukraine at low, low prices to various oligarchs," could be immediately resold "at market prices in Europe" and the difference could be pocketed.[51] One oligarch reported, according to Wagstyl and Warner, that in 2001 "it was impossible to approach a government official for any reason without also meeting with an organized crime member at the same time."[52] A distinguishing feature of Putin's rule has been "the capture of the state and its financial reserves by the cronies around Putin," which created an enormous "system that spans eleven time zones," with this system being assured of success because in this kleptocracy the state nationalizes the risk but privatizes the reward."[53] The one major requirement is for the oligarchs to remain loyal to Putin, who is the final arbiter and decision-maker of any issues that might arise. Through this system of reciprocal relating, Vladimir Putin has become tremendously wealthy, wealthy enough to be considered the world's richest person, with some suggesting his hidden wealth possibly approaches $200 billion.[54] This figure is a bit misleading, though, for although his greed has placed in his possession "over twenty official residences, fifty-eight planes,

---

49. Dawisha, *Putin's Kleptocracy*, 223.

50. Unger, *House of Trump*, 110.

51. Unger, *House of Trump*, 110.

52. Stefan Wagstyl and Tom Warner, "Gazpron's Secretive Ukrainian Partner Tells of Lone Struggle to Build Business," *Financial Times*, April 28, 2006, as cited in Unger, *House of Trump*, 111.

53. Dawisha, *Putin's Kleptocracy*, 331–32, 12.

54. Unger, *House of Trump*, 19.

and four yachts," most all of these items do not technically belong to him, but to the state, and when and if he leaves office, they will be left behind; he will, nevertheless, likely be able to take with him his collection of watches that is worth $700,000.[55]

Putin's kleptocracy or government ruled by thieves takes on a distinctive shape. In developing it, he utilized a secret weapon. Whereas many political leaders in our American tradition crack down on crime and attempt to snuff it out, Putin co-opted crime, weaponized it, with Russian gangsters becoming, essentially, Putin's enforcers, so that today the Mafia functions as "one of the branches of the Russian government": since gaining power "as prime minister in 1999 and then as president in 2000, Putin's greatest triumph is his extraordinary command over a Mafia state, a political system, that is effectively a government of, by, and for organized crime."[56] Experts estimate that annual bribery costs in Russia run well over $300 billion.[57] In some superficial ways the Russian people have benefited from the orderliness of Russia's governance; however, as a result of Putin's greedy kleptocracy, billions of dollars "that ordinarily would have been spent on education, transportation, health care and other services in Russia . . . have been stashed in offshore bank accounts, hedge funds, and luxury condos for Putin and his cronies who were allowed to make billions through drug trafficking, extortion, elaborate financial schemes, the sex trade, arms deals, and the like with just one fundamental condition: they work within Putin's rules to further his strategic goals."[58] For those who have been left behind in the country, with 35 percent of the nation's total wealth being owned by one hundred ten billionaires, the gap between the rich and the poor is among the greatest in the world.[59]

We have seen that as republics split off from the USSR, a large amount of money was stolen from the country and ended up in the hands of oligarchs in the kleptocracy established under Putin's crafty leadership. Donald Trump ends up benefiting tremendously from that situation, but background is needed to appreciate just how that happened.

---

55. Dawisha, *Putin's Kleptocracy*, 10.
56. Unger, *House of Trump*, 18.
57. Dawisha, *Putin's Kleptocracy*, 3.
58. Unger, *House of Trump*, 19.
59. Dawisha, *Putin's Kleptocracy*, 350.

Trump's family had relations with organized crime in New York City dating back three generations.[60] Fred Trump, Donald's father, was engaged in real estate projects that were tainted by scandal and often led to federal hearings and investigations over allegations of such charges as defrauding veterans in rental agreements and racist renting practices.[61] In a congressional hearing investigating fraud in the Federal Housing Administration, Fred "testified in Washington that he had brought on a brick contractor named William Tomasello as a minority partner in the Beach Haven venture [one of his two big Brooklyn housing projects, along with Shore Haven]. According to federal investigators, Tomasello had extensive organized-crime ties . . . [Fred indicated that] Tomasello was a ready source of construction funds at a time when Fred said he couldn't secure them elsewhere."[62] Through his real estate investments, Fred became wealthy, and while "in high school at New York Military Academy, Donald was so obsessed with money that he bragged about his father's wealth—he pegged it at $30 million—and boasted that it doubled every year."[63] Donald learned the real estate game by working with his father—running errands, hosing down construction sites, and collecting coins from the laundry rooms at the seven high-rises his father called Trump Village."[64] A few years later when he began his own career, he was comfortable in his surroundings, with an awareness of all the different players he needed to relate to in order to succeed, including those with mob associations. Assisting him in making his way to the top was his lawyer, Roy Cohn, who had gained a reputation as "a walking advertisement for every form of graft, the best-known fixer in New York": Cohn was so adept at what he did that Donald sometimes called him fifteen to twenty times a day for help on whatever the issue might be, and later in the oval office, President Trump has been heard to say, "Where's my Roy Cohn?"[65] Donald internalized and adopted as his own Cohn's credo: "Always attack. Never apologize. Attack. Attack. Attack."[66] As Donald continued his father's real estate business in Manhattan in the 1980s and 1990s, he "collaborated with a variety of unsavory players," such as crooked union officials" and

60. Unger, *House of Trump*, 20.
61. Unger, *House of Trump*, 21.
62. O'Brien, *TrumpNation*, 45.
63. Unger, *House of Trump*, 22.
64. Unger, *House of Trump*, 22.
65. Unger, *House of Trump*, 24–25.
66. Unger, *House of Trump*, 24.

"Mafia bosses and wise guys": his casino empire in Atlantic City began "by leasing property owned by two mob associates," and his relationship with Russsia-born Felix Sater, in particular, connected him more closely both to members of other assorted Mafia crime families and to individuals in the Russian mob syndicate.[67]

For over forty years the Soviet intelligence operation has had Mr. Trump on their radar. As early as 1977, Donald Trump came to the attention of intelligence "operatives of the Soviet Union and the Eastern Bloc"; that year he had married "Ivana Zelničková, a Czech national who had worked as a model in Canada and whose father was under surveillance by the Czech secret service, which, in turn, as a Soviet satellite, was in league with the KGB," and Trump was furthermore a "tempting target" because he "had transformed himself into a marketing phenomenon in which his self-promotion, however distasteful, generated a self-perpetuating, larger-than-life aura of success, wealth, status, and opulence."[68] Authorities wiretapped phone calls between Ivana and her father "to gather as much information about Trump as possible."[69] A decade later, in 1987, Trump made a trip to Moscow. That was made possible, as Trump proudly explains, because after conversing with the Russian ambassador, Yuri Dubinin, at a luncheon—"one thing led to another, and now I'm talking about building a large luxury hotel, across the street from the Kremlin, in partnership with the Soviet government. They have asked me to go to Moscow in July."[70] In January, 1987, Trump reports, he received a letter from Dubinin, "that began: 'It is a pleasure for me to relay some good news from Moscow.' It went on to say that the leading Soviet state agency for international tourism, Goscomintourist, had expressed interest in pursuing a joint venture to construct and manage a hotel in Moscow."[71] This led to the trip to Moscow to check out the possibility, with Trump likely not realizing "that Intourist was essentially a branch of the KGB whose job was to spy on high-profile tourists visiting Moscow," and that, while everything was free for Donald, so too was everything "subjected to twenty-four hour surveillance by the KGB."[72]

---

67. Isikoff and Corn, *Russian Roulette*, 84–85.
68. Unger, *House of Trump*, 38–39.
69. Unger, *House of Trump*, 42–43.
70. Trump with Schwartz, *Art of the Deal*, 27.
71. Trump with Schwartz, *Art of the Deal*, 364.
72. Unger, *House of Trump*, 49.

This meeting had happened because a year earlier Trump had shown a keen interest in learning all he could about Mikhail Gorbachev who had risen to power in 1985; with Gorbachev's more open approach to the West, "which eased the tensions of the Cold War, Trump became deeply infected with a severe case of Russophilia."[73] According to the *Hollywood Reporter*, this led Trump to orchestrate a meeting with Bernard Lown, a Boston cardiologist who had shared the Nobel Peace Prize with a Russian who was the personal physician of Gorbachev; since Lown had spent some time with Gorbachev, Trump wanted to learn from him all he could about the Soviet leader.[74] The article states that Trump's keen interest in this meeting with Gorbachev, recalled Lown, was explained with Trump's words: "'I intend to call my good friend Ronnie,' meaning Reagan, 'to make me a plenipotentiary ambassador for the United States with Gorbachev.'"[75] Dr. Lown was not aware "that Trump had retained the powerful lobbying firm of Black, Manafort & Stone shortly after it opened shop in 1980, and its three main partners—Charles Black, Paul Manafort, and Roger Stone—had just played vital roles in Ronald Reagan's ["Ronnie's"] 1984 landslide victory": Trump had told Lown "how within one hour of meeting Gorbachev, he would end the Cold War."[76] We see that Trump's fascination with Russia goes back over three decades.

In fact, in 1984 Trump's relating to members of the Russian Mafia began in earnest. That was in connection with finding buyers for luxury condos in Trump Tower, which offered a rare special feature: "Trump Tower was one of only two buildings in New York City that sold condos to buyers who used shell companies, such as limited liability companies, which allowed purchasers to buy real estate while concealing their identities."[77] With these lax regulations, Trump's condos were "an ideal vehicle through which criminals could put their dirty money into luxury condominiums while keeping their ownership anonymous"; in this capacity Trump served to help launder money for the Russian Mafia.[78] Unger estimates that at this

73. Unger, *House of Trump*, 43.

74. Scott Feinberg, "Donald Trump Angled for Soviet Posting in 1980s, Says Nobel Prize Winner," *Hollywood Reporter*, May 26, 1917, https://www.hollywoodreporter.com/news/donald-trump-angled-soviet-posting-1980s-says-nobel-prize-winner-1006312. See also, Unger, *House of Trump*, 44–45.

75. Feinberg, "Trump Angled for Soviet Posting."

76. Unger, *House of Trump*, 45.

77. Unger, *House of Trump*, 12.

78. Unger, *House of Trump*, 13.

Eternality or the Moment

time, the Russian Mafia "had grown to roughly nine thousand criminal gangs with thirty-five thousand members," including many who "were looking to transfer illicit funds into safe havens in the West"; with the Soviet Union's disintegration, hundreds of billions of flight capital in the hands of oligarchs and mobsters began to leave Russia, and Donald Trump stood with open arms ready to welcome them, asking no questions about shell companies, and assisting with laundering vast amounts of money while not disclosing identities.[79] Thomas Frank of *Buzzfeed News* reported that their investigators found that "More than one-fifth of Donald Trump's US condominiums have been purchased since the 1980s in secretive, all-cash transactions that enable buyers to avoid legal scrutiny by shielding their finances and identities. . . Records show that more than 1,300 Trump condominiums were bought not by people but by shell companies, and that the purchases were made without a mortgage, avoiding inquiries from lenders. Those two characteristics signal that a buyer may be laundering money, the Treasury Department has said in a series of statements since 2016."[80]

We know that Russia provided loans to Donald that were indispensable to his success, because after defaulting repeatedly he did not have access to money elsewhere. Speaking in Moscow in 2008 about the Trump Organization, Donald Trump Jr. claimed: "Russians make up a pretty disproportionate cross section of a lot of our assets. We see a lot of money pouring in from Russia."[81] He made a similar comment in a talk at a Manhattan real estate conference in the same year: "And in terms of high-end product influx into the US, Russians make up a pretty disproportionate cross-section of a lot of our assets; say in Dubai, and certainly with our project in SoHo and anywhere in New York. We see a lot of money pouring in from Russia."[82] Years later, in 2014, Eric Trump made a similar claim to James Dodson, a reporter for *Golf* magazine, stating "that the Trumps' golf courses are all financed by Russian banks—and that the Trump Organization has 'all the

---

79. Unger, *House of Trump*, 13.

80. Thomas Frank, "Secret Money: How Trump Made Millions Selling Condos to Unknown Buyers," *BuzzFeed*, January 12, 2018, https://www.buzzfeednews.com/article/thomasfrank/secret-money-how-trump-made-millions-selling-condos-to.

81. Harding, *Collusion*, 276.

82. Hazel Heyer," "Executive Talk: Donald Trump Jr. Bullish on Russia and Few Emerging Markets," eTurboNews, September 15, 2008, https://www.eturbonews.com/9788/executive-talk-donald-trump-jr-bullish-russia-and-few-emerging-ma. See also, Unger, *House of Trump*, 153.

money we need from Russia."[83] Unger claims that "Trump was $4 billion in debt when Russian money came to his rescue and bailed him out, and, as a result, he was and remains deeply indebted to them for reviving his business career and launching his new life in politics."[84]

Since Putin's maintenance of his power required controlling his oligarchs, he needed to keep track of their whereabouts and what they did with their money.[85] In Christopher Steele's 2016 dossier, he "alleges Trump has been severely compromised by Russia," and "that Trump unknowingly regularly supplied intelligence to Vladimir Putin."[86] This could be easily facilitated when Trump became involved with the real estate development company, Bayrock LLC, a "firm that had begun in Moscow during the tail end of communism. Its founder was Teyfik Arif, . . . a former bureaucrat who had worked in the USSR's commerce and trade department."[87] Upon arriving in New York, Arif "hired [Felix] Sater to manage the company. In 2003 Bayrock moved into offices in Trump Tower on the twenty-fourth floor, two floors below Trump's own premises. Sater, Arif, and Trump became partners."[88] With the Bayrock Group LLC being "largely staffed, owned, and financed by émigrés from Russia and the former Soviet Union," and "with its ties to the Kremlin, Russian intelligence, and possibly the Mob, Bayrock's looming presence in Trump Tower," suggests Unger, "should have had American counter-intelligence agents on high alert."[89] With his contacts in the Bayrock operation, Trump "was indirectly providing Putin with a regular flow of intelligence on what the oligarchs were doing with their money in the US . . . Now that Trump was getting investments from the Russians, Putin could keep track of where their money went because Bayrock kept a ledger that Moscow likely had access to. It wasn't just about buying condos": it was about "direct capital investment into various Trump projects."[90] Trump owed much to Putin, and from the consistent fawning over him that he has demonstrated since becoming our president, there is every reason to believe that he is still very much in Putin's debt. As we

83. Abramson, *Proof of Collusion*, 41.
84. Unger, *House of Trump*, 4.
85. Unger, *House of Trump*, 144.
86. Unger, *House of Trump*, 166.
87. Harding, *Collusion*, 292.
88. Harding, *Collusion*, 292.
89. Unger, *House of Trump*, 128.
90. Unger, *House of Trump*, 167.

have noted, while Special Counsel Robert Mueller's Report states that the investigation did not establish that members of the Trump campaign conspired or coordinated with the Russian government to interfere in the 2016 election, the level and degree of Trump's engagement with the Russians is surely a matter that will continue to be investigated for some time to come.

Kierkegaard and Kierkegaard-World

Correspondingly, how is it that divinity or God might be potently present in actuality and discernible according to Kierkegaard and Kierkegaard-world on eternality or the moment?

Going along with the expediency of the now is a mark of being bound by the momentary. For this reason, Kierkegaard was troubled by a popular satirical Copenhagen journal that lampooned respected intellectuals of the time under cover of offering literary and cultural analysis in a fun-loving manner. He did not respect this regularly published paper because its authors functioned anonymously and its satirical criticisms too often turned into mean-spirited and scurrilous attacks. The satiric weekly, *The Corsair*, was eventually called into question publicly by Kierkegaard and *The Corsair Affair* resulted, which has been called "the most renowned controversy in Danish literary history."[91]

The two central characters in this intriguing episode in Kierkegaard-world were Mëir Aron Goldschmidt (1819–1887) and Peder Ludwig Møller (1814–1865). Kierkegaard first met Goldschmidt in 1837 in the same house where he met Regine. Several years younger than Søren, Goldschmidt admired Kierkegaard's literary skills, and Kierkegaard, in turn, appreciated the talent and creativity of the innovative Danish journalist. In 1840, at the age of twenty-one, the young intellectual, who was Jewish and in 1845 published his first novel entitled *A Jew*, founded *The Corsair*, which, because of its criticisms of the king and the political establishment would lead to Goldschmidt's brief imprisonment on six different occasions.

---

91. Rubow, *Goldschmidt og Nemesis*, 188, and cited in Kierkegaard, *Corsair Affair*, vii.

Figure 7: Meïr Goldschmidt (1819–1887)

Kierkegaard's relationship with the other figure in the affair is much more negative. Møller, one year older than Kierkegaard, managed somehow to earn Kierkegaard's contempt, even though there is no evidence that they had any close association at the university.

Figure 8: Peder Ludwig Møller (1814–1865)

Møller's educational path was quite similar to Kierkegaard's; he received high marks on his examinations and in 1841 he "demonstrated his merits with a gold-medal-winning essay on French poetry, but he never completed his university degree."[92] Garff points out that this one whom Kierkegaard came to despise with a vengeance was a major lady's man, Copenhagen's Don Giovanni or Don Juan, having "scored several score [women] in Copenhagen," and the biographer claims that "Kierkegaard hated Møller because he, Møller, had precisely the body that Kierkegaard lacked," and Møller hated Kierkegaard "because Kierkegaard had precisely the writing that Møller lacked": Garff formulates the conflict between them in an admittedly "oversimplified way" by stating "that Møller wanted to write as Kierkegaard wrote and that Kierkegaard wanted to seduce as Møller seduced."[93] The oversimplifying maybe also involves a little distorting, although, according to Hannay and others, Møller "was reputedly the model for the seducer of the 'Diary'" in Kierkegaard's *Either/Or*, volume 1.[94] In spite of his exploits in sensuality and his being professionally unqualified, Møller maintained hopes of filling the professorial chair in aesthetics that had been filled by Adam Oehlenschläger (1779–1850), the great Danish poet and playwright who introduced romanticism into Denmark. Therefore, Møller knew that he had to protect what reputation he had left and not allow his work with Goldschmidt's *Corsair* to become known publicly.

Kierkegaard himself, or rather his pseudonyms, had been well received by the publication. Kierkegaard wasn't comfortable receiving this sort of endorsement from such a disreputable source, so some sort of statement was required. At the end of 1845, with the final touches on his manuscript of the *Postscript* about done, Kierkegaard submitted an article, "An Itinerant Aesthetician's Activity and How He Still Came to Pay for the Dinner," under his pseudonym Frater Taciturnus [Silent Brother], author of *Stages on Life's Way*, to the *Fædrelandet* [*The Fatherland*]; in the article he questioned why he had been given the dubitable distinction of not having been singled out for abuse by *The Corsair*. Frater wrote: "Would only that I might soon appear in *The Corsair*. It is really difficult for a poor author to be singled out like this on the Danish literary scene, so that he (assuming that we pseudonyms are all one) is the only one who is not abused there. If I am not mistaken, my superior, Hilarius Bookbinder, has been flattered in *The*

---

92. Garff, *Søren Kierkegaard*, 388.
93. Garff, *Søren Kierkegaard*, 390.
94. Hannay, *Kierkegaard*, 319.

Corsair, Victor Eremita even had to endure the disgrace of being immortalized—in *The Corsair*! And yet I have of course already been there, because *ubi spiritus, ibi ecclesia: ubi P. L. Møller, ibi 'The Corsair.'*[95] The Latin reads, "Where the spirit is, there is the Church: where P. L. Møller is, there is *The Corsair*." With this public disclosure of Møller's ties to the provocative journal, his hopes for a professorship were gone. This invitation for *The Corsair* to set their sights on Kierkegaard and attack him was repeated in another public statement, and soon it was obliged.

The attack went after Kierkegaard in different ways, making fun of his authorship, drawing attention to the clothes he wore and accentuating abnormalities of his physical appearance, and utilizing pictorial caricatures by a skilled cartoonist that seared images in people's minds that were not quickly forgotten. Sustained for several weeks, the assault left a deep impression on the many levels of Copenhagen society, so that if Søren ventured out for a walk he could count on being yelled at derisively by children and stared at in ways that were new by many he encountered. Kierkegaard's perception of the devastation might be somewhat overdrawn, but the pain ran deep. Hannay puts it well: "although the exchange was brief, its effect was long-lasting and the pillorying which Kierkegaard provoked from *The Corsair* made him a social outsider on a scale that he could scarcely have anticipated."[96] Goldschmidt sold his satiric weekly a few months after the campaign against Kierkegaard, perhaps in part because of second thoughts about having orchestrated the distasteful lampooning; he moved to Germany and Italy and returned a few years later. Møller, who "was an elegant polemicist with a perfectly perfidious pen," made his contributions to the onslaught, then resigned from *The Corsair*, went abroad and died in poverty a number of years later.

As for Kierkegaard, after the episode, he reflected on the action he had taken:

> I was very well aware of what I was doing, that I was acting responsibly, aware of my responsibility, that not to do it would have been irresponsible. I did it (and precisely in a newspaper, and precisely in a newspaper article that made contact with town gossip from start to finish), because to me it was very important to provoke attention upon this point, which is achieved neither by ten books that develop the doctrine of the single individual nor

---

95. Garff, *Søren Kierkegaard*, 394.
96. Hannay, *Kierkegaard*, 317.

by ten lectures on the subject, but in these days is achieved simply and solely by getting the laughter aimed at oneself, by making people somewhat angry, and then by getting them mockingly to reproach me again and again and continually for that—precisely for that which one wants inculcated and, if possible, brought to the knowledge of all.[97]

Concrete action had been required of him. To have refrained from that action would have been to turn away from what he considered an unsavory malignancy in society from which he could not disassociate himself; to remain silent would have meant capitulating to the momentary and dismissing the eternal.

Figure 9: Søren Kierkegaard (1813–1855)

The one called the Danish Socrates saw *The Corsair's* personal attack on him as illustrating the leveling done by the deadly abstract character of the public. To illustrate his meaning, Kierkegaard employs an allegory. He writes of a Roman emperor who is bored and desires to be entertained, to have an experience that will make him laugh; he has a dog, and he releases

---

97. Kierkegaard, *Point of View for My Work*, 114.

it to attack someone for fun.[98] In explaining the allegory's deeper sense, Kierkegaard remarks that the public keeps a dog for its amusement, and "the dog is the contemptible part of the literary world": "If a superior person shows up, perhaps even a man of distinction, the dog is goaded to attack him and the witty fun begins . . . The nasty dog tears at his coattails, indulges in all sorts of rough tricks—until the public is tired of it and says: That is enough now. So the public has done its leveling: the superior one, the stronger one has been mistreated—and the dog, well, it remains a dog which even the public holds in contempt."[99] The allegory's meaning is seen in the implied referents: The Roman emperor is the public, the dog is *The Corsair*, the attacked individual is Kierkegaard, and the public remains unrepentant because it did not do the dirty deed, for the dog or *The Corsair* as a third party did it, and the public can in addition declare the third party's actions reprehensible.

The Corsair Affair brought much suffering into Kierkegaard's life. The event, in fact, came to be a watershed occurrence in his life. In the writing on his authorship penned in 1848, Kierkegaard breaks down his literary output in terms of a first part, a last part, and a middle: "The first division of books is esthetic writing, the last division of books is exclusively religious writing—between these lies *Concluding Unscientific Postscript* as the *turning point*. This work deals with and poses *the issue*, the issue of the entire work as an author: becoming a Christian."[100] Contributing to this turning point was this painful affair: the experience brought about a time of accounting and reevaluating of his situation and general plan of attack. *The Corsair Affair* seems to have introduced a bit of realism into the mix for Kierkegaard. Reality was maybe harsher than he had realized. Change does not come easily. To put it into my terms, we can say that it's as though he came to realize that in the first part of his authorship, he had definitely gone deeper, but he hadn't managed to go forward the way he wanted and needed. He needed to adjust his strategy for the second part of his authorship. Inwardness and indirect communication now needed to be counter-balanced by tending more closely to external actions and a more direct form of communication. The second part of the authorship reflects

---

98. *Pap.* VII1 B 123 n.d., 1845–46, in Kierkegaard, *Two Ages*, Supplement: 136. See also Hannay's account of this, *Kierkegaard*, 335.

99. Kierkegaard, *Two Ages*, Supplement: 136–37.

100. Kierkegaard, *Point of View for My Work*, 31.

the incorporation of these adjustments to his literary game plan that now came to embody a heartier political dimension.

Greater clarity is needed in understanding eternity in its differentiation from the moment and greater attention is needed to be given to integrating that distinction into existence. For Kierkegaard and his world, the eternal is a nickname for God. Howard and Edna Hong offer an explanation of eternity: "The eternal as timeless being does not come into being but comes into time and space as a specific embodiment of the eternal. The moment, therefore, is an atom of eternity and has a significance qualitatively different from that of transient instants of time. Existence is a mode of being, but not all being is existence."[101] Therefore, in the *Postscript* "Johannes Climacus states that 'God does not think, God creates; God does not exist [*existere*], God is eternal.'"[102] In *The Concept of Anxiety*, Vigilius Haufniensis writes that inwardness "is the eternal or the constituent of the eternal in the human being"; and "whenever inwardness is lacking, the spirit is finitized."[103] Anti-Climacus in *Sickness*, therefore, insists that "one must become conscious of the fact that there is something eternal in the self."[104] Eternality's presence in the self is testimony to divinity's implanting holy desire within the human. In fact, in a *Postscript* draft Johannes claimed that "as knowing myself in relationship to God, . . . I am eternal."[105] The eternal is so engrained within the human that denying it does not get rid of it completely, but its annihilation best happens by immersion in the momentary.[106]

In Kierkegaard-world we read about time and eternity touching each other in time in the moment.[107] In that moment the eternal comes into time and space and fills it with meaning. But elsewhere the moment or instant stands over against eternity as its opposite. In a Christian discourse published in 1848, in his discussion of the joy in suffering only once but in being victorious eternally, Kierkegaard includes a differentiation between temporality and eternity. He writes: "Temporality itself, the whole of it, is

101. Kierkegaard, *Philosophical Fragments*, 280n25.

102. Kierkegaard, *Philosophical Fragments*, 280n25; and the reference is to Kierkegaard, *Concluding Unscientific Postscript*, 1:332.

103. Kierkegaard, *Concept of Anxiety*, 151.

104. Kierkegaard, *Sickness unto Death*, 61–2.

105. Kierkegaard, *Concluding Unscientific Postscript*, 2:34.

106. Kierkegaard, *Concept of Anxiety*, 152.

107. Kierkegaard, *Concept of Anxiety*, 87.

a moment; eternally understood, temporality is a moment, and a moment, eternally understood, is only once. Temporality futilely wants to make itself important, counts the moments, and counts and adds—when the eternal is allowed to rule, temporality never gets further than, never becomes more than, the one time. Eternity is the very opposite. It is not the opposite of a single moment in temporality (this is meaningless); it is the opposite of the whole of temporality, and with all the powers of eternity it resists temporality's becoming more."[108] So, temporality is a moment and the one time, while eternity is the opposite not of a single moment in temporality but of the whole of temporality. Therefore, "when a person does not draw her power from the eternal and acquire by communion with the eternal the power to hold temporality down, temporality steals her power from her and through this stolen power it now becomes some enormous something; it becomes her impatience, her despair, perhaps her downfall" as temporality, having become master, "makes her its slave."[109]

As we observe life in time, we can do so with the moment's view or with eternity's view. We can notice behaviors and accomplishments in the temporal realm that seem to have been impacted by attention to the eternal and those that have not. Judgments in this regard, Kierkegaard warns in his discourse on purity of heart, are not easy, because, as he says, as eternal willing manifests itself in the temporal, there is no one-to-one relation, with the eternal willing and the temporal manifestation corresponding like an echo to sound; if that were the case, temporality would be "the *uniform transparency* of the eternal" and discerning the relation between the two would be directly recognizable.[110] But in reality, temporality is, instead, "the *refraction* of the eternal," so the actual nature of eternal willing's relation to behaviors and accomplishments in time are less obvious and direct; and the more a striving person operates out of an intimate alliance with temporality instead of willing the eternal, the more she is likely to accomplish in the temporal sense.[111] Donald, for instance, in his own way, has accomplished a number of things in the temporal sense. Those who tend to the eternal do this in relation to particular situations that call for tailored responses; so the actions in temporality inspired by eternality cannot be standardized—they differ widely and possess unique qualities because of their individualized

---

108. Kierkegaard, *Christian Discourses*, 98.
109. Kierkegaard, *Christian Discourses*, 99.
110. Kierkegaard, *Upbuilding Discourses*, 89.
111. Kierkegaard, *Upbuilding Discourses*, 90.

character. To be expected, then, is a pluralism of eternity-inspired actions, the totality of which is eternity's refracted presence in the temporal flow. Maybe in our intensely broken and divided time, there are sprinkled hidden fructifying elements of refracted eternity that can be gathered up and put to use in the reunification project that necessarily awaits us if we are going to reclaim our democratic country.

Possibly greater clarity on the character of eternity's hidden presence in temporality can be gained by examining the link between eternity and love. In *Works of Love*, Kierkegaard writes that "the love that Christianity speaks of is known by its own fruit—that it has within itself eternity's truth ... Christian love is eternal ... Christian loves abides, and for that very reason it *is*."[112] Christian love experienced in our setting of temporality is also a refracted expression of eternity, so it is hidden and therefore is known only by its revealing fruits. Kierkegaard employs in this consideration one of his favorite terms, redoubling [*Fordoblelse*]. A temporal object such as a rock or a tree never has redoubling in itself, but the matter is different for human beings: "When, however, the eternal is in a human being, this eternal redoubles in her in such a way that every moment it is in her, it is in her in a double mode: in an outward direction and an inward direction back into itself, but in such a way that this is one and the same, since otherwise it is not redoubling. The eternal is not only in its characteristics but is in itself in its characteristics. It not only has characteristics but is in itself in having the characteristics."[113]

The same is to be said about love. For: "what love does, that it is; what love is, that it does—at one and the same moment. At the same moment it goes out of itself (the outward direction), it is in itself (the inward direction); and at the same moment it is in itself, it goes out of itself in such a way that this outward going and this returning, this returning and this outward going are simultaneously one and the same."[114] In this redoubling the magic of love is at work: "the one who loves is or becomes what she does. She has or rather she acquires what she gives."[115] In building up others, in loving others, we build up and love ourselves. And that building up and love—in both its outer manifestation of embracing the beloved or the neighbor and its inner manifestation of forming the heart of the lover—abides; and

---

112. Kierkegaard, *Works of Love*, 8.
113. Kierkegaard, *Works of Love*, 280.
114. Kierkegaard, *Works of Love*, 280.
115. Kierkegaard, *Works of Love*, 281.

it abides because it has the eternal within it. Love connects the temporal and eternity because love is eternity's bond.[116] It seems appropriate to add that Kierkegaard's logic of the redoubling of love applies equally well to the redoubling of hate: hatred or tearing down of others is at the same time hatred or tearing down of oneself.

One last quick point is that on Kierkegaard's view, the eternal is big on mercifulness and the momentary is big on the monetary or money. He declares that those who are into money usually don't have any real sense for eternity and in fact regard it as a delusion while they regard money as the true reality; and those who are into eternity cannot imagine money having a place within the eternal and regard it as a delusion. As Kierkegaard states it: "There is nothing of which you can be so sure that it will never enter heaven as—money. On the other hand, there is nothing of which heaven is so sure as mercifulness. So you see that mercifulness is infinitely unrelated to money."[117]

---

116. Kierkegaard, *Works of Love*, 6.
117. Kierkegaard, *Works of Love*, 319.

5

Subjectivity or Freedom

Trump and Trump-World

Fifth, why might it seem as if divinity, which implants in the human the desire for the divine or God, is not readily discernable in relation to Trump and Trump-world on subjectivity or freedom?

Donald Trump always gave some thought to going into real estate like his father. However, he also had an interest in film. Timothy O'Brien informs us that Trump's "imagination was, and remains, decidedly cinematic. Before heading off to college he was fairly certain that he wanted a career in show business, not real estate. He said he planned to attend the University of Southern California to study filmmaking and had already produced a Broadway show called *Paris Is Out*."[1] But Hollywood did not work out for him. Then, "just before he left for Fordham [University, which he attended for two years before transferring to the University of Pennsylvania's Wharton School of Business], Donald helped a Manhattan entertainment lawyer named Egon Dumler find an apartment and Donald said that the attorney, impressed with the depth of his real estate know-how, convinced him that his talents would be wasted on the West Coast. Donald said the lawyer told him that real estate, not movies, was his calling"; he thought about it and figured he'd do it: he would go into real estate and he would put show

---

1. O'Brien, *TrumpNation*, 53.

business into real estate, having the best of both worlds.² That's what he did, and many have been entertained by him ever since.

Given what we have uncovered about Donald Trump thus far, it should not be surprising to find that combining those two has led to a life that can be characterized as being committed to living the game of a conman. In his book *The Plot to Destroy Democracy*, Malcolm Nance offers this assessment. As a conman, he notes, Trump "also brought the persona of a larger than life cartoon—the 'professional' wrestler—to the campaign trail": "Before he entered politics, he was a man who had appeared on wrestling shows and enjoyed the spectacle of riling a crowd of young children and the great blue-collar worker. Trump played himself, an indifferent rich guy with a fake giant million-dollar check to the delight of the audience. He understood the pantomime of giving the public heroic characters and evil villains. All these Punch-and-Judy traits propelled him into the White House."³ "Trump sees everything through the narrow, blinkered framework of his role as a reality-TV game show host and pitchman," quips Rick Wilson.⁴ And this role that he has successfully executed within our Republic tells us something about those being conned, as David Cay Johnston explicates: "What every con artist knows: people see what they want to see, hear what they want to hear, believe what they want to believe, and let their hopes and wishes vanquish their skepticism. Unless and until some fact they cannot reconcile slaps them hard in the face, the con's marks will keep seeing the world through the credulous and distorted lens they fashioned for themselves."⁵ If a conman is a person who cheats or tricks people by gaining their trust and persuading them to buy into something that isn't true, then I guess "conman" works as a summative term for the fruits of the Donald's subjective freedom.

Another characteristic running deep within Trump's functioning as a subjectively existing free person is his transactional manner of relating. A close Trump associate reported to journalist Emily Jane Fox, "'Donald is the most transactional person you'll ever meet, and the most possessive too ... He's a narcissist, and a narcissist like that is incapable of understanding" a person's feelings.⁶ Another of Trump's longtime acquaintances remarked:

2. O'Brien, *TrumpNation*, 53.
3. Nance, *Plot to Destroy Democracy*, 30.
4. Wilson, *Everything Trump Touches Dies*, 52.
5. Johnston, *It's Even Worse*, 9.
6. Fox, *Born Trump*, 135.

"The only person Donald ever really loved was Donald."[7] Bobby Jindal, former Governor of Louisiana, once insightfully stated that he doubted if Trump ever read the Bible because: "HE ISN'T IN IT."[8] Steve Bannon, after having observed the President for a number of months, registered his view that Trump does not have any friends.[9]

The transactional manner is apparent in Trump's penchant for seeking relational leverage. Reince Priebus reported to Bob Woodward: "'The president's MO is to put people back on their heels. Put all the chips on the table. And then slowly but surely pick off each chip individually.' It could be a person, a policy, a country, a foreign leader, a Republican, a Democrat, a controversy, an investigation—Trump would try to leverage anyone, by any means, and at times he would succeed. 'He uses leverage in a way I've never seen before.'"[10]

When Melania first met Donald, he asked her for her number. She responded by asking him to give her his number. It was a little test. She wanted to see if he would give her his office line, in which case she would surmise that he really wasn't interested. At this point the storyteller adds, "She had no interest in doing business with him, though ultimately that is what all of Donald's relationships—romantic or otherwise—become, transactional."[11] Melania later told her friends that she wasn't interested in pursuing Donald, "especially knowing he'd cozied up to her after coming to the party with another woman."[12]

The transactional mode carried over into his relationship with his kids as well. When son Donald Jr. would report in to his father every morning before heading off to school, Donald Sr. would repeat the same maxims to him daily: "No smoking. No drinking. No drugs." And this was followed by: "Don't trust. Anyone. Ever." Then would come: "So, do you trust me?" And Jr. would say, "Of course, you're my dad," to which father Trump would reply, "What did I just say? My son's a loser, I guess, because he can't understand what I'm telling him." Jr. later said it was hard getting his father's meaning when he was four years old.[13]

---

7. Fox, *Born Trump*, 149.
8. I am indebted to Karl Netting for this information,
9. Woodward, *Fear*, 299.
10. Woodward, *Fear*, 288.
11. Fox, *Born Trump*, 158.
12. Fox, *Born Trump*, 158.
13. Fox, *Born Trump*, 265. Fox states that Donald Jr. told this account to "host Donnie

A classmate of Don Jr. at the University of Pennsylvania tells about Donald Trump coming to visit Don Jr. to take him to a basketball game. Donald knocked on the door. Don Jr. greeted "his dad, all set to go to the game in a Yankees jersey . . . Donald took one look at his son and slapped him across the face. Jr. flew to the ground as his classmates watched [from down the hall]. 'Put on a suit,' Donald hissed, 'and meet me outside.'"[14]

The person whose subjectivity is truly free has come to realize the important role played by the trans-moral conscience—or the conscience that has been freed from the tyranny of life's "ought," "must," or "should"—which freedom is an outgrowth of experiencing unqualified love. Donald Trump's imprisonment in his transactional world affords him no release from the retaliatory quid pro quo, tit for tat causal chain of actions that must be taken in service to, ultimately, his infinite need for ego gratification.

Freedom culminates in action as it passes through the mediating phase of decision-making. Even the casual observer of President Trump has noticed that, despite his reputation for declaring "You're fired" on *The Apprentice*, he has a hard time carrying through on the actual, personal decisiveness required to fire somebody.

Trump's indecisiveness can be dramatically seen in his inability to make a decision on marrying second wife Marla Maples. "The should-I or shouldn't-I indecisiveness that plagued Donald Trump—that continues to plague Donald Trump today—would have gone on forever if not for a red line drawn by Marla": She "delivered her man an ultimatum," we could say, a Kierkegaardian ultimatum: "either he married her by Christmas, or she would take his daughter and move out. She'd had enough . . . She wasn't going to spend another Christmas with Donald . . . without a wedding band on her finger." Under pressure, Donald finally decided to marry Marla.[15]

Frustrated Rex Tillerson unleashed criticism of Trump to his White House team, stating: "The president can't make a decision. He doesn't know how to make a decision. He won't make a decision. He makes a decision and then changes his mind a couple of days later."[16] Reince Priebus became aware of an important fact that one has to keep in mind to understand the way Trump made decisions: "The president has zero psychological ability

---

Deutsch in a 2008 episode of CNBC's *The Big Idea*." Fox, *Born Trump*, 265.

14. Fox, *Born Trump*, 249–50.
15. Fox, *Born Trump*, 144–45.
16. Woodward, *Fear*, 211.

to recognize empathy or pity in any way."[17] Omarosa agrees. She states, "Donald Trump's single greatest character flaw as a leader and human being is his complete and total lack of empathy."[18] She sees it as being "a function of his extreme narcissism": "Trump constructs his own reality to make himself look good, even in horrible situations, and then he repeats it over and over again until his distortion becomes the only version he knows. His lies and boasts are only, always, about making him look better . . . The difference between Trump and world leaders who may be a tad bit narcissistic is that he can't function unless everything is about him. He has to be at the center of everything. If he's not in the middle of it, he'll force himself in[to] the middle."[19]

The large bulk of human decisions are made with some degree of influence coming from the self-interest of the decider. That has been rather blatantly the case with Donald Trump, in decisions both big and small. People wondered when Trump fired "the head usher of the White House, Angella Reid, the first woman and second African American to hold the position," and she'd done so since 2011; the unofficial explanatory word on the firing was that "she wasn't very well liked," but likely the bigger issue was that "Trump didn't approve of her handling of his tanning bed."[20] Similar questionable features of Trump's decision to fire head usher Reid also seem to have been in play in his October 2018 decision in France to skip the World War I memorial ceremony because of concern over rain giving him a bad-hair day.

Most important political leaders in the modern world have recognized the need to receive information from many quarters and to garner assistance from wise counselors who offer reasons in support of the claims they set forth. The deliverances of commonsense are usually not completely discounted by the capable leader, but neither are they touted as being more trustworthy than the viewpoints of experts. "Grappling with the complexities of large-scale social and economic problems," argues Duncan J. Watts, a principal researcher at Microsoft Research and a professor at large at Cornell University, require "a scientific approach to decision-making, meaning one that starts from a position of epistemic modesty, seeks out competing explanations for observed phenomena, decides among these explanations

---

17. Woodward, *Fear*, 235.
18. Newman, *Unhinged*, 144.
19. Newman, *Unhinged*, 287.
20. Newman, *Unhinged*, 242–43.

on the basis of available evidence, and continually seeks to redefine its understanding of the world."[21] Things become a bit scary when one juxtaposes this sort of thoughtful decision-making to the "commonsense" approach of Donald, who insists "that he can learn any subject in minutes and that the best advisers reside in his head."[22] Trump's commonsense approach effectively utilizes "causal stories," that is, "plausible-sounding narratives that are dressed up to look like explanations"; they're intended to make us feel better by giving us the feeling that we've made sense of something, when, in actuality, these causal stories, which have the form of an explanation, ultimately mislead and disappoint because they don't explain the mechanism under question but just describe it.[23] Competent leaders need more than what a commonsense approach to decision-making can offer.

In chapter 1 our discussion mentioned the important role social media played in the 2016 election. It is worth digging deeper into the place of social media in our society today, because an analysis of it can give us a better handle on Trump-world. Two books are worth a closer look in this regard.[24]

First, Michael Patrick Lynch, Professor of Philosophy and Director of the Humanities Institute at the University of Connecticut, has written a provocative book on the way big data of the digital form of life is shaping human beings in new ways in our contemporary world. His book is entitled *The Internet of Us: Knowing More and Understanding Less in the Age of Big Data*. By big data, Lynch means three things: 1) the ever-expanding volume of data that currently surrounds us in Facebook pages, blogs, tweets, YouTube videos, etc., and that constitutes our digital form of life; 2) the analytic techniques used to extract information from that data; and 3) the gigantic firms like Google and Amazon and government agencies such as NASA that utilize data analytical techniques in carrying out their work and in the extraction process gain control of the information and knowledge, the ideas and actions consequently fueled by acquiring that cognitive content, and the power that accompanies controlling this knowledge and these

21. Watts, "Commonsense Presidency," 330.
22. Johnston, *It's Even Worse*, 140.
23. Watts, "Commonsense Presidency," 348.
24. In addition, for a helpful account of the rise of the Internet and the way this rather "lawless, unregulated, and unaccountable" reality provides the background for understanding how "disregard for restraints on conduct" has "come to characterize American domestic politics," see the brief but lucid discussion by Lepore, *These Truths*, 731–38.

Subjectivity or Freedom

ideas.[25] Lynch argues that in the world of big data, people are able to access the information they need very readily, without having to go to some place where they encounter others to check out or buy a book or whatever resources they are seeking. Nor do they have to wait in order to get that resource; it can be gotten quickly. The Web "allows us unprecedented control over the sources and types of information we receive, to dip into the flow of information where and how we wish, and to extract and isolate what interests us more quickly, all in the comfort of our pajamas . . ." And this can be done "without leaving our protective bubble, without sullying ourselves with the messy and inconvenient physical lives of others; it offers anonymity and friends we've never met."[26] This freedom of expression and consumption leaves us with "the risk of increased individual isolation."[27] Yet, Lynch thinks that the greater danger is that, yes, while having been given more ways of communicating that allow us to make contact with others all the time, the problem is that "we listen and talk to those in our circle, our party, our fellow travelers. We read the blogs of those we agree with, watch the cable news network that reports on the world in the way that we see it; and post and share jokes made at the expense of the 'other side.'"[28] Therefore, the real problem is not the isolation of individuals; rather, the vexing issue is that "the Internet is increasing 'group polarization'—that we are becoming increasingly isolated *tribes*."[29] Unfortunately, we are becoming more and more accustomed to this fragmentation because our participation in the digital form of life perpetuates and validates the perspective, ideas, and values of "my" group or tribe or party or polarized faction.

A basic distinction informing Lynch's view differentiates between receptive knowledge and reflective knowledge. When we are on the Web, we are usually operating in a receptive mode. We take in basic facts and information, and through this absorption process we gain receptive knowledge. This form of knowing we share with other animals who also process information. Receptive knowledge is not yet an intellectual cognitive grasping, just as it is also not really reflective. Lynch calls receptive knowledge

---

25. Lynch, *Internet of Us*, 8–9.
26. Lynch, *Internet of Us*, 42.
27. Lynch, *Internet of Us*, 42.
28. Lynch, *Internet of Us*, 42–43.
29. Lynch, *Internet of Us*, 43.

"Google knowing," which "tends to swamp other ways of knowing" and to which thereby we tend to give more of our attention.[30]

Lynch makes the case that receptive knowledge is not enough. It serves an important initial role in the knowing process, but needed is the important second element of engaging in reflection, which involves sorting out the true from the false, identifying reasons that one can own for responsibly believing something presenting itself as knowledge, and thus finding evidence for backing up what one is going to affirm as true. Being reflective in this way leads to knowing in a different way, for one here is not just being receptive; one is being reflective, and what one affirms or believes can now be acknowledged as a responsible act of judgment.[31] Both receptive and reflective knowledge need to be operative for a person to be functioning with understanding; for understanding is comprised of various cognitive capacities working in concert to provide a grasping not just of particular relational elements but of the structure of the whole, which data alone does not provide: the understanding, which cannot be outsourced because it involves a highly personal process of synthesis and integration, is so valuable because it allows us to explain things and to be able to give creative expression to "some of the deepest parts of our humanity."[32]

We can see that big data can make its contributions to society and to the political process, but those contributions are limited and should not mislead us into thinking that we do not need to go deeper beyond what they can deliver. Democracy, as viewed by Lynch, is "a space of reasons," and by this he means a space in which one's claims are backed up by reasons that are in keeping with shared principles or standards of what it means to know; as he writes: "To engage in democratic politics means seeing your fellow citizens as equal autonomous agents capable of making up their own minds. That means that in a functioning democracy we owe each other reasons for our political actions."[33] Former President James Buchanan 150 years ago called the United States Senate "the greatest deliberative body in the world." However, today it does precious little deliberating. For that institution to do better, we must recognize, first, the need to reintroduce more depth into the way we all know, and second, to recognize that beyond improving our knowing, we also need to reintroduce more depth into the

30. Lynch, *Internet of Us*, 30–31.
31. Lynch, *Internet of Us*, 39.
32. Lynch, *Internet of Us*, 163–64, 182–83.
33. Lynch, *Internet of Us*, 55, 58.

SUBJECTIVITY OR FREEDOM

way we all exercise our will and make decisions. Lynch claims, "institutions that encourage the use of critical thinking and the civil exchange of reasons are *doing the work of democracy*."[34] If we can together manage to increase "the use of critical thinking" and "the civil exchange of reasons" in the fullest sense of Lynch's phrases, we will have made significant progress on addressing the central problems of our time.

Second, Chris Hughes, who had roomed with Mark Zuckerberg and became wealthy as a result of being one of Facebook's first employees, purchased the *New Republic* in 2012. He hired a good editor and together they followed their idealistic dreams to make a great magazine. This lasted for a couple of years until the issue of the bottom line took center stage and the magazine was transformed into a technology company in which data-determining trending metrics dictated journalistic decisions. At that point the editor, Franklin Foer, left the magazine. He wrote a most insightful book based on his experiences entitled *World Without Mind: The Existential Threat of Big Tech*, which can shed light on the dynamic influence Silicon Valley has had on Trump-world.

Foer possesses Kierkegaard-like instincts for sniffing out nefarious forces undercutting individuality in our contemporary society. He focuses on the Big Tech Companies (BTC) and concentrates on four in particular, Google, Apple, Facebook, and Amazon, which he affectionately refers to as GAFA. The Kierkegaardian flavor can be discerned in some of his critical comments. The BTCs of GAFA "believe we're fundamentally social beings, born to collective existence. They invest their faith in the network, the wisdom of crowds, collaboration": they are "shredding the principles that protect individuality," he writes, and "the time has come to consider the consequences of these monopolies, to reassert our own role in determining the human path."[35]

In the 1950s and 1960s, Americans experienced a whole new way of relating to food. With the introduction of TV dinners, slices of cheese wrapped in plastic, convenient burgers and fries—a revolution in cuisine took place. Part of that revolution was the engineering of foods, which made us fat, and industrial farming, which could produce the large amount of meat and corn required by the new way of doing food. A transformation took place, but on the other side of it was unintended consequences—a

---

34. Lynch, *Internet of Us*, 61.
35. Foer, *World Without Mind*, 2–3.

revision in how we consume food and an estrangement from that which we eat.[36]

Foer sees something similar to this food revolution now restructuring "the production and consumption of knowledge": being impacted by the dominant tech firms are "our intellectual habits," "how we read and what we read," how we structure information (Google's sorting of the Internet), how we sort the news we encounter (Facebook's use of algorithms to understand our social circles), and how we engage the world of books (Amazon's influence on publishing through its dominating hold on that market). With this degree of impact, these companies are able to remake markets, developing techniques for creating "products that pander to the tastes of their consumers," with an eye on overhauling "the entire chain of cultural production, so that they can capture greater profits."[37]

The big tech companies pose a threat to two realities very dear to our topic of subjectivity and freedom, and that's contemplation, which is centered in our attention, and the reading of texts. That's because, first, as Foer points out: tech companies "have created a world in which we are constantly watched and always distracted. Through their accumulation of data, they have constructed a portrait of our minds, which they use to invisibly guide mass behavior (and increasingly individual behavior) to further their financial interests. They have eroded institutions—media, publishing—that supply the intellectual material that provokes thought and guides democracy. Their most precious asset is our most precious asset, our attention, and they have abused it."[38] One important way they have robbed us of our attention is by taking away the second valuable reality, the reading of texts. In the Middle Ages, the book made its appearance, and with the slow emergence of literacy beyond a small elite and the eventual invention of the printing press, public reading gave way to the book being made available to individuals. Foer sees this as a miracle, because it led to the holy event of silent reading: silent reading ushers us into a private, interior world that shuts out the external world with its social conventions nudging us to conform, bringing the individual to the fore, and allowing the mind to do its best thinking by facilitating the possibility of genuine "contemplation, moments of isolation, where the mind can follow its own course to its own

---

36. Foer, *World Without Mind*, 3–4.
37. Foer, *World Without Mind*, 4–5.
38. Foer, *World Without Mind*, 8.

Subjectivity or Freedom

conclusions."[39] We can acknowledge that we do benefit in certain instances from joining the crowd to "network, collaborate, create, and strategize in concert with others," but this ought not replace the magical powers emanating from the encounter that can happen when one, as Foer says, takes "regular refuge in the sanctuary of paper" in order through such "reading on paper" to be given "one of the few slices of life" that the big tech companies "can't fully integrate" via their algorithms and data-gathering to create "a portrait of our psyche" in order "to predict our behavior and anticipate our wants."[40] If cultured eating is now the organic alternative to the world of fast foods, so too is cultured reading now the organic alternative to the world of clickbait.[41] Contemplation and reading of text on paper is subversive in that it equips us for being able to resist the cultural forces pushing us to conform and undermining our individuality.

If one thinks of Trump's aversion to reading and his apparent reticence to spend time in contemplation, we can see that he might well be a victim of the BTCs. However, he also has received great benefit from being featured on the various forms of media they have created. Foer interprets him as being a culminating phenomenon of their tremendous sway over the cultural developments—both progressive and regressive—of society:

> Donald Trump is the culmination of the era. He understood how more than at any moment in recent history, media need to give the public what it wants, a circus that exploits subconscious tendencies and biases. Even if media disdained Trump's outrages, they built him up as a character and a plausible candidate. For years, media pumped Trump's theories about President Obama's foreign birth into circulation, even though they were built on dunes of crap. It gave endless attention to his initial smears of immigrants, even though media surely understood how those provocations stoked an atmosphere of paranoia and hate. Once Trump became a plausible candidate, media had no choice but to cover him. But media had carried him to that point. Stories about Trump yielded the sort of traffic that pleased the Gods of Data and benefited the bottom line. Trump began as Cecil the Lion [the animal killed by a Minnesota hunter, with the photo of the smiling hunter over the corpse of the lion generating 3.2 million stories in various media,

---

39. Foer, *World Without Mind*, 225–28.
40. Foer, *World Without Mind*, 227–28, 72, 187.
41. Foer, *World Without Mind*, 217.

thus providing the supreme example of "trending"], and then ended up president of the United States.[42]

Going deeper with contemplation and reading of texts, we might realize, with Foer, that: "The election of Donald Trump came with the shock of collective recognition that our media culture has decayed—and a sense that we need more committed protectors of truth than the feckless gatekeepers at Facebook and Google."[43] Kierkegaard is one such committed protector of truth who can help us in this regard, if, as Joakim Garff jestingly suggested in response to a paper I had given, we strive to "Make Kierkegaard Great Again."

Kierkegaard and Kierkegaard-World

Correspondingly, how is it that divinity or God might be potently present in actuality and discernible according to Kierkegaard and Kierkegaard-world on subjectivity or freedom?

Another central figure in Kierkegaard-world is Hans Lassen Martensen (1808–1884), the highly regarded theologian five years older than Kierkegaard who, upon Mynster's death, became the bishop of the Danish Lutheran Church. Martensen functioned as Kierkegaard's tutor early in his education, then as his professor, and finally as the target of his criticisms. Anachronistically, we could say that Kierkegaard saw Martensen as sort of a Trumpian. All the breaks seemed to fall Martensen's way in his career. He was given acclaim in his theological work, his writings were well-received, he was respected in the cultural establishment of Golden Age Denmark, and, not unimportantly, he consistently refused to give Kierkegaard the acknowledgment that the younger religious thinker would have very much appreciated receiving. I have made the case elsewhere that, despite the many obtrusive realities preventing an unperturbed and tranquil relationship between these two major figures of Danish history, Martensen actually

42. Foer, *World Without Mind*, 149.

43. Foer, *World Without Mind*, 221. Personally, it seems that, on the one hand, the venture of Amazon and Netflix into film production, with both of them investing billions of dollars in the last couple of years in this area, fits Foer's analysis of BTCs desiring to capture more and more markets and dominate the culture; on the other hand, these companies have created very high-quality series such as "The Magnificent Mrs. Maisel" (Amazon) and "Ozark" (Netflix) that are clearly a positive contribution to the culture. Their impact is ambiguous. We can be alert to the negative effects and do what we can to minimize them, while at the same time appreciate the positive effects.

Subjectivity or Freedom

mattered very much to Kierkegaard and that the younger thinker followed him closely, not merely the better to know the enemy but also to receive assistance in establishing the theological agenda of the day, to learn from him, and to appropriate ideas and principles of Martensen that he found helpful.[44]

Figure 10: Professor Hans Lassen Martensen (1808–1884)

The thinking of both Martensen and Kierkegaard placed the principle of personality at the center of their concerns. This meant that for both of them the notions of subjectivity and freedom were held in high regard. However, Martensen assessed the condition of the contemporary culture differently from how Kierkegaard assessed it. Martensen believed that, especially with the influence of romanticism, the pendulum had swung too far in the direction of subjectivity and that a corrective emphasis on objectivity was therefore required to bring the pendulum back to the center for a better balance. Kierkegaard, on the other hand, who, having written his dissertation on the concept of irony, knew full well the impact the romantics had

---

44. See Thompson and Kangas, *Between Hegel and Kierkegaard*, especially my Introduction, 1–71, and Thompson, *Following the Cultured Public's Chosen One*.

exerted on Danish culture, nevertheless believed that objectivity was still winning the day and a greater accent needed to be placed on subjectivity.

A closely related matter was the attention and standing that should be given to G.W.F. Hegel (1770–1831), the German philosopher whose "system" had been introduced into the Danish context by the labors of Johann Ludwig Heiberg (1791–1860), the great playwright, poet, and literary critic, and Martensen. Hegel—whom Kierkegaard came to vigorously oppose even as he appropriated much from him—is another major figure in Kierkegaard-world. Martensen did indeed insist that university students needed to read Hegel's writings and come to a basic understanding of them, since the Hegelian viewpoint was dominating the world of science, to such an extent that to be educated in that time required an accounting of Hegel. While Martensen advocated for making one's way through Hegel, he did not hold that one should stop with Hegel; he believed one needed to go beyond Hegel, because the great philosopher attributed too large a role to an autonomous view of reason and thinking and too little place to a theonomous view of faith and revelation. Martensen did appreciate Hegel's speculative method of doing philosophy and he, in fact, found it very useful in the doing of theology. Kierkegaard harshly criticized speculative theology because it spuriously claimed to "mediate" between important differences of the Christian gospel but held that this could be accomplished purely within the arena of thinking, with such mediations actually destroying those differences and leaving nothing for faith to affirm. Speculation, on Kierkegaard's view, was reducing religion to being merely a matter of objective science, and the place of passionate faith, the subjective side of religion, was being leveled to insignificance. It is in this setting that Kierkegaard makes his strident claim through Johannes Climacus in the *Postscript* that "truth is subjectivity."

In that writing, Johannes cursorily deals with objective Christianity in Part One on "The Objective Issue of the Truth of Christianity," a section of some forty pages. Then he proceeds to his robust treatment of subjective Christianity in Part Two on "The Subjective Issue, The Subjective Individual's Relation to the Truth of Christianity, or Becoming a Christian," a section of 570 pages. A rather famous passage in Part Two is where Johannes Climacus presents a question to the reader concerning truth. He writes: "If someone who lives in the midst of Christianity enters, with knowledge of the true idea of God, the house of God, the house of the true God, and prays, but prays in untruth, and if someone lives in an idolatrous land but prays with all the passion of infinity, although his eyes are resting upon the image of an idol—where, then is there more truth? The one prays in truth to God although he is worshiping an idol; the other prays in untruth to the true God and is therefore in truth worshiping an idol."[45]

Raised here is the question of the "what" and the "how." "What" deals more with the objective factors and "how" deals more with the subjective factors. The Christian individual prays with little or no passion, so the "how" is missing, even though he might perfunctorily and formally begin his prayer by addressing it to the true God, and therefore with the proper "what." The second individual, though addressing herself to an idol, an inappropriate "what," nevertheless does so with infinite passion, or with the "how" fully present. It seems that Johannes and Kierkegaard would give their preference to the person manifesting in her praying a subjectively intense passion for divinity or the divine, the appropriate "how" although addressed to an inappropriate "what," an idol. The penetrating subjectivity gains access to touching the divinity operating beneath the idol.

One can learn much about a person's theological perspective by discerning how they understand the relation between human freedom and divine action, especially the notion of divine omnipotence. For subjectivity and freedom to be given their due within a theological understanding, care has to be taken in the way in which the concept of divine omnipotence is formulated. An all-mighty deity cannot be conceived as holding literally all the power, for creatures need to be given power to exist. Kierkegaard engages in some careful reflection on this theme in a journal entry of 1846 that I hold to be one of his most beautiful statements. We see in this extended entry that Kierkegaard has an appreciation for the notion of divine self-limitation. He interprets the notion of divine omnipotence as the ability of God to limit Godself in bestowing freedom and independence to the human. He writes:

> The whole question of the relation of God's omnipotence and goodness to evil (instead of the distinction that God works good and merely permits evil) can perhaps be resolved quite simply in the following way. The highest thing after all that can be done for a being, higher than anything else one could do for it, is to make it free. The ability for doing precisely this belongs to omnipotence. This seems strange, since precisely omnipotence is supposed to make dependent. But if one is willing to think about omnipotence,

---

45. Kierkegaard, *Concluding Unscientific Postscript*, 1:201.

> one will see that precisely in this must lie in addition the determination to be able to take oneself back again in the expression of omnipotence in such a way that precisely therefore that which has come into existence by omnipotence can be independent. That is why one human being cannot make another human being completely free, because the one who has the power is actually imprisoned in having it, and therefore always still has a wrong relation to the one this human wants to liberate. Furthermore, in all finite power (talent, etc.) there is a finite self-love. Only omnipotence can take itself back while it gives away, and this relation is indeed precisely the independence of the recipient. God's omnipotence is therefore God's goodness. For goodness is to give away completely, but in such a way that by omnipotently taking itself back one makes the recipient independent. All finite power makes dependent, only omnipotence can make independent, from nothing bring forth that which receives continued existence in itself by the fact that omnipotence continuously takes itself back. Omnipotence does not come to rest in a relation to another, for there is no other commensurate with itself; no, it can give without really giving up the least of its power, i.e., it can make independent. This is the incomprehensible, that omnipotence not merely is able to bring forth the most imposing of all things: the visible totality of the world, but is able to bring forth the most frail of all things: an independent being who is directly over against omnipotence. Consequently, that omnipotence, which with its gigantic hand wreaks such havoc on the earth, can in addition make itself so light that the one coming into existence receives independence. — It is only a sorry and secular representation of power's dialectic, that depicts power as greater and greater in proportion to the extent to which it can compel and make dependent. No, Socrates understood it better: that the art of power is precisely to make free. But in the relation between human and human it [making free] is never able to be done, even though it always is necessary to stress again and again that this is the highest; only omnipotence is in truth capable of it.[46]

The art of [genuine] power is to make free. We could say that this art is what Kierkegaard's authorship is all about. This differs radically from Trump's view that the art of power is to evoke fear. Kierkegaard, of course, intends his language to lift up a personal God; that is apparent in his tying omnipotence to goodness. It is more explicitly apparent in a magnificent

---

46 *Pap.* VII1 A 181 n.d., 1846; Kierkegaard, *Journals and Papers* 2, 1251, to which I have made minor changes.

passage in the *Christian Discourses* where the language of omnipotence is tied to that of love. Kierkegaard here reflects on God's love which makes the human into something in relation to Godself, using the same formulation as was used in the previous passage: "Oh, what wonderful omnipotence and love! A human cannot bear to have his 'creations' be something in relation to himself; they are supposed to be nothing and therefore he calls them, and with disdain, 'creations.' But God, who creates from nothing, omnipotently takes from nothing and says, 'Become'; God lovingly adds, 'Become something even in relation to me.' What wonderful love; even God's omnipotence is in the power of love."[47] We have in Kierkegaard, then, the omnipotence of love as a way of talking about God's self-limitation.

This way of thinking receives a distinctive formulation by Kierkegaard, but it is present elsewhere in Kierkegaard-world. Martensen expressed this viewpoint as well. For him, the logic of divine love leads him to the notion of divine self-limitation, for the divine needs to limit Godself to make room for human freedom. Martensen clearly affirmed the notion of divine self-limitation in his *Christian Dogmatics* and elsewhere. He writes in his *Dogmatics*: "God limits God's power, as God from the depths of God's eternal life calls forth a world of created beings, which God produces in a derivative sense to have life in themselves; but exactly by this fact that God is the power in a free world, God reveals the inner greatness in God's power. For that power is not the true power, which does not tolerate any free movement outside itself, because it itself will immediately be everything and do everything; but that power is the true power, which creates freedom, and which nevertheless is able to make itself all in all."[48]

The notion of divine self-limitation had also received expression by Mynster. He wanted to write a devotional book and in preparation for that he worked out a systematic theology, the *Fundamentals of Christian Dogmatics*, a manuscript of some 400 pages, which he never published, although it was later included in his published miscellaneous writings. In that writing he states: "Although every power is grounded in God, and every manifestation of power is dependent on God, we ought yet by no means say that everything that happens is the work of God's omnipotence. If the world and God are not identical, if there is life and existence that is

---

47. Kierkegaard, *Christian Discourses*, 127. I am indebted to Paul Sponheim for drawing my attention to this passage.

48. Martensen, *Den christelige Dogmatik*, 98. English translation: *Christian Dogmatics*, 81. This is my translation from the Danish edition.

not God's, then this life and this existence certainly has its ground in God's omnipotence, but the Omnipotent One, in the very same moment it called forth the life outside Godself, must limit Godself, and only by this self-limitation of God [*Guds Selvbegrændsning*], which again is grounded in God's love, is the creature's life, above all the rational creatures' self-consciousness and freedom, explainable."[49]

This viewpoint is reaffirmed in his 1833 two-volume devotional writing that became the most popular book of its kind in that time in Denmark. Mynster declares in a section on "God, the Omnipresent, the Omnipotent": "But in spite of all this I still say the words: omnipotent God! say it with the fullest conviction, know, feel, believe it deep in my soul, that God is omnipotent. I believe that there is no power in heaven and on earth except that which God gives, and that if God withdrew God's power, then the creature would be capable of nothing more, since it would dissolve into nothingness. I believe that God, in sparking the rational life in the creature's breast, therewith gave the creature freedom, therewith in a way *limited Godself* [*begrændsede sig selv*]—an expression that can be ridiculed only by that person who will have all freedom abolished in God's kingdom."[50] Kierkegaard's thought on this critical theme of divine self-limitation likely benefited from the views of both Martensen and Mynster in Kierkegaard-world.

Johannes Climacus is the pseudonym of Kierkegaard-world who deals most fully with the notion of subjectivity. Kierkegaard points out in a journal entry of 1845: "by subjectivity is meant not what is called a subject as such but to become subjective or the developed subjectivity."[51] In the *Concluding Unscientific Postscript*, Johannes provides an account of this development. Subjectivity develops because subjective existence is marked by a continued striving.[52] The subjective thinker's final reference point is always existence, concrete existing.[53] The subjective thinker gains concretion through passion, for existence involves passion.[54] The human possesses gifts and a task for utilizing those gifts: "Every human being must be assumed to possess essentially what belongs essentially to being a human being. The subjective

49. Mynster, *Grundrids*, 6:66.

50. Mynster, *Betragtninger*, 1:70.

51. *Pap.* VI B 40:32 n.d., 1845 in *Concluding Unscientific Postscript, Vol.* 2 Supplement: 54–55.

52. Kierkegaard, *Concluding Unscientific Postscript*, 1:121–22.

53. Kierkegaard, *Concluding Unscientific Postscript*, 1:357.

54. Kierkegaard, *Concluding Unscientific Postscript*, 1:350–51.

thinker's task is to transform herself into an instrument that clearly and definitely expresses in existence the essentially human."[55] Therefore, "the subjective thinker as existing is essentially interested in her own thinking, is existing in it."[56] Becoming is the primary concern: "Subjective thinking invests everything in the process of becoming and omits the results," or in other words, is unconcerned about her place within the wider realm of the world-historical.[57]

Climacus clarifies that the inward reflection of the subjective thinker is a double-reflection that first thinks the universal, but in existing in that thinking, makes a second reflective movement that brings the universal thinking into touch with existence, so that it culminates in a form of reflection in service of acting in one's existence.[58] We see then that reflection is important for the subjectively existing thinker, but reflection is not able to bring closure to the issue it is being confronted with—for it is resolution or decision that accomplishes that.[59] Climacus identifies a hierarchy or a chain of dependency that is at play. He writes: "Christianity is spirit, spirit is inwardness, inwardness is subjectivity, subjectivity is essentially passion, and at its maximum an infinite, personally interested passion for one's eternal happiness."[60] When subjectivity is missing from this sequence, then passion departs as well, and with passion's departure goes the infinitely interested passion, and with that loss is lost decision too.[61] That's why the claim is made that "all decision is rooted in subjectivity."[62] If life's task is to observe reality or to speculate about reality, then there's no great urgency to make a decision; but if life's task is to do something with oneself, to choose oneself, through how one exercises one's freedom, then there is some urgency.[63]

The possibility of freedom within the human is "to be able."[64] This capacity includes the ability to choose oneself, and when this choice is made a

---

55. Kierkegaard, *Concluding Unscientific Postscript*, 1:356.
56. Kierkegaard, *Concluding Unscientific Postscript*, 1:73.
57. Kierkegaard, *Concluding Unscientific Postscript*, 1:73.
58. Kierkegaard, *Concluding Unscientific Postscript*, 1:73.
59. Kierkegaard, *Concluding Unscientific Postscript*, 1:116.
60. Kierkegaard, *Concluding Unscientific Postscript*, 1:33.
61. Kierkegaard, *Concluding Unscientific Postscript*, 1:33.
62. Kierkegaard, *Concluding Unscientific Postscript*, 1:33, 129.
63. Kierkegaard, *Concluding Unscientific Postscript*, 1:33.
64. Kierkegaard, *Concept of Anxiety*, 49.

new reality comes into existence. In "The Balance between the Esthetic and the Ethical in the Development of the Personality," in volume 2 of *Either/Or*, we find a few relevant passages on freedom worthy of noting. We read that with the new birth of freedom there comes to be an identity with new attending responsibilities: "When the passion of freedom is awakened, it is jealous of itself and by no means allows what belongs to a person and what does not to remain unspecified and confused."[65] When the choice of one's self takes place, a personality emerges: In one way, she remains the same, but in another manner, "she becomes another, for the choice penetrates everything and changes it."[66] The change from this choice involves as well a change in status, from finite to infinite: "Her finite personality is now made infinite in the choice, in which she infinitely chooses herself."[67] The result is the biggest prize, the capacity that gives humanity its distinctiveness: its ability to decide or to cut off possibilities from the realm of infinite possibilities—as free: "Now she possesses herself as posited by herself—that is, as chosen by herself, as free."[68] So to the question, "What is this self of mine?" the answer comes: "It is freedom." Choosing oneself brings an eternal, infinite, absolute validation of the personality:

> She chooses herself—not in the finite sense, for then this "self" would indeed be something finite that would fall among all the other finite things—but in the absolute sense, and yet she does choose herself and not someone else. This self that she chooses in this way is infinitely concrete, for it is she herself, and yet it is absolutely different from her former self, for she has chosen it absolutely. This self has not existed before, because it came into existence through the choice, and yet it has existed, for it was indeed "herself."[69]

However, to clarify that the view being affirmed here is a theonomic rather than an autonomic one, the author adds: "But I don't *create* myself—I *choose* myself."[70] Within the Kierkegaard world, we see, one turns inward, discovers freedom, and "comes to know freedom as one's bliss," recognizing both that "the greatness of freedom is that it always has to do only with

---

65. Kierkegaard, *Either/Or*, 2:223.
66. Kierkegaard, *Either/Or*, 2:223.
67. Kierkegaard, *Either/Or*, 2:223.
68. Kierkegaard, *Either/Or*, 2:223.
69. Kierkegaard, *Either/Or*, 2:215.
70. Kierkegaard, *Either/Or*, 2:215. I have added the emphases.

itself," and that "the greatness of a human being depends simply and solely on the energy of the God-relation."[71]

To help us go deeper in our national political situation, we can draw on a distinction Kierkegaard makes in his 1844 discourse "To Need God Is a Human Being's Highest Perfection."[72] The title expresses the view prevailing throughout the discourse: A human being is great and at his or her highest when he or she corresponds to divinity or God by being nothing at all.[73] This view makes life more difficult, but apart from arriving at this view of oneself, a human lives a delusion, because it is only in and through this deeper view that one learns to know oneself.[74]

The distinction the author sets forth is between two selves: a first self that tends to the business of carrying on in the world without too much interest in being side-tracked from accomplishing significant goals by having to reflect on more profound, ultimate concerns; and a deeper self that is honed in on the eternal claim being made on it and does not deviate from attending to the resulting high calling to perfection that demands being needful of divinity.[75] The first self feels the lure of engaging in purposefulness; the deeper self feels the more profound lure of engaging in non-purposefulness or purposelessness: "The first self sits and looks at all the beckoning fruits, and it is indeed so clear that if one just makes a move everything will succeed, as everyone will admit—but the deeper self sits there as earnest and thoughtful as the physician at the bedside of the sick, yet also with transfigured gentleness, because it knows that this weakness is not unto death but unto life."[76] These two selves—the eager-beaver first self anxious to make its mark on the world and the contemplative deeper self holding out for relating to the eternal that brings a deeper joy—are at odds within a person.

Heidegger's existential philosophy, which calls for care that takes one's life project seriously, seems to sum up rather nicely what Kierkegaard speaks of as the functioning of the first self. This self engages in the external world with a sense of purpose, a set of plans, and an expectation for productivity; it creates its life's meaning through fruitful laboring as

---

71. Kierkegaard, *Concept of Anxiety*, 108–10.
72. Kierkegaard, *Eighteen Upbuilding Discourses*, 297–326.
73. Kierkegaard, *Eighteen Upbuilding Discourses*, 311.
74. Kierkegaard, *Eighteen Upbuilding Discourses*, 312.
75. Kierkegaard, *Eighteen Upbuilding Discourses*, 314.
76. Kierkegaard, *Eighteen Upbuilding Discourses*, 315.

guided by its structured project. By all appearances, Donald Trump's life seems to be governed by the first self without much qualification coming to it from the second, deeper self. Investment in existence in this fashion pays dividends, as good work is rewarded monetarily, a wholesome family life can be supported, and the sense of well-being includes pride in having shown self-determination in making oneself into a successful person and an upstanding member of society. The first self becomes the master, and it earns recognition from the world for its world-affirming attitudes and actions.

Kierkegaard would not want to declare the good introduced into the world by the industrious first self described in the above paragraph as being of little or no value. His problem would not be with what it tended to and did but with what it did not tend to and thereby did not do. The deeper self is more clear-eyed and doesn't get enticed by the glorious trappings of committing oneself and all one is about to existing in externalities. Rather, it attunes itself to the call of the eternal and comes to appreciate that its genuine need is for divinity, for acknowledging that before the divine it is nothing. The deeper self, then, realizes that in choosing the road of making oneself into a self-made person of project-conquering, one will never come to view oneself according to human perfection, for choosing that dreamy road of self-creation precludes choosing the more grounded road of a higher empowerment or potentiation by life's ultimate reality.[77] And deciding on this second road surely involves a clear-cut either/or: "instead of gaining the whole world, to gain himself; instead of becoming the master, to become one in need; instead of being capable of all things, to be capable of nothing at all."[78] The deeper self, despite the difficulty of its challenge, does not give ground: it continually provides its testimony to the first self, attempting to convince it to relativize its commitment to the world by acknowledging the truth "that in regard to the external a person is capable of nothing at all," for with that acknowledgment one really does know oneself.[79] For Kierkegaard, this coming together of the two selves can and does happen. He writes: "When the first self submits to the deeper self, they are reconciled and walk on together."[80] This reconciliation is an authentic self-knowledge

---

77. Kierkegaard, *Eighteen Upbuilding Discourses*, 313.
78. Kierkegaard, *Eighteen Upbuilding Discourses*, 314.
79. Kierkegaard, *Eighteen Upbuilding Discourses*, 319.
80. Kierkegaard, *Eighteen Upbuilding Discourses*, 316.

Subjectivity or Freedom

because it is a coming to know oneself in the appropriate way, and in so doing one comes to know the divine.[81]

At this point in the discourse Kierkegaard employs language that comes close to describing *divinitas*, the divinity or the Godhead that is the ground of being supporting one's life at every turn:

> The person who knows herself in the way mentioned is well aware that God does not dwell in temples, but she also knows that God is with her at night when sleep refreshes and when she awakens in an alarming dream, is with her in the day of need when she is searching for comfort, in the tumult of ideas when she listens in vain for a liberating word, in mortal danger when the world does not help, in her anxiety when she is working out her soul's salvation in fear and trembling. She knows that God is with her in the moment when anxiety rushes upon her with lightning speed, when it already seems too late, and there is no time left to go to the house of the Lord; then God is with her, swifter than the light that pierces the darkness, swifter than the thought that chases away the fog—present, yes, present as swiftly as one can be who was already present.[82]

The life in which the first self and the deeper self are recognized is more difficult than a life carried out merely on first-self terms, but it is also a life that "acquires ever deeper meaning and purpose."[83] And the person keeping the focus on divinity or the divine, comes to realize that she, although being capable of nothing at all, with the divine "is capable of more and more—that she is capable of overcoming herself, since with the help of God she is indeed capable of this!"[84] The nihilistic language of becoming nothing again becomes lucidly demarcated as being not an enervating nihilism but an empowering nihilism. One becomes nothing before the divine, yes; however, in so doing, one becomes something. This is language of divinity resurrecting.

Divinity is ever about its task of eliciting the creative advance, utilizing its power of creative transformation to move the creation toward greater wholeness. On Kierkegaard's vision, there is glory to be promoted. This is not, though, a passive glory contemplated and celebrated from afar by a distant, nonparticipating observer. Instead, it is an active glory in which

---

81. Kierkegaard, *Eighteen Upbuilding Discourses*, 321.
82. Kierkegaard, *Eighteen Upbuilding Discourses*, 322–23.
83. Kierkegaard, *Eighteen Upbuilding Discourses*, 324.
84. Kierkegaard, *Eighteen Upbuilding Discourses*, 324.

the creature participates. He writes near the end of the discourse: "Just as knowing oneself in one's own nothingness is the condition for knowing God, so knowing God is the condition for the sanctification [or making whole] of a human being by God's assistance and according to God's intention. Wherever God is in truth, there God is always creating. God does not want a person to be spiritually soft and to bathe in the contemplation of God's glory, but in becoming known by a person God wants to create in her a new human being."[85] Divinity resurrects. Divinity brings new life into people's lives and into conflictual situations. Irenaeus and Augustine proclaimed in the ancient world long ago that the glory of God is the human being fully alive. It seems that Kierkegaard, in his own manner, is declaring that truth no less in the modern world.

The relevance of Kierkegaard's discussion of two selves to our polarized and partisan national dilemma shouts out at us.

---

85. Kierkegaard, *Eighteen Upbuilding Discourses*, 325.

6

Possibility or the Future

Trump and Trump-World

Last of all, why might it seem as if divinity, which implants in the human the desire for the divine or God, is not readily discernable in relation to Trump and Trump-world on possibility or the future?

It's interesting that Trump "claimed during the campaign that he possesses 'the world's greatest memory'";[1] but I haven't heard or seen him saying anything about his capacity for expectation, the polar term to memory. I think that's because Donald is oriented to the past rather than to the future. Wilson insightfully states, "The Trump train stops in a Podunk future that looks like 1930, not 2030."[2] And Johnston points out numerous ways that Trump has "demonstrated his backward perspective on the world and his rejection of ideas, science, and technologies that move our species forward. Just as he promotes coal and rejects electricity made from wind, solar, and other renewable sources. Trump's vision is not about the future but about a mythical past, at best a romantic nostalgia."[3] Trump's "'Make America Great Again' is a retrospective, pessimistic throwaway, a callback to an imagined past."[4]

1. Johnston, *It's Even Worse*, 239.
2. Wilson, *Everything Trump Touches Dies*, 89.
3. Johnston, *It's Even Worse*, 179.
4. Wilson, *Everything Trump Touches Dies*, 88.

"Nostalgia," the late historian and cultural critic Christopher Lasch has suggested, "freezes the past in images of timeless, childlike innocence."[5] The emphasis on nostalgia is a powerful political tool that meshes nicely with a politics of fear. John Fea, historian of Christian evangelicalism, explains: "A politician who claims to have the power to take people back to a time when America was great stands a good chance of winning the votes of fearful men and women. In the end, the practice of nostalgia is inherently selfish because it focuses entirely on our own experience of the past and not on the experience of others."[6] For instance, many African Americans think that, overall, it was not better to be black back in some nostalgic yesteryear, as some African-American ministers have articulated: "'The best time to be black in the United States is right now!' When African Americans look back, they see the oppression of slavery, the burning crosses, the lynched bodies, the poll taxes and literacy tests, the separate but unequal schools, the 'colored-only' water fountains, and the backs of buses."[7] For them, "Make America Great Again"? I don't think so.

With a nostalgic emphasis, the administration's plans for the future don't have to be taken that seriously. Rick Wilson sums it up: "Trump's actual vision for America is a dimwitted slogan, not a plan," and it's "dazzlingly superficial."[8] A typical Trump plan, suggests the best-selling author David Cae Johnston, consists of "slogans and claims without substantive policy proposals."[9] Wilson accentuates just how negative this view is, describing "Down-note Trumpism" as being "fundamentally pessimistic: it's a picture of America in decline, of evil foreigners beating us at trade, of problems only a strongman can solve, and the idea that the amorphous 'left' is winning all the battles."[10] This fear-mongering works. Trump, unfortunately, has "trained his docile followers to believe in an America that is weaker, sadder, and smaller than we really are."[11] Trump's preoccupation with fear and revenge leaves no room for him to speak of hope and the imminent coming of new possibilities.

---

5. Lasch, *True and Only Heaven*, 118, as cited in Fea, *Believe Me*, 9.
6. Fea, *Believe Me*, 159.
7. Fea, *Believe Me*, 155.
8. Wilson, *Everything Trump Touches Dies*, 88.
9. Johnston, *It's Even Worse*, 186.
10. Wilson, *Everything Trump Touches Dies*, 89.
11. Wilson, *Everything Trump Touches Dies*, 89.

His focus instead is negative and selfish. "Trump's vision is for his brand, his company, and his bottom line, not the United States of America."[12] An author who has studied him for years indicates that Trump "has reduced his life philosophy to a single word—revenge": "'I love getting even,' Trump advised in one of his books, adding 'go for the jugular, attack them in spades!' Repeatedly he has said in talks and in his books that destroying the lives of people he considers disloyal gives him pleasure. That Trump does not recognize ethical limits on conduct, the propriety George Washington modeled, derives from his fundamental character, narcissism. But unlike the mythic figure who came to a tragic end drowning in the pool that mirrored his visage [Narcissus], Trump's narcissism has so far helped him get to where he has for decades said he belonged—in the White House."[13]

With revenge front and center for Trump, with no readiness to join forces with those who used to be our allies, it is easy to comprehend why things aren't going smoothly for him in our intricately complex and interdependent world. Trump is quick to take and slow to give. He has "rejected the idea of turning the other cheek, saying that those who do so are 'fools' and 'idiots.'"[14] Albright reminds us of the nearby presence of fascism, that authoritarian statist posture supported by "the theory that nations are entitled to take what they want for no other reason than that they want it" and that perspective also has no time for golden rules.[15] As informed by revenge, Trump's outlook on international associations "offers no incentive for friendship": "no trust, no special relationships, no reward for helpfulness, and no penalty for cynicism—because cynicism is all we promise and all we expect."[16] It's no wonder that with his negative mindset and jaundiced outlook, his reception in the international sphere has resulted in a loss of credibility for America as a whole and for all its citizens, as former friends and allies have pulled back their allegiance to us while hoping that world order might return to greater normality with an eventual changing of the guard.

Great power resides in the one who leads from the White House. Jon Meacham helps us to remember just how much good could be accomplished

12. Wilson, *Everything Trump Touches Dies*, 88.
13. Johnston, *It's Even Worse*, 7.
14. Johnston, *It's Even Worse*, 7.
15. Albright, *Fascism*, 218.
16. Albright, *Fascism*, 218.

right now under different circumstances. He reminds us that Truman knew "the presidency offers possibilities for such action that are both dazzling and daunting. 'The President,' Woodrow Wilson wrote, 'is at liberty, both in law and conscience, to be as big a man as he can,' and Meacham sadly but realistically adds, "or as small."[17] He adds another fitting truth to mention in our particular time, marked as it is by a high level of selfishness: "Leadership is the art of the possible, and possibility is determined by whether generosity can triumph over selfishness in the American soul."[18] It will be reassuring when generosity is once again able to triumph in our midst.

As we consider the *topos* of possibility or the future, I think it is necessary to say more about Alexander Dugin (1962–), the Kremlin intellectual whom some have called the most dangerous philosopher in the world.[19] I hesitate to deal with him in any detail because of being perceived as affirming and endorsing Dugin and his ideas, which I definitely am not doing. Some of his ideas are fanciful and some are scary to consider. Yet, in spite of that, Dugin is being taken seriously in many quarters of the Russian government, not least amidst the leaders in foreign policy, the military apparatus, and the office of President Putin. Therefore, with one eye on the future, an account of him is necessary—not to promote his ideas but to better understand an influential figure in Trump-world.

In hearing this academic declare, "The American Empire should be destroyed," it is easy to be drawn into Dugin's world to see what drives him to make such a claim. Dugin speaks ten languages, has served as a translator for German, French, and English, has published writings in philosophy, history of religions, geopolitics, and sociology in Russian, Serbian, English, Italian, Spanish, and Turkish, is a guest columnist in several newspapers, currently heads up a publishing house called Arktogaia [North-land], and broadcasts regularly on TV and radio.[20] Dugin is a very eclectic thinker. He pulls together sources that don't easily coalesce into a coherent whole. This

17. Meacham, *Soul of America*, 259.

18. Meacham, *Soul of America*, 258.

19. Paul Ratner, "The Most Dangerous Philosopher in the World," *Big Think*, December 18, 2016, https://bigthink.com/paul-ratner/the-dangerous-philosopher-behind-putins-strategy-to-grow-russian-power-at-americas-expense. The descriptive statement of this article announces, "The work of Kremlin-approved philosopher Alexander Dugin provides key insights on the longterm strategy behind Russian hacks of the American elections."

20. "Alexander Dugin," *Geopolitica.RU*: https://www.geopolitica.ru/en/person/alexander-dugin?page=1, accessed on January 24, 2019.

Russian super-patriot has a mystical bent to him that draws him to occultism, and while these emphases have been somewhat downplayed as he has become more popular among people of power, they still hover behind his theoretical views and his practical aims. The two major elements of his position are Traditionalism and Neo-Eurasianism, with the former equipping him with a world view and the latter with a practical orientation.

Traditionalism is a movement dating back to the 1920s and 1930s but embraced by it are ideas of Renaissance scholars of the fifteenth century, in particular Marsilio Ficino (1433–1499): "Ficino's promotion of the *prisci theologi*—the 'ancient theologians of pagan antiquity'—had a profoundly significant influence on the Renaissance" and established "Ficino's role as the ideological ancestor of Traditionalism (also called 'Perennialism')."[21] A central idea of Ficino that became a fundamental claim of Traditionalism is "that different religions were divinely-inspired, with various 'heathen' nations receiving their own salvific revelations from God."[22] Dugin has stated that when he was 17 to 18 years old it struck him how the world was absolutely empty and disgusting; this void needed to be filled by something, but all the alternatives available did not fill the emptiness. But then he became acquainted with Traditionalism: "The only thing which could fill this gigantic inner emptiness which I had was the total rejection of everything modern within the framework of ultra-revolutionary non-conformist intellectualism of [René] Guénon and [Julius] Evola."[23] This encounter gave him at an early age a philosophical position and his own intellectual agenda. He would later translate extracts from the works of these great Traditionalist theoreticians Guénon and Evola, and also from such "soft" Traditionalists as Mircea Eliade and Carl Jung.[24]

René Guénon (1886–1951), "an early twentieth-century French occultist and metaphysician who was raised a Roman Catholic, practiced Freemasonry, and later became a Sufi Muslim," developed a philosophy of antimodernism of the "Traditionalism"-variety.[25] According to Joshua Green, "Guénon was a 'perennial' Traditionalist, a believer in the idea that certain ancient religions, including the Hindu Vedanta, Sufism, and medi-

---

21. Heiser, "American Empire Destroyed," 15–16.

22. Heiser, "American Empire Destroyed," 18.

23. Heiser, "American Empire Destroyed," 33–34, as cited originally in Umland, "Post-Soviet 'Uncivil Society,'" 147.

24. Heiser, "American Empire Destroyed," 25.

25. Green, *Devil's Bargain*, 204–5.

eval Catholicism, were repositories of common spiritual truths, revealed in the earliest age of the world, that were being wiped out by the rise of secular modernity in the West. What Guénon hoped for, he wrote in 1924, was to 'restore to the West an appropriate traditional civilization.'"[26] The antimodernist tone of Guénon attracted a number of followers who made attempts to restore lost values to the world. One of these was Evola. Julius Evola (1898–1975), an Italian political philosopher, opposed democracy because of its inverting of the natural order through its egalitarianism that gives a voice to all in choosing a leader rather than allowing the powerful, disciplined warriors to be in charge. He advocated for an authoritarianism that maintains traditions of family, beliefs, and culture, for these elements of traditional civilization are able to nurture a connection to the transcendent; modernism, on the other hand, with its modern transportation, media, and technology dehumanizes people, divorcing them from the richness of the real world and eternal values.[27] While Guénon became a devout Muslim primarily focused on spiritual transformation, the black sheep Traditionalist Evola "took concrete steps to incite societal transformation": "By 1938, he had struck an alliance with Benito Mussolini, and his ideas became the basis of Fascist racial theory; later, after he soured on Mussolini, Evola's ideas gained currency in Nazi Germany."[28] Alexander Dugin, "Vladimir Putin's chief ideologist," "developed a Russian-nationalist variant of Traditionalism known as Eurasianism."[29]

Eurasianism, has been called the "armed doctrine" of Traditionalism, which identifies it as the practical counterpart of Traditionalism that is implementing its ideas into the socio-political world. Eurasianism is the political expression of Traditionalist doctrine.[30] Informing this strategy for praxis or action is the merger of a mythical narrative and a geopolitical understanding. The mythical narrative is connected with "two men—Jörg Lanz von Liebensfels (1874–1954) and Guido von List (1848–1919)—linked with the mystical racialist madness which spread in early twentieth century Germany."[31] Mattias Gardell characterizes this "zootheological" theory that vilified non-Aryans and set them over against the Aryans in a

26. Green, *Devil's Bargain*, 204–5.
27. Koffler, *Bannon*, 114–15.
28. Green, *Devil's Bargain*, 205.
29. Green, *Devil's Bargain*, 207–8.
30. Heiser, "American Empire Destroyed," 41.
31. Heiser, "American Empire Destroyed," 51.

Gnostic dualism: "Merging Theosophy and Gnosticism with anthropology and zoology Lanz formulated the 'theozoological' theory as the 'scientific' basis for a dualistic relation in which Aryans and non-Aryans were identified as carnal representations of the metaphysical principles of good and evil locked in a battle for world dominion. Lanz believed that the blond, blue-eyed Aryan was descended from an omniscient divine race that originally populated Arkotogäa, a mythic Aryan motherland in the North Pole region. When Aryan women engaged in sexual relations with 'daemon' races, the original race lost its superhuman powers."[32] Heiser and Nicholas Goodrich-Clarke before him point to the similarities between Lanz's neo-gnostic, racist, occultist religion that desired to dispose of inferior races and "the later practices of Himler's SS *Lebensborn* maternity organization, and the Nazi plans for the disposal of the Jews and the treatment of the enslaved Slavic populations in the East."[33]

In his "Arctogaia Manifesto" Dugin affirms the existence of a mythical polar continent that he thinks is relevant to the contemporary world. He explains: "Literally 'Arctogaia' means 'The North Land.'"[34] It is "a mythical continent, that in former days was situated on the North Pole, but long ago disappeared from physical reality and so from short-lived human memory": also vanishing at that time was the World Tree, "a spiritual axis of Being" that "gave to all traditions and religions a light-bearing and operative-transformative sense."[35] The men of Arctogaia "totally affirm the alternative world," the world of Tradition, the world of Arctogaia; "Arctogaia, the elite of the absent continent, the princes of the non-existent country, spreads in all directions," and "for the people of Arctogaia, every man is a potential Angel and his consciousness is a flower."[36] However, over against Arctogaia stands the Antichrist, which "has geopolitical, immanently social meaning," for "the most 'perfect' and 'complete' form of the historical realization of this sinister personage is the liberal West"; "the resistance to the power of the atlantic 'evil empire,' USA and the liberal capitalistic model," that is

---

32. Gardell, *Gods of the Blood*, 22.

33. Heiser, "American Empire Destroyed," 51–52, and Goodrick-Clarke, *Occult Roots of Nazism*, 97.

34. Heiser, "American Empire Destroyed," 53.

35. Heiser, "American Empire Destroyed," 53.

36. Heiser, "American Empire Destroyed," 53–54.

"fighting with us" must continue, for "a moment will come, and we'll overpower them," and "this victory will be the last and the final" one.[37]

Dugin joins this mythic view with a geopolitical view to constitute Eurasianism, or Neo-Eurasianism, as it is now often called, to differentiate Dugin's perspective from that of Eurasian thinkers of the early twentieth century. Charles Clover, former *Financial Times* Moscow bureau chief, informs us that the British geographer Sir Halford Mackinder gave rise to geopolitical theory in a 1904 lecture in which he argued that Russia, not Germany, was Britain's most worrisome opponent because its possession of the world's largest landmass, the "Heartland" of Eurasia, gave it an impregnable fortress that made it the greatest land power, and land power will win out over sea power, with which Britain and the United States are associated.[38] A half century later this geopolitical claim was being used to justify language of Russia's version of "Manifest Destiny."[39] As geography rather than economics was now viewed as the primary determinant in a nation's long-term potential for dominance, hope was given to a nation that had lost to the West in the Cold War and had turned to a new era of universal tolerance and democracy. Alexander Dugin, with his having become connected with Kremlin officials and with the publication of his *The Foundations of Geopolitics*, Clover explains, made geopolitics mainstream and provided "a how-to manual for conquest and political rule in the manner of Niccolò Machiavelli," and the hardliners enthusiastically incorporated it as a feature of their worldview and guide for future action.[40] In *Foundations*, Dugin called for thwarting "the conspiracy of 'Atlanticism' led by the United States and NATO" to contain Russia's engagement beyond its immediate vicinity; consequently, the task was simply to "put the Soviet Union back together" and then to "use clever alliance diplomacy focused on partnerships with Japan, Iran, and Germany to eject the United States and its Atlanticist minions from the continent."[41] Essential to creating Eurasia, though, Dugin counsels, is rejecting a narrow nationalist agenda; this was the mistake made by Hitler when he tried to make Europe German

---

37. Heiser, *"American Empire Destroyed,"* 53–54.

38. Clover, *Black Wind, White Snow*, 232. The remainder of this paragraph is dependent on Clover's interpretation of Dugin's work, since I have not had occasion to learn Russian and Dugin's major work on geopolitics has not yet been translated from Russian into English.

39. Clover, *Black Wind, White Snow*, 232.

40. Clover, *Black Wind, White Snow*, 236, 234.

41. Clover, *Black Wind, White Snow*, 235.

rather than European: Russia needs to make a Eurasian Empire, not a Russian one.[42] Dugin wrote: "The Eurasian Empire will be constructed on the fundamental principle of the common enemy: the rejection of Atlanticism, the strategic control of the USA, and the refusal to allow liberal values to dominate us."[43]

Paul Ratner reports that Dugin's book on geopolitics is assigned as a textbook in Russian military universities.[44] In that book the current opponent is portrayed as "not just the United States, but Atlanticism, the axis of cooperation between Europe, US and Canada that crosses the Atlantic Ocean. These maritime, liberal nations value individuality and market forces"; over against Atlantis there is Eurasia that "represents the conservative philosophy of land-locked continentalism, which according to Eurasians, has among its values a hierarchical structure, law and order, traditionalism and religion."[45] The battle, then, is between Atlantis and Eurasia, viewed as the war between maritime and land-based nations.[46] Alexander Reid Ross identifies this contestation as the basic emphasis of Dugin's 2009 *The Fourth Political Theory*, in which he calls an end to the three classical theories of liberalism, communism, and fascism, and offers in their place his fourth theory, which is essentially "a 'crusade' against the 'enemy' that distorts tradition and a pursuit of the rebirth of the archaic and futuristic at once": "This purportedly nonfascist ideological space," continues Ross, "provides ample room for the denial of 'fascism' while producing its ideology under other names."[47]

To cast Dugin's view in theological terms, the category that must be used is eschatology, which refers to discourse about the last things or the end. Dugin's mythic narrative is telling the story of good forces battling against evil forces and the final result being a victory of the good. For Dugin, though, this mythic account is tied to his geopolitical account of the contemporary world: he sees his eschatology as needing to be actualized in the here and now of the real world. His eschatology, therefore, becomes a realized or immanentized eschatology. As he writes in *The Fourth Political Theory*:

42. Clover, *Black Wind, White Snow*, 235.
43. Clover, *Black Wind, White Snow*, 235.
44. Ratner, "Most Dangerous Philosopher."
45. Ratner, "Most Dangerous Philosopher."
46. Ratner, "Most Dangerous Philosopher."
47. Ross, *Against the Fascist Creep*, 323–24.

> The end times and the eschatological meaning of politics will not realize themselves on their own. We will wait for the end in vain. The end will never come if we wait for it, and it will never come if we do not. This is essential because history, time, and reality have special strategies to avoid judgment Day, or rather, they have a special strategy of a reversionary manoeuvre [sic] that will create the impression that everyone has come to a realization and an understanding . . . If the Fourth Political Practice is not able to realise the end of times, then it would be invalid. The end of days should come; but it will not come by itself. This is a task, it is not a certainty. It is active metaphysics. It is a practice.[48]

The mythic vision of a cosmic battle and victory needs to be translated into life in the present, and engaging in the battle with all the shrewdness and power that can be mustered is required for the victory to be gained. To this end, Dugin urges specific action: "It is especially important to introduce geopolitical disorder into internal American activity, encouraging all kinds of separatism and ethnic, social and racial conflicts, actively supporting all dissident movements—extremist, racist, and sectarian groups, thus destabilizing internal political processes in the U.S. It would also maybe make sense simultaneously to support isolationist tendencies in American politics."[49]

Roger Griffin regards "the mythic core" of fascism as being "a fascist form of palingenetic ultranationalism [reborn or recreated super-nationalism]," which "means fascism is an ideology that draws on old, ancient, and even arcane myths of racial, cultural, ethnic, and national origins to develop a plan for the 'new man.'"[50] Ross suggests that Dugin's view is "unquestionably palingenetic ultranationalism" and fits as well "Umberto Eco's evaluation of syncretic 'Ur-Fascism'—the mythical understanding that all things return to one underlying spiritual essence, 'a *fuzzy* totalitarianism, a collage of different philosophical ideas, a beehive of contradictions' involving traditionalism, irrationalism, identitarianism, elitism, belief in life as struggle, and the characterization of the enemy as at once both powerful and inferior.'"[51]

---

48. Dugin, *Fourth Political Theory*, 183, as quoted in Heiser, "American Empire Destroyed," 201–2.

49. Dugin, *Foundation of Geopolitics*, 367, as quoted in Ratner, "Most Dangerous Philosopher." This important book on geopolitics has not yet been translated into English.

50. Griffin, *Nature of Fascism*, 26, and quoted in Ross, *Against the Fascist Creep*, 4–5.

51. Ross, *Against the Fascist Creep*, 199; the Eco reference is to Umberto Eco,

Possibility or the Future

It is clear from the preceding quote that Dugin's ideas have been heeded by Putin and his world. The relationship has not always been fully harmonious between these two, but it seems that they are currently most respectful of one another. They are on the same page in wanting to make Russia great again. It appears that Dugin's immanentized eschatology, which articulates a rather complete vision of possibility and the future, will have a role to play in bringing that about.

One last scholar is worth being considered in Trump-world on this topic of possibility or the future. That is Timothy Snyder, Levin Professor of History at Yale University, and his book *The Road to Unfreedom: Russia, Europe, America*. Incidentally, the author discusses Dugin at a number of points in his book, but he dismisses him in a rather offhanded fashion, viewing his life work as bringing fascism to Russia, and depicting his "Eurasian" Nazism as merely reviving or remaking Nazi ideas for Russian purposes with the Eurasian movement leading to an empire for Russia and merely nation-states for everyone else: in short, Dugin is a racist, anti-Semitic, extremely nationalistic fascist.[52] Turning now to the primary purpose of the book, Snyder is startled by a politics of irresponsibility that he sees having emerged over the past decade of the twenty-first century. At the heart of this transformation has been an alteration to our experience of time and our relation to the future: these have undergone a change, for the worse. He identifies two different experiences that have tended to prevail; they each have their own characteristics and qualities, but they share the feature that they are pulling us away from the present and away from responsible action within it, and to this extent they are ushering us into a new unfreedom. Snyder documents this new form of politics as it has appeared in Russia and as it is now making its way into Europe and America; and he ably and aptly draws lines of connection among these three. He labels the two unfortunate and inappropriate experiences of time and relating to the future—the politics of inevitability and the politics of eternity; although, it should be noted that Snyder's view of eternity is negative and therefore differs greatly from that of Kierkegaard.

The politics of inevitability, on the one hand, tells the tale of "the end of history," which conveys "a sense that the future is just more of the present, that the laws of progress are known, that there are no alternatives, and

---

"Ur-Fascism," *New York Review of Books*, June 22, 1995, http://www.nybooks.com/articles/1995/06/22ur-fascism.

52. Snyder, *Road to Unfreedom*, 47–48, 68, 88–89, 91.

therefore nothing really to be done."⁵³ In this optimistic view, "inevitability promises a better future to everybody" and "no one is responsible because we all know that the details will sort themselves out for the better."⁵⁴ Developing from this politics were the stories of America and Europe, with America's capitalist narrative running from the market to democracy to happiness and with Europe's historical narrative running from the nation to peacefulness (learned from war) to prosperity.⁵⁵ In America, the power of the politics of inevitability weakened with such setbacks as the financial crisis of 2008 and the growing gap in economic inequality: "fewer Americans believed that the future held a better version of the present."⁵⁶ A different politics slowly became more convincing.

The politics of eternity, on the other hand, which is an experience of time ushered in by the collapse of the politics of inevitability, does not promise everybody a better future as inevitability politics does, but rather it "places one nation at the center of a cyclical story of victimhood. Time is no longer a line into the future, but a circle that endlessly returns the same threats from the past."⁵⁷ In this scenario, "no one is responsible because we all know that the enemy is coming no matter what we do. Eternity politicians spread the conviction that government cannot aid society as a whole, but can only guard against threats. Progress gives way to doom."⁵⁸ We learn much about the eternity being talked about here when we hear that eternity begins with the end of factuality, its replacement by a knowing cynicism, and "the regular manufacture of crisis" keeps citizens uncertain and allows their emotions to be managed and directed.⁵⁹ Snyder describes the tactics used by the politician of eternity: "In power, eternity politicians manufacture crisis and manipulate the resultant emotion. To distract from their inability or unwillingness to reform, eternity politicians instruct their citizens to experience elation and outrage at short intervals, drowning the future in the present. In foreign policy, eternity politicians belittle and undo the achievements of countries that might seem like models to their own citizens. Using technology to transmit political fiction, both at home and

---

53. Snyder, *Road to Unfreedom*, 7.
54. Snyder, *Road to Unfreedom*, 8.
55. Snyder, *Road to Unfreedom*, 7.
56. Snyder, *Road to Unfreedom*, 7.
57. Snyder, *Road to Unfreedom*, 8.
58. Snyder, *Road to Unfreedom*, 8.
59. Snyder, *Road to Unfreedom*, 160, 162.

abroad, eternity politicians deny truth and seek to reduce life to spectacle and feeling."[60] In Russia, "Killing the political future forced the political present to be eternal; making an eternity of the present required endless crisis and permanent threats."[61] This form of politics has moved, or at least has gained an initial foothold, beyond Russia. It sounds all too familiar for those of us who have been residing in Trump-world for over two long years now.

Snyder characterizes the way each of these political viewpoints translates facts into narratives and how they operate with specific propaganda styles. But the purpose in writing his book is "to win back the present for historical time, and thus to win back historical time for politics," and to recognize that "what has happened in Russia"—"the stabilization of massive inequality, the displacement of policy by propaganda, the shift from the politics of inevitability to the politics of eternity"—"is what might happen in America and Europe."[62] There is wisdom in Snyder's words: "To experience its destruction is to see a world for the first time. Inheritors of an order we did not build, we are now witnesses to a decline we did not foresee."[63] A harsh and poignant experience of what has been lost makes one appreciate what one once had. Snyder thinks that "a history of disintegration"—which many of us believe is precisely what we have been experiencing in our context, to which disintegration my writing of this little book, at least in part, is a response—"can be a guide to repair. Erosion reveals what resists, what can be reinforced, what can be reconstructed, and what must be reconceived."[64] I hope that what we are about here is exactly such resisting, reinforcing, reconstructing, and reconceiving. Nothing less is required in order "to resuscitate history,"[65] or as I maintain, to resurrect history and democracy. Snyder underscores the polar relation that exists between institutions and virtues: "If institutions are to flourish, they need virtues; if virtues are to be cultivated, they need institutions."[66] I think that our consideration of Kierkegaard and Kierkegaard-world on selected topics has directed us to some virtues that might be helpful in dealing with the political challenge of

60. Snyder, *Road to Unfreedom*, 8.
61. Snyder, *Road to Unfreedom*, 48.
62. Snyder, *Road to Unfreedom*, 9–10.
63. Snyder, *Road to Unfreedom*, 277.
64. Snyder, *Road to Unfreedom*, 13.
65. Snyder, *Road to Unfreedom*, 13.
66. Snyder, *Road to Unfreedom*, 13.

resurrecting the institution of democracy lying before us. To the Kierkegaardian treatment of the sixth topic we now turn.

Kierkegaard and Kierkegaard-World

Correspondingly, how is it that divinity or God might be potently present in actuality and discernible according to Kierkegaard and Kierkegaard-world on possibility or the future?

During the last couple of years of his life, in looking to the future and considering the possibilities before him, Kierkegaard felt a profound sense of urgency to do what he could to bring about a change in the church. This led to what came to be called his "attack on Christendom." The term "Christendom," of course, was not confined to a narrow understanding of the church; rather, it referred to the religious legitimation of the socio-political, cultural establishment of the time in Denmark, and more particularly, Copenhagen. But the attack was focused on established Christianity, and particularly on two figures we have already encountered—Mynster and Martensen. Martensen became bishop of the Lutheran Church of Denmark after Mynster's death. Kierkegaard's harsh criticisms of the Christian church took place in 1854 and 1855. Some have viewed this later attack on established Christianity by Kierkegaard as being out of character with his normal way of operating. According to that view, normally, the naturally prone-to-critique Kierkegaard holds in check his public criticisms of Christianity, but not so in the case of the attack. Normally, in the pseudonymous writings of the first part of his authorship at any rate, Kierkegaard is concerned to use indirect rather than direct communication, but in the case of the attack his communicating is very direct. Normally, Kierkegaard did not very often mention explicitly in his public writings the great clique or coterie of the established order—J. L. Heiberg, J. P Mynster, and H. L. Martensen, but in the attack especially the latter two figures are quite overtly denounced.

I think, over against this view of the attack as being discontinuous with the earlier Kierkegaard, that it is more in continuity with his previous public and private writings than is often realized. Martensen's writings all along had been affirming the Christian church and objectivity as themes that needed to be lifted up at a time in which individuality and subjectivity were receiving excessive emphasis. Martensen had been consistently eliciting negative responses from Kierkegaard and these critical assaults constitute a "pre-attack" of established Christianity which blossoms into a full-fledged attack at the end of his life. Kierkegaard's final attack is best understood, then, not as an outburst that explodes out of nowhere but rather as an organic outgrowth of his earlier critical labors. In terms of contemporary emergence theory, the form of emergence involved here is of the weak rather than strong variety, since the new property of attack can be accounted for on the basis of elements at the preceding pre-attack level.

As we have articulated, Kierkegaard saw contemporary culture as destroying persons, and validating that culture was the established Christianity of Christendom. Constitutive elements of modern culture—"the public," "the press," "the crowd," "the numerical," and "the professor"—ought to properly be seen as including "the church" as well. On Kierkegaard's view, all of these elements were functioning in concert to level life by shrinking the scope and squelching the passionate intensity of human freedom. Martensen shared aspects of Kierkegaard's analysis of the contemporary cultural configuration, though Kierkegaard was much more the prophetic gadfly for his time, likely because he more sensitively and profoundly discerned just how devastatingly these elements were insidiously shaping human existence in deleterious ways. Martensen's terms of analysis are often used by Kierkegaard, though just as often in support of an opposite judgment. We have seen that both realized the crucial place of subjectivity, but Martensen was attempting to provide a corrective of his own to what he saw as an overemphasis on subjectivity, by emphasizing objectivity. This disagreement over subjectivity and objectivity was at the center of Kierkegaard's problem with Martensen. A further reality complicit in the leveling of subjectivity's passion required criticism, and that was "the church." On Kierkegaard's view, if Christianity had been replaced by Christendom, which to his mind it surely had, then, the corrective required is the reintroduction of Christianity into Christendom, and it is precisely this which Kierkegaard's attack attempted to accomplish.

Figure 11: Bishop Hans Lassen Martensen (1808–1884)

Quickly recounting eight important events of 1854 conveys the basic temporal development that led to the attack, which is directed most pointedly toward Martensen. The first of these events is the death of Jacob Peter Mynster, which took place on January 30, 1854. This figure, we remind ourselves, held importance for both Kierkegaard and Martensen. The second event is the memorial service for Mynster that was held on February 5, 1854. At that service, the theme of "witness to the truth," which held special significance for both Kierkegaard and Martensen, was applied to Mynster, and Kierkegaard regarded this application as absolutely outrageous. Event three is the funeral for Mynster that was conducted on February 7, 1854.

Figure 12: Søren Kierkegaard (1813–1855)

Informing Martensen's handling of this event is likely the same thoughts on the significance of Mynster's life that he articulated in a talk he later gave to the Society of Scientists, in which he characterized Mynster's understanding of the age of modernity as the age of humanity, noting how Mynster understood humanity as being mutually correlated to Christianity. In Kierkegaard's eyes, of course, as we have noted, Mynster's theological understanding of the relation of Christianity to culture had contributed precisely to the problem that needed to be addressed. Event number four is Martensen being named Mynster's successor as bishop of Sjælland, the prime bishop's chair of the Danish Lutheran Church, by the king on April 15, 1854. This added another gold star to Martensen's résumé, providing yet one more reason for Kierkegaard's irritation with and resentment toward his former teacher. Event five is Martensen being installed as bishop of Sjælland on June 5, 1854, which calls to mind Martensen's 1843 writing on Christian baptism, in which he presents his theological understanding of the church, and the many critical comments on that writing that Kierkegaard entered into his journals. The sixth event is the beginning of Kierkegaard's official attack on establishment Christianity on December 18, 1854. It can be pointed out that the many criticisms Kierkegaard sets forth over the next months, by way of a series of pamphlets that he published at his own expense, were very hard-hitting blows intended to be a corrective prompting change. It is worth recalling that Martensen, himself, had published an 1842 article on "The Religious Crisis of the Present" in which—in response to the threats to the state church on the left by such Hegelians as Feuerbach and Strauss and on the right by avid zealous sectarians—he recognized that a corrective was required and that this corrective should take the form of the church instituting a self-criticism. Martensen believed that only a critique from the inside would be able to afford the church a genuine advance in spiritual self-consciousness. Event seven is the ordination service Martensen conducted for two bishops on December 26, 1854, in which he again preached on "the witness to the truth" theme, and which again roiled Kierkegaard's hostile juices. The eighth and final event is Martensen's single response to Kierkegaard's attack, published in the *Berlingske Tidende* on December 28, 1854. Martensen remained silent during the attack, making no further response to his critic, Kierkegaard, who died on November 11 of the next year.

A couple of quotations from *The Moment*, convey a flavor of Kierkegaard's literary attack on Christendom. One can see that he utilizes humor as well as various rhetorical devices to make his points. The first quote is from issue number 5 of *The Moment*:

> Since long robes have now become the professional apparel for pastors, one can also be sure that this implies something, and I think that by paying attention to what it implies one can interpret very characteristically the nature or odious practice of official Christianity.
>
> Long robes involuntarily prompt the thought that there is something to hide; when one has something to hide, long robes are very appropriate—and official Christianity has a great deal to hide, because from start to finish it is an untruth, which therefore is best hidden—in long robes.[67]

The second quote is from a little piece entitled "That 'Christendom's' Crime is Comparable to Wanting to Appropriate an Inheritance Unjustifiably" that is included in issue number 10 of *The Moment*:

> Christianity is a gift, if you will, stipulated for humanity according to the testament of the Savior of the world. But there is a responsibility; with regard to Christianity, the relation is this: the gift and

---

67. Kierkegaard, *Moment and Late Writings*, 199.

> the responsibility correspond to each other altogether equally; to the same degree that Christianity is a gift it is also a responsibility.
>
> "Christendom's" skullduggery is to accept the gift and say good-bye to the responsibility, to want to be the heir to the gift but without accepting the responsibility, to want to make it appear as if humanity is indeed the heir whom the Savior of the world himself has in his will designated as the heir, whereas the truth is that only with the observance of the responsibility is humanity or, more correctly (since, precisely because it is a responsibility, an abstraction such as "humanity" can at most be called the heir only figuratively), each individual within humanity the heir.[68]

Kierkegaard's attack on Christendom, did not appear out of the blue; there were earlier "pre-attacks" that shared resemblances with the later full-blown attack. In both instances, Kierkegaard was actualizing possibilities that he hoped would make a positive impact on the future.

In the world of Trump, the province of the imagination is the past, and the domain of the future is fear. In the world of Kierkegaard, the province of the imagination is the future, and the domain of the future is possibility.[69] According to Kierkegaard's estimation, the importance of the imagination cannot be over-emphasized because it is the human's means of access to the future's possibilities. Thompson and Cuff highlight how Kierkegaard's pseudonym Anti-Climacus had recognized the imagination as "the medium for the process of infinitizing," as the capacity for all capacities of the self, as that in knowledge from which the categories derive, as "the rendition of the self as the self's possibility," as "the possibility for any and all reflection," and as that whose intensity "is the possibility and intensity of the self."[70] The imagination is a multi-faceted human faculty or medium. It functions to pull us forward; as Kierkegaard writes in a journal entry: in imagination, "everyone, even the most capable, is usually a good distance beyond himself or beyond what she is in act and actuality."[71] As the imagination reaches out ahead into the future it lures us to live life forward. This is what Kierkegaard means in a later, 1854, entry: "Imagination is what providence uses to take men captive in actuality [*Virkeligheden*], in existence [*Tilværelsen*], in order to get them far enough out, or within, or down

---

68. Kierkegaard, *Moment and Late Writings*, 336.

69. See Thompson, "Interpreting God's Translucent World."

70. Thompson and Cuff, *God and Nature*, 258, and these various dimensions of the imagination refer to Kierkegaard, *Sickness unto Death*, 30–31.

71. *Pap.* VIII1 A 292 n.d. 1847; Kierkegaard, *Journals and Papers* 1, 1049.

into actuality. And when imagination has helped them get as far out as they should be—then actuality genuinely begins."[72] The power of the ideal, the possible, draws us out, enabling us to go deeper into what might be, so that we are able to go forward, into actuality. If Donald's thinking naturally orients him to fear, to the past, and to living life backwards, Søren's thinking naturally orients him to hope, to the future, and to living life forward.

Kierkegaard links possibility to the future in *Works of Love* : "To hope relates to the future, to possibility."[73] Dealing with possibility's future involves "a duality, the possibility of advance or of retrogression, of rising or falling, of good or of evil"; then this is spelled out further by instructing us on some fine points concerning eternity's relation to time's three modes of past, present, and future: "The eternal *is*, but when the eternal touches the temporal or is in the temporal, they do not meet each other in the *present*, because in that case the present would itself be the eternal. The present, the moment, is over so quickly that it actually does not exist, it is only the boundary and therefore is past, whereas the past is what was present. Therefore, when the eternal is in the temporal, it is in the future. This, of course, is why we call tomorrow the future, but we also call eternal life the future. The possible as such is always a duality, and in possibility the eternal always relates itself equally to its duality."[74] The present moment cannot accommodate the eternal because about when it is ready to do that it is over as the present moment and has moved into the past. The past is done, no longer alive, now marked by necessity rather than possibility, and thus it is no candidate for entertaining the eternal. Therefore, by default, the future is the mode of temporality that can accommodate the eternal.

The category of expectation then comes into the picture. It too is marked by the same duality as is possibility. Kierkegaard continues: "When a person to whom the possible pertains relates herself equally to the duality of the possible, we say: She *expects*. To expect contains within itself the same duality that the possible has, and to expect is to relate oneself to the possible purely and simply as such. Then the relationship divides according to the way the expecting person chooses."[75] At this point, as if responding to Trump, Kierkegaard goes on to differentiate between hope and fear: "To relate oneself expectantly to the possibility of the good is to *hope*"; "to re-

---

72. *Pap.* XI1 A 288 n.d., 1854; Kierkegaard, *Journals and Papers* 2, 1832.
73. Kierkegaard, *Works of Love*, 249.
74. Kierkegaard, *Works of Love*, 249.
75. Kierkegaard, *Works of Love*, 249.

late oneself expectantly to the possibility of evil is to *fear*."[76] These different postures in relating to possibility are gigantic, for as soon "as the choice is made, the possible is changed, because the possibility of the good is the eternal": "by the decision to choose hope, one decides infinitely more than it seems, because it is an eternal decision; . . . in the differentiation (and the choice is indeed differentiating) the possibility of the good is more than a possibility, because it is the eternal."[77]

In an 1844 upbuilding discourse entitled "The Expectancy of Eternal Salvation," Kierkegaard introduces another duality in relation to expectation. He claims that the expectancy of an eternal salvation is dual in that "it works in heaven and it works on earth."[78] With the consequence of this expectancy being twofold, he turns first to a consideration of "the meaning of this expectancy for the present life." And it is that side of the duality, the side addressing how the expectancy of eternal salvation comes to bear on our life in the secular world, which I want to consider. This secular expectancy does not present imagery of a heavenly scene; it's not by-and-by-in-the-sky language of expectation concerning the last things, the type of religious language that Karl Marx characterized as lingo of the end times that draws believers away from the pressing realities of this world. No, this expectancy doesn't lead to eschatological escapism, as some have called it, but rather directs us to temporality or to that time in which we live out our everyday lives. Here our imagination is directed not to the imagery of heaven, but to imagery of the temporal world, our contemporary world that is full of concerns and conflicts and conversations and considerations. We are to have expectations for this worldly, earthly, secular life that we carry out under the conditions of time and space, no less than we are to have expectations for heaven. Kierkegaard thinks it is good to focus on our expectations for our life together in time.

Most all of us have our daily expectations. For some, it's living the life of the student, going to classes and in the setting of those classes relating as best can be done to the intellectual expectations that have been established. The same goes for people working in offices; in that setting there are the challenges and expectations of the workplace that come to bear on workers. Participation on sports teams or in clubs or associations carries with it peculiar expectations as well. But in this particular time in our country,

---

76. Kierkegaard, *Works of Love*, 249.
77. Kierkegaard, *Works of Love*, 249–50.
78. Kierkegaard, *Eighteen Upbuilding Discourses*, 259.

many are also feeling, or should be feeling, an expectation that might well be new for a large number, and that is the expectation to do what can be done politically to make a difference in our challenging times. That might be to participate in a political organization or an action group of some kind, or simply to make sure to vote in elections.

We have the privilege of living in a democracy, a democratic republic in which we have elections to determine whom we want to represent us. Elections can give us hope. If one group of people is disappointed by the current government, it can work to change things politically. So expectation or hope is written right into our form of government. If people are upset, they can do something about it the next time elections come around. They can elect a different sort of representative and bring what they take to be a needed correction to the group or party that is currently in control.

Many were saying that the mid-term election of November 2018 would possibly be the most important mid-term of our lifetimes. There were record numbers of early voters and voter registration numbers were up substantially as well. Pollsters reported that an unusually large number of House, Senate, and state governor contests were too close to call. Many people stayed up late watching the results as they came in. We can be sure that, upon learning results, there was some mourning and crying and pain, as fervent supporters found out that their candidate had lost. Others were shouting joyfully because of a key victory. But the results mattered deeply to people. And that's as it should be. That is because the secular expectations that are disappointed or fulfilled in elections—while not having a heavenly consequence—do carry a holy dimension. For these temporal decisions can make a difference in the degree of wholeness that is being created for people in society. Also, these temporal decisions in turn shape the real-life decisions that will consequently be made on issues that matter to people.

Divinity, divine love, is at work in every cranny of life to creatively nurture the lives of creatures toward greater wholeness. For humans, that means nourishing freedom by doing what can be done to present possibilities for richer lives. But the divine has to work within the structures that are in play, and some structures are better than others for facilitating more abundant living; and some political figures are more fit than others for introducing structures that do more to empower the movement of life toward greater fullness. Therefore, part of the divine work of loving us is to call us to discern which leaders are going to serve the creative advance in such a way that the earth's creatures will experience greater well-being.

Possibility or the Future

That means that we've got significant responsibility, because there is a divine expectation for us to be competent, compassionate co-creators with divine love. Kierkegaard's upbuilding admonition in our time would be: to keep in mind that divine love forcefully urges us every day to get involved, to exercise our freedom, and to make a difference. He might even urge us to listen carefully, so that we might be able to hear that gentle but persistent divine voice calling to us, saying: "Doggone it, get involved! Because it's the responsible, loving thing to do."

Vigilius Haufniensis of Kierkegaard-world, pseudonym of *The Concept of Anxiety*, writes, "The possible corresponds exactly to the future, and the future is for time the possible."[79] Then Anti-Climacus brings the "God" word into the conversation (which we can replace with the divine or divine love), writing in *Sickness*: "She who does not have a God does not have a self, either . . . Since everything is possible for God, then God is this—that everything is possible . . . To pray is also to breathe, and possibility is for the self what oxygen is for breathing . . . The existence of God means that everything is possible, or that everything is possible means the existence of God."[80]

Sometimes big things come out of little things. I have found rather big and significant a little phrase that Kierkegaard wrote onto a slip of paper on March 19, 1837. "That which I transcribe here was on a scrap of paper," he says, "and antedates my acquaintance with the younger Fichte [Immanuel Herman Fichte (1797–1879), son of Johan Gottlieb Fichte (1762–1814)], of whose works I have hastily read only *Idee der Personlichkeit*; no doubt it [the jotting] was written in February [of 1837]."[81] The short phrase stated is, "God is the actuality of the possible."[82] Or, I like, "God is the actuality of possibility." I want to attribute this thought to Kierkegaard, although all that I can be sure of is that he was intrigued enough by it to jot it down on a piece of paper and a month later to enter it into his Journal. We surely can safely assume, though, its place in Kierkegaard-world, and it does nicely

---

79. Kierkegaard, *Concept of Anxiety*, 91.

80. Kierkegaard, *Sickness unto Death*, 40.

81. Kierkegaard, *Kierkegaard's Journals and Notebooks* 1:35; Kierkegaard, *Journals and Papers* 2, 1190.

82. The Danish reads, "Gud er det Muliges Virkelighed." Therefore, this translation, "God is the actuality of the possible," is the most accurate. However, the use of "possibility" instead of "the possible" makes for a little more alluring phrase with little loss of meaning and better fits the topic under consideration. For a more extended discussion of God in relation to possibility, see my *Following the Cultured Public's Chosen One*, 169–80.

sum up what Kierkegaard says about possibility in relation to the divine. This is a construal of the divine that I think communicates a notion of God that serves an understanding of the divine as love. It speaks of the divine as Possibilizer, which—if we follow Plato's suggestion that we ought to become like the divine—presents us with the task of possibilizing in relation to the other. Possibilizing is what love is all about. But just what does such possibilizing mean?

Again, in *Works of Love*, we learn more. He states there that love hopes the other person will have access to the possibility of the good: "Lovingly to hope all things signifies the relationship of the loving one to other people, so in relation to them, hoping for them, he continually holds possibility open with an infinite partiality for the possibility of the good. That is, he lovingly hopes that at every moment there is possibility, the possibility of the good for the other person."[83] Love both hopes and acts; without hope, love cannot engage in loving action. To enlarge possibility for a person or a situation, there are many things that can be done. But possibilizing is surely an essential part of loving, for expanding possibilities oftentimes serves as a key ingredient in allowing freedom to function. For Kierkegaard, "the highest one human being can do for another is to make her free, help her to stand by herself"; and to do this ethically and lovingly, "the helper must be able to make herself anonymous, must magnanimously will to annihilate herself," so "that it remained hidden from the person helped that he was helped and how."[84] To possibilize is to expand possibility, to infinitize, to potentiate, in brief, to enlarge the other's freedom. Possibilizing unlocks the potential of freedom so that it can be acted on and contribute to the movement of the self into greater fullness of life. To possibilize is to love. Possibilizing carries within it the divine power of resurrection.

Divinity is situated at the heart of life for Kierkegaard, and as eternity, it holds in dynamic unity the interdependent realities of love, hope, and possibility. As he states, the less love there is in a person, the less of the eternal there is in that one as well, and if there is less of the eternal, then there is also less possibility, or less of a sense of possibility in that person, because possibility appears as the eternal touches in time the eternal in the human, so that if there is nothing eternal in that person, then the eternal's touching that one is in vain and there is no possibility.[85] It sounds in this statement

---

83. Kierkegaard, *Works of Love*, 253.
84. Kierkegaard, *Works of Love*, 286.
85. Kierkegaard, *Works of Love*, 258.

Possibility or the Future

as though a condition is in place for being able to receive possibilities, and this is quite enigmatic. One suggestion for a possible way to interpret this is to view the condition as being established by the difference between the possible and the actual. The less love, the less of the eternal, and the less possibility, that's the formula in place, because possibility comes when what we might call the transcendent eternal touches what we might call the immanent eternal. But if the immanent eternal is the desire implanted in the human by divinity, and this implanted desire is a potential to be actualized, then, when it is actualized and takes the shape of love, there is more of a basis to the eternality present within the human, so there is more of the immanent eternal to be touched by the transcendent eternal, and thereby more possibility can come to the person, because the actualization of the desire in love gives greater substantiality to the eternal. Divinity's implanted desire is potential love, and such potential love possesses enough of the eternal for it to be touched by the eternal to receive more possibilities, but when such potential love becomes actual love, further possibilities can be received.

A similar dynamic is at work in Kierkegaard's treatment of the distinction between originality and acquired originality. He mentions these two in reflecting on what can be learned from the lily in the field and the bird of the air. The lily and the bird possess at first hand "the direct and first originality," but "the acquired originality" is different: "the acquired originality" is "simplicity," and "the simplicity is that the teacher herself is what she is teaching."[86] These two, the lily and the bird, in their simplicity "are completely present to themselves in being today."[87] As the human being learns from these two about "becoming completely present to oneself in being today," the matter becomes more complicated because of the difference between potentiality and actuality for humans. We have originality implanted within ourselves, but it is present as a potential that needs to be actualized. When that actualization comes about, though never a finished result but ever requiring fresh repetition, then, acquired originality is at hand. This is in keeping with what has been stated throughout our discussion. We have affirmed an original desire, a desire-longing-for-the-divine or love, implanted within the human as desire or longing or would-be love, but this is a potentiality that needs to be actualized. When that actualizing happens, then it takes on the character of an "acquired originality" that thereby gives

---

86. Kierkegaard, *Without Authority*, 38.
87. Kierkegaard, *Without Authority*, 39.

shape in one's actual existence to what one is in one's (potential) essence. All this is possible because divinity or the divine, who is love, works as one's coworker to empower one to progressively move toward becoming more fully one who is love, which is to progress toward becoming more like the divine, a lover. The lover has become completely present to herself in being today.[88]

And the lover hopes. Kierkegaard asserts that the person who loves knows the personal joy of eternity vouching for her that there is always hope: "the one who truly loves, does not hope *because* eternity authenticates it to her, but she hopes *because* she is one who loves, and she thanks eternity that she dares to hope."[89] For Kierkegaard, then, participating in a relationship with the divine is at the same time opening oneself to the infinite arena of possibility, being able to breathe with ease because of the lightness of the possible, venturing with zest and verve because of living forward into an open future, and being energized by hope because of being buoyed up "with the help of the eternal, that is, with the help of the possibility of the good."[90]

---

88. See the rich discussion of this theme of acquired originality in the article, "To Become Love Itself: Charity as Acquired Originality in Kierkegaardian Christianity," in *Kierkegaard Studies Yearbook*, forthcoming 2019.

89. Kierkegaard, *Works of Love*, 259.

90. Kierkegaard, *Works of Love*, 250.

Conclusion

The question being held before us in this book is, "How is divinity at work in the world, and in particular, in our American context to resurrect democracy? How can divinity's implanting of desire within the human make a discernible difference in improving our situation of democratic discourse and institutions being undercut and devastated?" Having engaged in a brief comparison of Trump and Trump-world over against Kierkegaard and Kierkegaard-world, we can conclude that the former is not a clone of the latter. Instead, we find these two being very much at odds with one another. In all six areas we looked at, Donald consistently manifested himself in ways that lifted up himself and his infatuation with glamor, glitz, and glory that were maybe powerful in a superficial sense but not conducive to standing up as hot spots of divine disclosure in our contemporary context. On the other hand, Søren drew us much closer to the subtle aspects of operating as full human beings and directed us to places—which Trump would judge as weak and impotent—where we could encounter in, with, and under our deepest, most elemental human experiences the actual presence of the divine being discerned. If we take a step back from this analysis, it seems that Kierkegaard is giving us clues to features of our humanity that are essential to pay attention to if we are going to develop into free and responsible human beings, the kind of folks that make for good citizens in a democracy.

Of course, we are currently suffering from constitutional dysfunction[1] and polarization of our society, and these two closely-related factors of our

---

1. Balkan, "Constitutional Rot," 20, clarifies that constitutional dysfunction is a problem of representation: over time our political system has become less democratic [i.e., less responsive to popular will and popular opinion] and less republican [i.e., that representatives are less devoted to the public good, and less responsive to the interests of the public as a whole, as opposed to a small group; and when the latter happens, we

time are not going to be easily overcome. A counter-move in the November 2018 midterms brought a rebalancing of sorts in the powers that be. New congressional investigations are being undertaken in 2019. But the gigantic task facing us all is to regain the capacity for being civil and gracious, not just to our political colleagues, but most especially to those on the other side of the divide. We don't require, nor should we want, complete unanimity or uniformity as a nation, but we do require enough civility to sponsor compromise and compassion by which we can jointly arrive at consensus. To listen one last time to a journal entry not of the Don but of the Dane, "Where reconciliation takes place, there the altar is, and reconciliation itself is the only gift that can be offered upon the altar of God."[2] Divinity, construed as the divine, is manifested in reconciliation being instantiated.

In drawing our discussion to a close, the focus falls on addressing the challenge of reclaiming the institution of democracy. In approaching this task, we ought not allow ourselves to be naïve or sanguine. David Runciman, Professor of Politics at Cambridge University, can help to brace us for dealing realistically with the daunting possibility that democracy might be coming to an end. Runciman's analysis leads him to the view that democracy will very likely not come to a sudden end but will rather limp along, enjoying some occasional successes while suffering notable setbacks. He is very pessimistic about democracy fully winning the day again; instead he forecasts that "slowly but surely, democracy will come to an end," even though it "will certainly have a drawn-out demise"; but he thinks this political institution is a relative good whose demise ought not to be equated with our demise, because we are not to be equated with democracy: "its salvation is not our salvation," and "we could save democracy and destroy the world."[3] He warns that if we remain insistent on affirming the sacrosanct status of democracy, we might be blinded from better alternatives that could possibly be brought into being.[4] He closes his book by claiming that "Western democracy will survive its mid-life crisis," maybe being chastened a little by it, but not likely being revived by it; for, as he coyly

---

have an oligarchy].

2. Kierkegaard, *Works of Love*, Supplement: 420: *Journals and Papers* 2, 1208 (*Pap.* VIII1 A 115) n.d., 1847.

3. Runciman, *How Democracy Ends*, 216–17.

4. Runciman, *How Democracy Ends*, 217–18.

CONCLUSION

contends, in our current situation we are not experiencing "the end of democracy," but we are experiencing "how democracy ends."[5]

As we proceed with our conclusions we can acknowledge with Runciman that democracy is a political institution whose goodness and worth are relative rather than absolute, that we need to be realistic and somber about our abilities to revive it back to its full health, and that we should not be closed off from new ideas that might transform it into a stronger structure for organizing and facilitating the deliberations of our political life. On the other hand, we ought not be too quick to throw up our hands in disgust and despair and throw in the towel prematurely on this critical challenge facing us.[6]

An interesting distinction is made in *How to Save a Constitutional Democracy* by Gingsburg and Huq. Although democracy has been known to be a government of, for, and by "the people," they want "to avoid the loaded and hazardously totalizing term *the People*" and to speak instead of "the *participants in a democracy*."[7] For them, as we recall, a "liberal constitutional democracy is a system that involves three discrete and mutually

---

5. Runciman, *How Democracy Ends*, 218.

6. My focus in this book falls predominantly on the contributions that can come from changes at the personal or individual level under the tutoring of Søren Kierkegaard. A book that focuses more on larger forces and dynamics at play in our situation is Gardels and Berggruen, *Renovating Democracy*. These authors call for changes at a more systemic level as guided by their belief that democracy needs to be renovated so that it can address "the uncertainties posed by the great transformations under way, from the intrusions of globalization on how sovereign communities govern their affairs, to such rapid advances in technology as social media and robotics, to the increasingly multicultural composition of all societies." Gardels and Berggruen, *Renovating Democracy*, 5. They hold that renovation rather than rebellion, populism, or reform is the required course of change for modern societies, and renovation, which mixes creation and destruction, saving what is of value and discarding what is outmoded, can be best applied to renovating democracy, the social contract, and global interconnectivity in three ways: first, by "empowering participation without populism by integrating social networks and direct democracy into the system through the establishment of new mediating institutions that complement representative government"; second, by "reconfiguring the social contract to protect workers instead of jobs while spreading the wealth of digital capitalism by providing all citizens not only with the skills of the future but also with an equity share in 'owning the robots'"; and, third, by "harnessing globalization through 'positive nationalism' at home, global cooperation where necessary, and partnership where interests converge to temper the strategic rivalry between China and the United States." Gardels and Berggruen, *Renovating Democracy*, 6–7. This important book was published just as I was sending my manuscript to press. I wish I could have incorporated some of its ideas into my account.

7. Ginsburg and Huq, *Constitutional Democracy*, 238.

reinforcing elements, each of which must be safeguarded: electoral competition, associational and speech rights, and the rule of law, understood not so much as the superiority of judges as the broader ideas of bureaucratic autonomy and rule-following."[8] While these three ingredients are necessary, they are not sufficient for sustaining a democracy; for these University of Chicago law professors recognize that "there is no democracy without a decent measure of popular commitment to democracy."[9] Such popular commitment means participation in the democratic process. These scholars emphasize that, in the end, even "constitutions cannot save democracy: Only (small d) democrats can," or those who are prepared as participants to put democracy into practice.[10] I agree with these authors that this emphasis on participating in a liberal constitutional democracy is key, and I agree with them that such commitment is legitimated by the moral superiority of this form of government, which flows from its (at least theoretical) commitment "to a principle of political equality in which each citizen's voice counts to the same extent."[11] My effort here is in keeping with this turn to the practical.

There is need for us to mobilize one another in the belief and hope that some reviving of democracy might still be possible, and that reviving will happen through more effective participation in the practice or praxis of democracy. I'm calling that reviving—"resurrecting." That entails making bold to speak of divinity and the holy desire implanted within each of us to construe the divine and to embrace the divine as the reality of love. Injecting religion into the situation at this point does not mean shifting our attention to another realm of reality. That would not be very Kierkegaardian. As Johannes Climacus reminds us: "It shows greater respect for the religious to demand that it be installed in its rights in everyday life rather than affectedly to hold it off at a Sunday distance."[12] This sort of language, theological language, gives us access to a resource—the divine loving power of creative transformation—that can provide a basis for affirming the possibility of resurrection.

Of course, resurrection language, while being present in more than one religious tradition, enjoys the most central place in that monotheistic

---

8. Ginsburg and Huq, *Constitutional Democracy*, 238.
9. Ginsburg and Huq, *Constitutional Democracy*, 238.
10. Ginsburg and Huq, *Constitutional Democracy*, 240, 10.
11. Ginsburg and Huq, *Constitutional Democracy*, 24.
12. Kierkegaard, *Concluding Scientific Postscript*, 1:313.

CONCLUSION

religion focused on the one whom Alfred North Whitehead refers to as "the brief Galilean vision of humility" that "flickered throughout the ages, uncertainly," and was an expression of divine love.[13] We can learn a couple of things from this tradition on resurrection. First, while it is the resurrection of this one that this religion celebrates, within that religion the term resurrection came to apply as well to the new resurrection life this living one was engendering within communities of followers. I want to emphasize that second meaning of resurrection in our particular situation: as we make claims of resurrecting democracy, we are referring to happenings that can take place here-and-now within our everyday experiences. Second, within this religion, the stories of resurrection arose in response to death by crucifixion of the Galilean lover, and these stories included the wounds of this death as an important part of their communication of new life.[14] As we speak of resurrecting democracy, we want to acknowledge the extremely negative, hate-filled events that have taken place in recent years under the name of democracy, with many now bearing deep scars and wounds of those events and bringing the afterlife of their crosses into the current context, and we want to be sure not to leave those wounds behind, but to carry them forward as part of the wholeness-restoring process of resurrecting democracy. The resurrecting we are striving to nurture and facilitate is finally a mystery, a mystery grounded in the divine loving power of creative transformation, but it's also a mystery in which we can play a role in helping to become a reality as we take seriously our status as coworkers with divine love.

Wendell Berry, poet, novelist, and nonfiction writer, published in 1971 a powerful poem entitled "Manifesto: The Mad Farmer Liberation Front," the ending line of which reads "Practice resurrection."[15] I regard that exclamation as a beautiful admonition. I want to utilize that phrase in our discussion of divinity resurrecting democracy. It appropriately puts the stress on the action of human freedom: if a difference is to be made in our situation, it is going to be a difference made by those of us citizens who are desiring a change of quality in our political life. Many presidential candidates for 2020 are being quick to say as they announce that they are in the running, "We can do better than this!" We surely can, and one significant way to do that is to tend to the task of practicing resurrection.

13. Whitehead, *Process and Reality*, 342–43.
14. Rambo, *Resurrecting Wounds*.
15. Berry, "Manifesto."

What follows is a run-down of Kierkegaardian insights that emerged in our discussion of the six topics—sixteen insights into actions that can be seen to possess power for resurrecting democracy. Since the NCAA Division I Men's Basketball Tournament expanded its field to 64 teams in the 1980s, the regional semifinal round of March Madness has been called the "Sweet 16." That term, the Sweet 16, works well for designating Kierkegaard's sixteen insights, for they do sweeten the possibility of resurrecting democracy. Each of the book's six topics will be considered in turn, to identify these sixteen places where Kierkegaard or Kierkegaard-world has helped us to go deeper in order to go forward.

Narrativity or story. One place where a clue to resurrection possibility lies latently present is in Kierkegaard's awareness that the story he told in his authorship needed to be comprehensive enough to cover the full range of concerns. That was one of the reasons for employing pseudonyms in his authorship: to be able to present many different perspectives for his readers to entertain. Attempts to truncate the story, to radically curtail it and reduce it to a bumper sticker slogan for attacking one's opponents, is to reduce it to false news. Truth demands appropriate breadth of the story line so that factual evidence can substantiate claims made. One dimension of operating truthfully in storytelling is to make the effort to tell the whole story, to be inclusive in scope so as to avoid cherry-picking from the facts of the story to bolster one's preferred version of it, but also so as to relate to as many listeners and readers as possible by giving them points of connection to the story being told. That applies as well to the telling of our national story. We need to be aware of the longer temporal reach of our history so that we can know that the chaotic disfunction currently befuddling us has from time-to-time visited us previously but also that our history is marked by significant periods when genuine bipartisanship worked extremely well. To realize things have not always been the way they are—that they have become this way through actions by people like us—creates space for thinking seriously about changing how we relate to one another for the better. We have fantastic national historians—Jon Meacham, Doris Kearns Goodwin, Michael Beschloss, and Jill Lepore, to name a few—who can provide us with that larger perspective through their comprehensive storytelling, and we should access their narratives as background for relating more effectively in our encounters with others.

Insights for practicing resurrection can also be identified in relation to the imparting or telling of our story, and this gives us the second point of the Sweet 16. Kierkegaard was highly conscious of both the content of his story and the style of communicating his story, and resurrecting power for relating to others can be gained by tending to both of these areas. The content for him was addressed to single individuals with the intent of moving them to take the relationship with themselves seriously, so as through their personal self-relation or conscience to realize that they possessed the power to give shape to themselves. Kierkegaard's second focus, on the style of communication, is again basically treating the communication recipient with respect and dignity, wanting to relate in one's storytelling in a way that establishes connections to where that person is at in life so that there might be interest piqued by which the story can be better appropriated. This style concern is again taking the individuality of the recipient seriously in all its personal dimensions. Both of these concerns call in different ways for acknowledging the humanity of the other. Such relating possesses potency for breathing new life into situations that were previously close to dead. Narratives, thoughtfully communicated, can embody resurrection power if they inspire individuals to become more centered and courageous, which can create greater personal integrity and weaken if not break the binding power of tribal or partisan inclinations.

Interiority or earnestness. This topic too makes suggestions for practicing resurrection. To journey into one's interiority and to become a person of earnestness is essential for going more deeply into life. Earnestness gives one a sense of ownership about who one really is and a grounding for making judgments concerning the extent to which behaviors or statements are in accord with the actual state of affairs or with what ought to be the case. Without earnestness a person will not possess the wherewithal to function critically in relation to the world. With earnestness one is equipped with potential for being a prophet or prophetess. In Kierkegaard's case, his criticism was directed most forcefully against what he perceived to be disfunctions, aberrations, or abuses in cultural and religious life. However, his insights into the value of earnestness surely also are relevant for practicing resurrection through critically speaking truth to power in the political arena. His example can be extended to a political ideology critique that employs a hermeneutics or interpretation theory of suspicion to expose self-serving, party-serving, or even Russia-serving interests at play in political principles, policies, and practices.

Kierkegaard, of course, advocated for the critical scrutiny nurtured by earnestness to be directed inwardly no less than outwardly. Because of the propensity for human selfishness, he believed that the individual needs to distrust oneself and to be suspicious of oneself. In our extremely partisan environment, it is hard to imagine a more potent weapon to utilize in practicing resurrection than the regular administration of a heavy dose of self-scrutiny upon one's psyche, to examine closely the true motives, intentions, and goals of one's behaviors. The Danish Socrates knew that his namesake's claim that "the unexamined life is not worth living," applied no less to life in mid-nineteenth-century Copenhagen than it did to life in fifth-century BCE Athens; and we know that the claim is every bit as relevant in our own time, when it seems that those in political skirmishes who genuinely "know themselves" are not great in number. There are plenty of folks who in all seriousness are being driven to push for their goals, but it's so often shorn the benefit of earnestness, which sees to it that the ends being pursued are appropriately scrutinized so that the means of action being engaged are justified.

But then there is that other factor that Kierkegaard insists must necessarily accompany earnestness, and that is—jest, our fifth item of the Sweet 16. Earnestness without jest is overbearing; jest without earnestness is triviality. But earnestness and jest working in conjunction is resurrection power. Jest or humor can be disarming. In a tense conversation, an injection of humor can completely change the tone and dynamics of a situation. Why? Because jest or humor gives a respite from the intensity of the earnest interchange. It can indicate that the business-as-usual tone that has prevailed in a particular situation is now going to change. It relativizes the seriousness of the exchange between the conversationalists. It lightens the gravity and lowers the temperature of the situation so that dialogue partners are put at ease. In this way it can elevate the discussion to a higher level. Jest or humor can communicate that, in actuality, respect for the humanity of the discussants in some ways is more important than the particular issue under consideration. After the encounter, the moment or moments of jest will stand out as possibly the most enjoyable instances of the discussion, and this will leave a positive trace in the memory of the event. For instance, in the midst of Flightgate—the episode of the double leak by the administration about

Conclusion

the planned congressional trip to Afghanistan, which made untenable the prospect of either a government flight or a commercial flight because of the danger it brought on the ground, since it gave a heads-up to the Taliban that American officials were coming—a reporter asked the leader of the trip whether she thought this action was retaliation for her letter to Trump postponing his State of the Union speech. Her response was uproariously understated. House Speaker Pelosi responded, "I don't think the president would be that petty, do you?" Kierkegaard understands all forms of the comic, including jest or humor, as residing in contradiction. In this case, Pelosi's statement is so humorous because of the contradiction she sets in play between saying that he wouldn't be that petty while knowing, along with everybody else in the universe, that of course he would be that petty. This is a creative reply that serves the situation much better than if she had lambasted the president for undercutting an important mission and preventing her and her team from carrying out their duty, which would have only further deteriorated her relationship with the president. Jest or humor, when coupled with the gift and skill of knowing when they can best be used, is one of the most powerful tools in practicing resurrection.

Normativity or measure. Honoring the rule of law, one would think, is a minimal requirement that one should be able to expect every politician to ascribe to. But in these times it is far from anything that can be taken for granted, especially when one understands that rule to include unwritten, procedural laws (of the type being suggested in this Conclusion) as well as written laws. Operating with full sensitivity to this essential ingredient of an adequately functioning democratic institution is a mark of distinction that separates those who gain the respect of others because of being able to be counted on as individuals who embody the virtue of justice and fair play. To be just is to respect the norms, principles, and laws, written and unwritten, as well as to be a good listener, so that the cries of those suffering from outdated or unjust laws can be heard and efforts to create new, more just laws can be made. As the Kierkegaardian theological thinker Reinhold Niebuhr pointed out: the human's "capacity for justice makes democracy possible," but the human's "inclination to injustice makes democracy necessary."[16] Those unafraid to stand for justice are those who acquire the

---

16. Niebuhr, *Mighty Works on Religion and Politics*, 354, in Meacham, *Soul of America*, 10.

social capital that can be judiciously and effectively expended in practicing resurrection.

Item seven of the Sweet 16 concerns measure. The effective practitioner of resurrection is one who worries less about judging others and more about judging her- or himself. But judging of the self can vary greatly depending on the measure that one employs for doing the judging. If the measure one uses calls for living up to a low bar, then the passion required to meet the ideal is minimal. On the other hand, if the measure used is high, so that much will be expected, then the greater passion called forth will lead to a fuller life. If the measure or criterion over against which I live out my life is divinity or the divine who is love, then the passion I will be lured into to become a lover will be very great, as will be the intensity of my living and the meaningfulness of my life. With people expecting much of themselves as concerns the criterion they choose for the instrument to nurture and educate the desire implanted within them, the chances for there being significant numbers of those willing to become coworkers with divinity resurrecting democracy will increase substantially.

Understanding Kierkegaard's stages on life's way can assist us in identifying where we are in our individual lives and how we might desire to re-situate ourselves into another stage of life. But we might also want to evaluate our performance on the stage in which our lives are being played out, that is, the setting of family, work, recreational, and cultural involvements in which we are entangled. How is my performance faring on that stage or on those stages? Here different norms, ideals, criteria must be employed, but careful scrutiny can lead to judgments about the contributions I am making to my variegated social world as well as the shortcomings in that arena that I might be able to identify. We are all actors on a stage or stages, and we can learn about our performance in those various settings if we are willing to open ourselves to giving ourselves a critical review. Some things might be gained by this different sort of rating our engagement with other performers on the stages, things that might strengthen our practicing resurrection.

Eternality or the moment. Kierkegaard made clear that in his vision of eternality, the moment does not accommodate the eternal in one standard fashion, making for a conformity of instantiations of eternity. Instead of such a "*uniform transparency* of the eternal" there is a "*refraction* of the eternal," making for a pluralism of eternity-inspired actions. Open and

Conclusion

unguarded readiness and willingness to embrace this variegated plurality of eternal manifestations can be a form of practicing resurrection. To sponsor, endorse, encourage, support, and promote diversity is to contribute to life's fullness, since a basic formula for fullness is the experience of unity-amidst-diversity. Fostering conversations where the voices of all parties are heard is key to a healthy democracy. The garden of diversity is a kaleidoscope of varying flowers and shrubs, each of them beautiful in its own way, and no precinct of the garden should be prejudged as having nothing to contribute to the beauty of the whole. Those resurrecting democracy find ways to lift up the voices of every citizen and those aspiring-to-become-a-citizen.

The Sweet 16's tenth point concerns countering abuses of the momentary. Trump and Putin drew our attention to one particular reality that can easily gain undeserved, inordinate power and disrupt if not destroy the institution of democracy, and that is—money. The momentary loves the monetary. Corruption has been rampant in the Trump administration since the very beginning, in fact even during the campaign. Legislators need to devise programs that will benefit the common good, and this deserves to be their top priority. But a close second is to utilize their oversight authority to engage in serious investigations of the numerous instances of conflict of interest, dishonesty, greed, and abuse in what some have labeled a predator's ball of corruption that has been hosted by the White House. Violations of corruption need to be exposed and legislation to make reforms to the system to restrain such corruption needs to be passed. Furthermore, the more the effects of large injections of money into the political process can be excised, the better off that process will be as concerns its democratic functioning. Besides differentiating itself decidedly from money, the eternal is seen by Kierkegaard as loving mercifulness. Mercifulness is the opposite of money, but it is also the opposite of meanness, wickedness, cruelty, heartlessness, callousness, ruthlessness, nastiness, and spitefulness. In our time, the time of Trump, the abuses committed in association with the three words that energized Trump's campaign, "Build the wall," are going to eventually be brought fully into the light and all of us will have tremendous guilt and shame to bear for not having been more creative to find ways to stop our government's policies and practices, formal and informal, that dehumanized and harmed thousands of innocent victims whose only "crime" was seeking asylum in our country. A society is only as good as the way it treats "the least of these"; our country recently has fallen far in this regard. Practicing resurrection needs to inform work on arriving at an appropriate immigration policy that doesn't dismiss the issue of border security, but which also upholds our long-standing tradition of being a wonderful, welcoming beacon of freedom and democracy for those seeking safe harbor. Resurrecting our immigration policy is an essential part of resurrecting our democracy.

Subjectivity or freedom. Freedom and love are the two greatest treasures of the human, and the former is the means for arriving at the latter. In the case of divinity, divine love and the resulting divine self-limitation is the means for bestowing freedom on the human. And in the case of humanity, human love and the resulting self-limitation is the means for bestowing— as best can be done in the human context—freedom on the other human. Self-limitation, in both cases, involves holding back one's efficacy so as to make room for the other to operate without feeling dependent. In both cases, as well, the true art of power is to make free, not to make beholden or subservient; and such power is an expression of love. A healthy democracy strives to ensure, protect, and nurture human freedom while creating conditions for human freedom to be able to eventuate in love and thus to arrive at its proper destination. Practicing resurrection requires the practitioner to be cognizant of the necessity of these two polar realities to find their fundamental place in human lives and to be passionately active to redress situations where they are being crushed, diminished, or inhibited.

The tension between society's forces emphasizing subjectivity and those accenting objectivity is present today no less than in Kierkegaard's day. Today, the GAFA big tech companies are gaining greater and greater prominence in our lives and their data-analyzing, algorithms, and psycho-profiling are giving objectivity and group-think the upper hand over subjectivity and individuality. Practicing resurrection will be best done by those who desire on occasion to commune reflectively in solitude with text on the written page and thus to cultivate their subjectivity; however, so will they operate respectfully toward factual, evidence-based knowledge that is produced by experts, and recognize that such objective knowledge needs to have its place in public deliberation leading up to the making of important political decisions, for the commonsensical approach that deprecates objective knowledge is too often merely a disguise for rampant ignorance. Those whose lives demonstrate a good balance between objectivity and subjectivity are going to be better candidates for becoming adept and sound contributors to resurrecting democracy.

Conclusion

Freedom's deeper source is the focus of the Sweet 16's thirteenth item. Kierkegaard acknowledged that autonomy as self-rule or self-determination is a crucial dimension of our humanity. However, he recognized that autonomy can easily bring with it an inflation of the self that leads it into a disrelation with itself. Therefore, while he affirmed autonomy, he also affirmed theonomy. Theonomy refers to divine-rule or to the divine as grounding the human's autonomy, empowering it to be able to exercise its self-determination. For him, then, the divine does not negate freedom but makes it possible for freedom to operate as it should. In this vision, the autonomous self, if in touch with the full reality of the situation, acknowledges that its freedom is dependent on the divine. That is why he writes that "I don't create myself, I choose myself." Nobody else can choose myself. I must do that and as I do my freedom is constituted. And yet, that act is not an act of self-creation, for the divine reality is present, sustaining me as I engage in that action. It is this affirmation of theonomy as empowering autonomy that also leads to Kierkegaard's nihilism. It is a religious nihilism that calls the human to recognize that before divinity, the human self is nothing. We have encountered this religious nihilism repeatedly in our considerations of Kierkegaard. To be underscored once again, though, is that Kierkegaard's nihilism is not of the enervating sort, but rather empowering in character. The acknowledgment of the nothingness of one's self ends up being a means leading to the acquiring of the full access to the resources of divinity which empower one to become someone of great stature and accomplishments. Such a religious nihilist makes the best practitioner of resurrection.

This topic's final suggestion for practicing resurrection is Kierkegaard's thought that we can benefit from distinguishing between two selves—a first self and a deeper self. We recall that his first self is the self caught up in the routine activities of bourgeoise existence, with the customary commitments to concerns such as family, job, friends, social groups, cultural institutions, etc. This self's life is marked by meaning and purpose, as it strives to make a decent living and accomplish the many goals it has established for itself within the world-historical arena. The deeper self, on the other hand, has a larger perspective that informs it, so that, with its consideration of relating to the eternal coming into the picture, the enterprising life of the first self is judged to be missing the point a bit, for it seems to have lost itself in secondary concerns and forgotten about that in life which is most important. The good created by the first self is appreciated by the deeper self, but the relativity of that good is also recognized, and so the deeper self desires that its counterpart-self would enter into a harmonious relationship with it. When that happens, so that the first self operates with the perspective of the deeper self, then the self is healthy, powerful, and able to have great effects marked by decision-making informed by the wisdom and care of a broader, religious perspective. The self, whose life benefits from such an intimately working partnership of the first and deeper selves, will be a very judicious and efficacious practitioner of resurrection.

Possibility or the future. How we should be oriented to the future provides us with the fifteenth item of the Sweet 16. Trump and Kierkegaard gave us a stark contrast in how they think we should relate to the future. Trump, on the one hand, operates out of a politics of fear that affords a huge place to the negative features of life that are looming over us in frightening ways and encroaching upon the security of our daily existence. Kierkegaard, on the other hand, advocates a theology of hope that carries with it political implications that, in dwelling on the possibility of the good, create space for functioning optimistically with expectations of always being able to ameliorate deficiencies in the situation so that the human project might be better carried out, rather than continually running scared to the salvific actions of a political strongman to stave off the dark, lurking possibilities of evil. This theology of hope, while not discounting the heavenly dimension, can serve a secular expectation that practicing resurrection in the here-and-now can produce real-life, flesh-and-blood changes in such down-to-earth areas as the political institution of democracy. A lively sense of hope is one of the results of love, our next and final Kierkegaardian insight that can bear resurrecting fruits.

Throughout the book an emphasis has been placed on divinity's implanted desire within the human, which lures the human toward the infinite or ultimacy and leads to imagining construals of the divine, best of which are those centering on love. The human is drawn to the divine, and as the divine is construed in relation to love, the human comes to love love. A love-focused construal of the divine, in Kierkegaard's case, led him to tie this loving divine reality to possibility. We examined the way in which Kierkegaard understands the divine as embodying possibilities. The divine as the actuality of possibility can breathe freshness into any situation by bringing new possibilities into the mix with new life often being the result. The divine power of creative transformation at work in the world is always manifesting love. Its possibilizing work, that is, its work of presenting new

Conclusion

possibilities to situations in which they are needed, by drawing on the divine storehouse of infinite possibilities, expands human freedom where humans are present. This enhancement of freedom via enlarging of possibility is the work of love. Possibilizing that takes place by divine agency can also take place by human agency; while human possibilizing is not as effective as divine possibilizing, it can nevertheless accomplish much. We, in our loving, possibilize for the other, which contributes to the unlocking of their potential. And of course, on Kierkegaard's view, this human possibilizing is an expression of love, which finally is most appropriately seen as being a participation in divine possibilizing or divine love. Human possibilizing is a significant means of mediating divine possibilizing. In interactions political or otherwise, just about every movement, action, decision one makes can be sanctified by considering how it can be brought forth in a way that serves the loving venture of possibilizing. Of all the Sweet 16 contributions Kierkegaard makes to our trumping of Trump by providing us ideas for practicing resurrection, I think number sixteen, this loving activity of possibilizing, is the greatest.

I close this little book with a winsome story about an incident that occurred in Fergus Falls, Minnesota—which happens to be the hometown in which my wife and I grew up. We have fond memories of this town, back then, of 12,608 people, not including the 2,000 or so residents of the state mental hospital, which serviced those with "psychological problems," covering everything from those who needed electric shock therapy to those suffering from alcoholism. The town was tranquil, the schools were strong, homes were comfortable with yards well-kept, there was little to no crime, and people generally got along very well. I have jestingly referred to this community as a "Scandinavian ghetto," since just about everybody's last name ended in "son," and many of Norwegian extraction thought that those with a Swedish background represented the genuine "other" and vice versa. I remember in junior high being proud of the article on religion in *Time* magazine featuring Fergus Falls, because of its thirty-three churches, which included in downtown Fergus our church, Bethlehem Lutheran (2,500 members), First English Lutheran a block away (2,500 members), Augustana Lutheran a block the other way (1,000 members), and Zion's Lutheran four blocks yet another way (600 members). We had Tuesday school—as did I think many American small towns in the 1950s—when students in the elementary schools were to report after lunch to their church at 1:00 p.m. for three hours of instruction in the Bible, the creed, the commandments, the sacraments, prayer, and singing. So we would ride our bikes or trudge our way on foot through the snow en route to our "church home," while the two or three students with no church connection in a classroom would get to be involved in alternative activities.

Well, Fergus Falls recently made it into national and international news because of a story that appeared in Germany's *Der Spiegel*, one of the most respected publications in Europe. It seems that about the time of the Trump inauguration, the news magazine dispatched a reporter to the United States to get a story about the impact of the Trump campaign on a community in the middle of the country. The reporter selected Fergus Falls, where he spent a number of weeks acquiring information for his story. The reporter was one of the magazine's best writers, a winner of multiple awards and a journalistic idol of his generation.

Reporters Matt Furber and Mitch Smith of the *New York Times* informed the world that Claas Relotius, the *Spiegel* reporter, had fabricated a story to make it more sensational rather than writing an accurate, factual narrative.[17] As they state, this reporter "could have written about the many residents who maintain friendships across partisan lines, about the efforts to lure former residents back to west-central Minnesota or about how a city of roughly 14,000 people maintains a robust art scene"; "he could have described local landmarks like the giant statue of Otto the Otter," "the Minnesota-shaped welcome sign," or "the expansive prairie that surrounds the town." To the contrary, Mr. Relotius chose to invent "a condescending fiction," portraying "Fergus Falls as a backward, racist place whose residents blindly supported President Trump and rarely ventured beyond city limits. He concocted characters, roadside signs and racially tinged plotlines."

My point in communicating this story is to highlight the way the people of this community handled the situation. First, they showed ingenuity and creativity in doing fact-checking in relation to the claims that had been made and ascertaining precisely what this reporter had done. But, most importantly, they have responded to the situation in a wholesome way. As the *Times* indicates: "As upset as Fergus Falls residents were with their treatment—upset enough to compile a point-by-point rebuttal of Mr. Relotius's story—many of them have also been willing to accept apologies, set the record straight and forge ahead, almost sanguine about the whole ordeal."

---

17. Matt Furber and Mitch Smith, "A Besmirched Town Rights the Wrongs, And Then Forgives," *New York Times*, December 28, 2018.

Conclusion

In fact, the magazine sent another reporter to Fergus to chronicle the missteps Relotius had made, and he "suggested that Fergus Falls might be 'the most forgiving city in the Western Hemisphere.'" The fabricating reporter has been fired for what was discovered to be a long history of fraudulent story-writing, and Fergus Falls makes its way into the future, confident that it is a community where people are ready to share with each other the commitment to maintain their city as a place in which people can trust one another, work together to advance goals, and forgive when need be to move on in a positive fashion. Our hometown community made us proud, and it deserves to be lifted up as an exemplary group of people who mustered up the will to forgive one who did them wrong and in the process practiced resurrection in a way that brought new life to their city.

As we bring this little book to a close, it seems that we have managed to go a bit deeper into the issues and the incredible challenge that lies before us. We have also pointed to some ways that we might practice resurrection, and in so doing—go forward. We can make a difference. To help in that regard, I urge you to take a break from time to time in your busy schedule to ask yourself sixteen Kierkegaardian questions that have been formulated in relation to Kierkegaard's Sweet 16 insights into practicing resurrection. These questions appear in Appendix A, which is entitled "The Sweet 16 Questions for Going Deeper in Order to Go Forward." Other optional titles for these questions facilitating personal interrogation are: "16 Ways to Help Divinity Resurrect Democracy," "Kierkegaardian Top 16 List," "The Sweet 16 Inquiries to Facilitate Resurrecting Democracy," and "16 Elements of a Personal Examination of Conscience." There is also, at the end of these 16 questions, "A Prayer for Any Time," which can be utilized as desired. I encourage you to engage in this self-examination exercise periodically. And if you're a politician, I beg you to do so.

Appendix

Sweet 16 Questions for Going Deeper in Order to Go Forward

Or 16 Ways to Help Divinity Resurrect Democracy

Or Kierkegaardian Top 16 List

Or The Sweet 16 Inquiries to Facilitate Resurrecting Democracy

Or 16 Elements of a Personal Examination of Conscience

1. Is the narrative or story I share comprehensive enough to cover the full range of concerns, including factual evidence for the claims of truth I am asserting?
2. Am I always respectful of the freedom of the recipients of or listeners to my story?
3. Do I have the earnestness and courage of conviction to be myself and prophetically speak truth to power?
4. Am I being appropriately distrustful and suspicious of myself in striving to know myself?

Appendix

5. Am I remembering the importance of jest or humor as essential sidekicks of earnestness?

6. Do I consistently honor the rule of law in written and unwritten form and embody the virtue of justice and fair play?

7. What is my measure, or over against what ultimate reality am I living my life?

8. How do I assess my performance, especially in relation to other performers, on the stage of my life in political and other situations?

9. Am I a respecter, defender, and promoter of pluralism and diversity, vestiges of eternality's refracted manifestation in time?

10. Does the corruption and wickedness in the White House fill me with a desire for change and prompt me to work for that change?

11. Does my life demonstrate my affirmation of true power as the art of making free?

12. Have I got an appropriate balance in my accommodating of the objective and subjective aspects of my life?

13. Have I chosen myself by choosing freedom, and am I a religious nihilist who knows the empowerment this nihilism brings?

14. Am I nurturing my deeper self as well as my first, eager-beaver self and striving to have them operate in concert?

15. In relation to the future, am I living out of fear and the possibility of evil or out of hope and the possibility of the good?

16. Do I love divinity by loving love? Am I loving by possibilizing for others?

A Prayer for Any Time

O Holy Godhead, Mysterious Divinity, Source of the universe
and all reality,
Open our hearts and minds to sense the desire you have planted
deep within us.
May that desire impassion us to question and to quest,
so that our intellects affirm ideas and stories that align us with truth,
our wills affirm values and virtues that align us with goodness,
and our construals of you do justice to you, who lures us into truth
and goodness.
We give you thanks that, residing in you, our understanding can serve
well our existing,
and we can live our free lives as lovers, in harmony with you,
the Fullness of Love.
Amen.

Bibliography

Abramson, Seth. *Proof of Collusion: How Trump Betrayed America.* New York: Simon & Schuster, 2018.
Albright, Madeleine. *Fascism: A Warning.* New York: HarperCollins, 2018.
Backhouse, Stephen. *Kierkegaard: A Single Life.* Grand Rapids, MI: Zondervan, 2016.
———. *Kierkegaard's Critique of Christian Nationalism.* Oxford: Oxford University Press, 2011.
Balkan, Jack M. "Constitutional Rot." In *Can It Happen Here? Authoritarianism in America,* edited by Cass R. Sunstein, 19–35. New York: HarperCollins, 2018.
Berry, Wendell. "Manifesto: The Mad Farmer Liberation Front." In *The Country of Marriage.* New York: Harcourt Brace Jovanovich, 1971.
Clover, Charles. *Black Wind, White Snow: The Rise of Russia's New Nationalism.* New Haven, CT: Yale University Press, 2016.
Dawisha, Karen. *Putin's Kleptocracy: Who Owns Russia?* New York: Simon & Schuster, 2014.
Dooley, Mark. *The Politics of Exodus: Søren Kierkegaard's Ethics of Responsibility.* New York: Fordham University Press, 1999.
Dugin, Aleksandr. *The Foundation of Geopolitics: The Geopolitical Future of Russia [Osnovy geopolitiki: Geopoliticheskoe budushchee Rossii].* Moscow: Arktogeya,1997.
———. *The Fourth Political Theory.* Translated by Mark Sieboda and Michael Millerman. London: Arktos, 2012.
Faris, David. *It's Time to Fight Dirty: How Democrats Can Build a Lasting Majority in American Politics.* Brooklyn: Melville House, 2018.
Fea, John. *Believe Me: The Evangelical Road to Donald Trump.* Grand Rapids, MI: Eerdmans, 2018.
Feldman, Noah. "On 'It Can't Happen Here,'" In *Can It Happen Here? Authoritarianism in America,* edited by Cass R. Sunstein, 157–74. New York: HarperCollins, 2018.
Foer, Franklin. *World Without Mind: The Existential Threat of Big Tech.* New York: Penguin, 2017.
Fox, Emily Jane. *Born Trump: Inside America's First Family.* New York: HarperCollins, 2018.
Frum, David. *Trumpocracy: The Corruption of the American Republic.* New York: HarperCollins, 2018.
Gardell, Mattias. *Gods of the Blood: The Pagan Revival and White Separatism.* Durham, North Carolina: Duke University Press, 2003.

Bibliography

Gardels, Nathan, and Nicolas Berggruen. *Renovating Democracy: Governing in the Age of Globalization and Digital Capitalism.* Oakland: University of California Press, 2019.

Garff, Joakim. *Kierkegaard's Muse: The Mystery of Regine Olsen.* Translated by Alastair Hannay. Princeton: Princeton University Press, 2017.

———. *Søren Kierkegaard: A Biography.* Translated by Bruce H. Kirmmse. Princeton: Princeton University Press, 2005.

Ginsburg, Tom, and Aziz Z. Huq. *How to Save a Constitutional Democracy.* Chicago: University of Chicago Press, 2018.

Goodrick-Clarke, Nickolas. *The Occult Roots of Nazism.* New York: New York University Press, 1992.

Green, Joshua. *Devil's Bargain: Steve Bannon, Donald Trump, and the Storming of the Presidency.* New York: Penguin, 2017.

Griffin, Roger. *The Nature of Fascism.* New York: Routledge, 1994.

Hannay, Alastair. *Kierkegaard: A Biography.* Cambridge: Cambridge University Press, 2001.

———. *Papers and Journals: A Selection.* London: Penguin, 1996.

Harding, Luke. *Collusion: Secret Meetings, Dirty Money, and How Russia Helped Donald Trump Win.* New York: Vintage, 2017.

Hayden, Michael V. *The Assault on Intelligence: American National Security in an Age of Lies.* New York: Penguin, 2018.

Heiser, James D. *"The American Empire Should Be Destroyed": Alexander Dugin and the Perils of Immanentized Eschatology.* Malone, TX: Repristination, 2014.

Holmes, Stephen. "How Democracies Perish." In *Can It Happen Here? Authoritarianism in America,* edited by Cass R. Sunstein, 387–427. New York: HarperCollins, 2018.

Hughes, Carl S. *Kierkegaard and the Staging of Desire: Rhetoric and Performance in a Theology of Eros.* New York: Fordham University Press, 2014.

Isikoff, Michael, and David Corn. *Russian Roulette: The Inside Story of Putin's War on America and the Election of Donald Trump.* New York: Twelve, 2018.

Johnston, David Cay. *It's Even Worse Than You Think: What the Trump Administration Is Doing to America.* New York: Simon & Schuster, 2018.

Judis, John B. *The Populist Explosion: How the Great Recession Transformed American and European Politics.* New York: Columbia Global Reports, 2016.

Kazin, Michael. *The Populist Persuasion: An American History.* New York: Basic Books, 1995.

Keller, Catherine. *Intercarnations: Exercises in Theological Possibility.* New York: Fordham University Press, 2017.

Kierkegaard, Søren. *Christian Discourses/The Crisis and A Crisis in the life of an Actress.* Edited and translated by Howard V. Hong and Edna H. Hong. Princeton: Princeton University Press, 1997.

———. *The Concept of Anxiety: A Simple Psychologically Orienting Deliberation on the Dogmatic Issue of Hereditary Sin.* Edited and translated by Reidar Thomte in collaboration with Albert B. Anderson. Princeton: Princeton University Press, 1980.

———. *The Concept of Irony: With Continual Reference to Socrates.* Edited and translated by Howard V. Hong and Edna H. Hong. Princeton: Princeton University Press, 1989.

———. *Concluding Unscientific Postscript to Philosophical Fragment.* 2 vols. Edited and translated by Howard V. Hong and Edna H. Hong. Princeton: Princeton University Press, 1992.

Bibliography

———. *The Corsair Affair and Articles Related to the Writings*. Edited and translated by Howard V. Hong and Edna H. Hong. Princeton: Princeton University Press, 1982.

———. *Eighteen Upbuilding Discourses*. Edited and translated by Howard V. Hong and Edna H. Hong. Princeton: Princeton University Press, 1990.

———. *Either/Or*. 2 vols. Edited and translated by Howard V. Hong and Edna H. Hong. Princeton: Princeton University Press, 1987.

———. *For Self-Examination/Judge for Yourself*. Edited and translated by Howard V. Hong and Edna H. Hong. Princeton: Princeton University Press, 1990.

———. *Kierkegaard's Journals and Notebooks*. Princeton: Princeton University Press, 2000– . The lone reference to this work cites volume number and page number.

———. *Letters and Documents*. Translated by Henrik Rosenmeier. Princeton: Princeton University Press, 1978.

———. *The Moment and Late Writings*. Edited and translated by Howard V. Hong and Edna H. Hong. Princeton: Princeton University Press, 1998.

———. *Philosophical Fragments/Johannes Climacus*. Edited and translated by Howard V. Hong and Edna H. Hong. Princeton: Princeton University Press, 1985.

———. *The Point of View for My Work as an Author: A Direct Communication, Report to History*. Edited and translated by Howard V. Hong and Edna H. Hong. Princeton: Princeton University Press, 1998.

———. *Practice in Christianity*. Edited and translated by Howard V. Hong and Edna H. Hong. Princeton: Princeton University Press, 1991.

———. *Prefaces/Writing Sampler*. Edited and translated by Todd W. Nichol. Princeton: Princeton University Press,

———. *The Sickness unto Death: A Christian Psychological Exposition for Upbuilding and Awakening*. Edited and translated by Howard V. Hong and Edna H. Hong. Princeton: Princeton University Press, 1997.

———. *Søren Kierkegaard's Journals and Papers*. Edited and translated by Howard V. Hong and Edna H. Hong. Bloomington, IN: Indiana University Press, 1967–1978. Cited by volume number and entry number.

———. *Søren Kierkegaards Papirer*. Edited by P. A. Heiberg, V. Kuhr, and E. Torsting. Copenhagen: Gyldendal, 1909–1948. The abbreviation is *Pap.*, which is followed by reference to volume, section, and number in the standard Danish edition, e.g., *Pap.* X5 A 13.

———. *Stages on Life's Way*. Edited and translated by Howard V. Hong and Edna H. Hong. Princeton: Princeton University Press, 1988.

———. *Three Discourses on Imagined Occasions*. Edited and translated by Howard V. Hong and Edna H. Hong. Princeton: Princeton University Press, 1993.

———. *Two Ages: The Age of Revolution and the Present Age, A Literary Review*. Edited and translated by Howard V. Hong and Edna H. Hong. Princeton: Princeton University Press, 1978.

———. *Upbuilding Discourses in Various Spirits*. Edited and translated by Howard V. Hong and Edna H. Hong. Princeton: Princeton University Press, 1993.

———. *Without Authority*. Edited and translated by Howard V. Hong and Edna H. Hong. Princeton: Princeton University Press, 1997.

———. *Works of Love*. Edited and translated by Howard V. Hong and Edna H. Hong. Princeton: Princeton University Press, 1995.

Bibliography

Kirmmse, Bruce H. *Encounters with Kierkegaard: A Life as Seen by his Contemporaries.* Collected, edited, and annotated by Bruce H. Kirmmse and Virginia R. Laursen. Princeton: Princeton University Press, 1996.
Koffler, Keith. *Bannon: Always the Rebel.* Washington, DC: Regnery, 2017.
Lasch, Christopher. *The True and Only Heaven: Progress and Its Critics.* New York: Norton, 1991.
Lepore, Jill. *These Truths: A History of the United States.* New York: Norton, 2018.
Levitsky, Steven, and Daniel Ziblatt. *How Democracies Die.* New York: Crown, 2018.
Llosa, Mario Vargas. *The Storyteller: A Novel.* New York: Picador USA, 1989.
Lynch, Michael Patrick. *The Internet of Us: Knowing More and Understanding Less in the Age of Big Data.* New York: Liveright, 2016.
Marantz, Andrew. "How Fox and Friends Rewrites Trump's Reality." *The New Yorker*, January 15, 2018.
Martensen, H. *Den christelige Dogmatik.* Copenhagen: C. A. Reitzel, 1849. English translation: *Christian Dogmatics.* Translated from the 1856 German and edited by W. Urwick. Edinburgh: T. & T. Clark, 1878.
Meacham, Jon. *The Soul of America: The Battle for Our Better Angels.* New York: Random House, 2018.
Mynster, J. P. *Betragtninger over de christelige Troeslærdomme [Reflections on the Doctrines of the Christian Faith].* 2 vols. Third printing. Copenhagen: Deichmanns, 1846.
———. *Grundrids af den christelige Dogmatik [Fundamentals of Christian Dogmatics]. Blandede Skrivter [Miscellaneous Writings]* 6. Edited by J. H. Paulli, 1–400. Copenhagen: Gyldendal, 1857.
———. *Meddelelser om mit Levnet.* Copenhagen: Gyldendal, 1854.
Nance, Malcolm. *The Plot to Destroy Democracy. How Putin and his Spies Are Undermining America and Dismantling the West.* New York: Hachette, 2018.
Newman, Omarosa Manigault. *Unhinged: An Insider's Account of the Trump White House.* New York: Gallery, 2018.
Niebuhr, Reinhold. *Mighty Works on Religion and Politics.* Edited by Elisabeth Sifton. New York: The Library of America, 2015.
Nussbaum, Martha C. *The Monarchy of Fear. A Philosopher Looks at Our Political Crisis.* New York: Simon and Schuster, 2018.
O'Brien, Timothy L. *TrumpNation: The Art of Being the Donald.* New York: Werner Business Books, 2005. Reprinted with a new introduction by Timothy L. O'Brien. New York: Hachette, 2016.
Pattison, George. *Kierkegaard's Upbuilding Discourses: Philosophy, Literature, Theology.* London: Routledge, 2002.
Plum, Niels Munk. *Jakob Peter Mynster: Som Kristen og Teolog.* Copenhagen: G.E.C. Gad, 1938.
Rambo, Shelly. *Resurrecting Wounds: Living in the Afterlife of Trauma.* Waco, TX: Baylor University Press, 2017.
Rorty, Richard. *Achieving Our Country: Leftist Thought in Twentieth-Century America.* New York: Harvard University Press, 1987.
Ross, Alexander Reid. *Against the Fascist Creep.* Chico, CA: AK, 2017.
Rubow, Paul. *Goldschmidt og Nemesis.* Copenhagen: Munksgaard, 1968.
Runciman, David. *How Democracy Ends.* New York: Basic Books, 2017.
Schelling, F.W.J. *Of Human Freedom.* Translated by James Gutmann. Chicago: Open Court, 1936.

Bibliography

Schweizer, Peter. *Secret Empires: How the American Political Class Hides Corruption and Enriches Family and Friends.* New York: HarperCollins, 2018.

Sims, Cliff. *Team of Vipers: My 500 Extraordinary Days in the Trump White House.* New York: Thomas Dunne, 2019.

Snyder, Timothy. *The Road to Unfreedom: Russia, Europe, America.* New York: Tim Duggan, 2018.

Sponheim, Paul R. *Speaking of God: Relational Theology.* St. Louis: Chalice, 2006.

Stewart, Jon. *Kierkegaard's Relations to Hegel Reconsidered.* Cambridge: Cambridge University Press, 2003.

Strauss, David. "Law and the Slow-Motion Emergency." In *Can It Happen Here? Authoritarianism in America,* edited by Cass R. Sunstein, 365–85. New York: HarperCollins, 2018.

Sunstein, Cass R. *Can It Happen Here? Authoritarianism in America.* New York: HarperCollins, 2018.

Thompson, Curtis L. *Following the Cultured Public's Chosen One: Why Martensen Mattered to Kierkegaard.* Copenhagen: Museum Tusculanum, 2008.

———. "Interpreting God's Translucent World: Imagination, Possibility, and Eternity." In *Translucence: Religion, the Arts, and Imagination,* edited by Carol Gilbertson and Gregg Muilenburg, 3–37. Minneapolis: Fortress, 2004.

Thompson, Curtis L., and David J. Kangas, translators. *Between Hegel and Kierkegaard: Hans L. Martensen's Philosophy of Religion.* Oxford: Oxford University Press, 1997.

Thompson, Curtis L., and Joyce M. Cuff. *God and Nature: A Theologian and a Scientist Conversing on the Divine Promise of Possibility.* New York: Bloomsbury, 2012.

Tolstrup, Christian Fink. "Jakob Peter Mynster: A Guiding Thread in Kierkegaard's Authorship." In *Kierkegaard and His Danish Contemporaries,* edited by Jon Stewart, 267–88. Surrey: Ashgate, 2009.

Trump, Donald J., with Tony Schwartz. *The Art of the Deal.* New York: Ballantine, 2015.

Umland, Andreas. "Post-Soviet 'Uncivil Society' and the Rise of Aleksandr Dugin—A Case Study in Extraparliamentary Radical Right in Contemporary Russia." PhD diss., Trinity College, 2007.

Unger, Craig. *House of Trump, House of Putin. The Untold Story of Donald Trump and the Russian Mafia.* New York: Dutton, 2018.

Ward, Vicky. *Kushner Inc.: The Extraordinary Story of Jared Kushner and Ivanka Trump.* New York: St. Martin's, 2019.

Watts, Duncan J. "The Commonsense Presidency." In *Can It Happen Here? Authoritarianism in America,* edited by Cass R. Sunstein, 329–64. New York: HarperCollins, 2018.

Wendling, Mike. *Alt Right: From 4chan to the White House.* London: Pluto, 2018.

Westphal, Merold. *Critique of Reason and Society.* University Park: Pennsylvania State University Press, 1991.

Whitehead, Alfred North. *Process and Reality: An Essay in Cosmology.* Corrected Edition. Edited by David Ray Griffin and Donald W. Sherburne. New York: Free Press, 1978.

Wilson, Rick. *Everything Trump Touches Dies: A Republican Strategist Gets Real About the Worst President Ever.* New York: Free Press, 2018.

Woodward, Bob. *Fear: Trump in the White House.* New York: Simon & Schuster, 2018.

Index

Abramson, Seth, 13n2, 14, 20–21, 97–98n83, 181
abstraction, abstract
  "world-historical" as, x
  of culture's leveling forces, 3
  thinking deals in, 22
  avoiding, 22
  government as, 65
  irony's, of humanity, and humor's of the God-relationship, 73
  of intellectual comprehension, 74
  character of the public, 103
  as "humanity," 131
active measures, 88
aesthetic
  writings, 27–30
  stage of life, 71–74, 81, 128
African Americans 62, 113, 134
Albright, Madeleine, 17–18n20, 57, 62, 67n44, 68n50, 135
Alt-Right, 63–66
anthropology, 16, 140
Antichrist (Dugin), 139
Anti-Climacus, 70, 81, 105, 151, 155
Apprentice, The, 112
Arif, Teyfik, 98
Aristotle, 30–31, 83
Attack upon Christendom, 146–50
Augustine, 85

Backhouse, Stephen, 48, 55n89, 181
Balkan, Jack, M., 159n1
Bannon, Steven, 17, 29, 33, 65–66, 111
Barr, William, ix, 13
Barron, James, 34–36

Bayrock Group LLC, 98
becoming a Christian, 28, 104, 122
Berggruen, Nicolas, 161n6
Berry, Wendell, 181
Beschloss, Michael, 164
Bible, 36, 84, 111, 174
big data, 115, 116, 117
Big Tech Companies, 114–19. big data, 114–16, 184
  Google, 114, 116, 117, 118, 120
  Apple, 117
  Facebook, 114, 117, 118
  Amazon, 114, 117, 118
Black Lives Matter, 64
Bookbinder, Hilarius, 56, 144
Breitbart News, 19, 65–66

Cambridge Analytica, 18
Chabad-Lubavitch movement, 42–43
character-traits
  Trumpian
    self-promoting, 11, 36
    narcissistic, 4, 110, 113, 135
    selfish, 70, 134, 135, 136, 166
    lying, 14, 113
    conman 110
    indecisive, 112
  Kierkegaardian
    earnest, 10, 34, 53, 166
    conscientious, 12, 165
    an individual, 54, 72
    truthful, 32, 130
    decisive, 72, 77, 127
Christ, 50, 53
  Inc., 5, 8, 33, 52

187

Index

Christ *(continued)*
    the Word, the prototype, 7
    paradoxical, incarnate, 78
    Galilean lover, 164
    the historical Jesus as the, 77
Christendom
    Søren attacking, xiii
    absent New Testament Christianity, 5
    replaced an eviscerated Christianity, 51
    habitual and unchanging, 52
    dehumanizes by lowering the measure, 79
    corrective, 81
    legitimates establishment, 146
    attack, was blossoming of previous actions, 147
    compared to inheriting, 150
    negative attack for positive results, 151
Climacus, Johannes, 30, 44, 45, 52, 53, 54, 74–77, 80, 105, 122–23, 126, 127, 162
Clover, Charles, 181, 140–41
Cohn, Roy, 94
Cold War, 96, 140
comic, 167
commonsense, 113–14
communication, direct and indirect, 27–28, 104
Congress
    intensity of new House, 2
    and Newt Gingrich, 59–60
    investigations of, 87, 94, 160
    Flightgate, 167
    Senate, 60, 61, 116, 154
conman, 110
conscience
    question of, 32
    Mynster on, 50–51
    ripped from conservatism, 68
    trans-moral, 112
    and liberty, 136
    personal self-relation, 165
Constantinople, 39–40
construal
    imaginative shaping, 10
    refine, 30
    earnestness and, 54
    in world religions, 74
    of Religiousness A, 77
    as Possibilizer, 156
    best ones center on love, 10, 172, 179
Conway, Kellyanne, 15
Cooper Ray, 61
Copenhagen
    mid-century, Golden Age, 3
    University of, 27
    pseudonym usage, 30
    as social gathering, 31
    and Michael Kierkegaard, 48
    and imaginative walks, 49
    Church of Our Lady, 49
    and *The Corsair*, 99
    and Peder Ludwig Møller, 101
    disrupted societally, 102
    Christendom and, 146
    and earnestness, 166
Coppins, McCay, 59–60
Corn, David, 13n3, 19n28, 20n33, 37–38
corrective, 81, 121, 147, 150
corruption, 69, 70, 90, 169, 178
coworker, 158, 163, 168
creation
    and nature, 10, 74
    self- 73
    new, 78
    one's works, x, 125
    and destruction, 161n6
creative advance, 7, 84, 154
creative transformation, 11, 74, 84, 162, 163, 172
crisis, 1, 6, 54, 144, 145, 150, 160
criterion, 3, 79, 80, 168
Cuff, Joyce M., 8n8, 151, 185
cynicism, 135, 144

Danish Socrates, 10, 103, 166. *See also* Socrates
Dawisha, Karen, 87, 93, 181
defiance, 81
Der Spiegel, 174
despair, 46, 81, 106, 161
Deutsch, Donnie, 111–12n13

Index

dialectic, dialectical
  Kierkegaard's skill in, 22
  tension between aesthetic and religious concerns of Kierkegaard's authorship, 29
  of earnestness and jest, 54
  reflection, 54
  within the human's normative structure, 75
  of paradoxicality in Religiousness B, 77
  of inward deepening in Religiousness A, 77
  in second place in Religiousness B, 78
diversity, 2, 66, 169, 178
divine, the
  instead of God, 9
  and divinity, 10
  construals of, 10, 30, 172
  and love, 10, 162, 163
  desire for, 12, 33, 44, 56, 82, 109, 133
  divinity nurtures us into, 20
  relating to, 32
  coming to exist, 53
  as manifested, 74
  and interiority, 76
  and nothing, 76, 80, 130, 131, 171
  makes capable, 76, 131, 171
  and guilt, 77
  in Religiousness A, 77
  and faith, 81
  passion for, 123, 168
  limits itself, 125
  and knowing, 131
  as loving, 154, 158
  and structures, 154
  and expectations, 155
  and possibility, 156, 158, 172, 173
  as resurrecting, 156
  as coworker, 158
  and experiences, 159
  and loving love, 172
divine self-limitation, 123–26, 170
divinity
  as the loving power of creative transformation, xi
  and dawn, 3, 5
  as Godhead, 9
  implants desire, 12, 22, 33, 44, 56, 78, 82, 105, 109, 133, 157, 159, 172
  and Meister Eckhart, 10
  resurrects by love, 11, 131
  and Providence/Governance, 29, 47
  nurturing, 29, 154
  enfolding, 30
  and self-involvement, 29–30
  manifested, 32, 160
  actual, 12, 33, 44, 56, 82, 109, 133
  and Mynster, 51
  and encounter, 54
  and Trump, 56, 84
  and being, 74
  and commitment, 75
  empowering, 74, 131, 171
  and shadow, 77
  second, 78
  and power, 81
  and ultimacy, 84
  and eternality, 105
  as divine love, 154, 158
  and life, 156
  working, 159
  speak of, 162
  passion for, 123
  and touching, 123
  and practicing resurrection, 163
  and nothing, 129, 171
  and need, 129–30
  and ground of being, 131
  and creative advance, 131, 154
  is love, 168
  coworker, 168
  and freedom, 70
  mysterious, 179
Dooley, Mark, 55, 181
dossier, of Christopher Steele, 98
Dubinin, Yuri, 95
Dugin, Alexander, 136–37, 139–43

earth, 36, 124, 126, 153, 154, 172
Ebodi, Shirin, 83
Eco, Umberto, 142–43n52
economy, economics
  growth, 12

Index

economy, economics *(continued)*
　global, 58
　Russian, 68
　and justice, 59
　post-industrial, 63
　and politics, 63
　and justice, 59
　crimes of, 91
　complexity of, 113
　and geography, 140
　and inequality, 144
egalitarianism, 138
elections, 1, 2–3, 154
　and Russian interference, 13, 19, 21, 87, 99, 136n19
　and Republican interference, 61–62
　2016, ix, 1, 13, 20, 43, 57, 58, 87, 114
　2018, 61–62, 66–67, 154, 160, 174
　2020, 61–62, 84, 163
Eliade, Mircea, 137
environment, 83–84, 120, 122, 169
equality
　political, 5, 162
　ideal of, 57
　gender, 65
　freedom and, 68
　America's inequality, 144
　Russia's inequality, 145
eros, 78, 182
eschatology
　and expectation, 152–53
　escapism, 153
　realized or immanentized of Dugin, 141–43
establishment
　as of the status quo, 54, 58, 62, 64, 67
　Danish political, 99
　Danish cultural, 120
　Danish socio-political, cultural, 146
　of Christianity,149,
　as of innovating, 161
ethical
　writings, 27
　stage of life, 68, 71–75, 79, 81, 128, 135, 156
Eurasianism, 138, 140
evil
　and purpose, 10
　in pantomime, 110
　and God, 123
　foreigners as, 134
　good and, 139, 141, good or, 152
　possibility of, 153, 172, 178
Evling, Ron, 66–67
Evola, Julius, 137–38
exceptionalism, 69
existence
　leveling of, 4, 147
　God's, 10
　of reality, 15
　take seriously one's, 22
　choice and, 32
　and the single individual, 32
　and unhappiness, 46
　a child's 47
　thought and, 52
　faith and, 52
　freedom and God's, 53
　jest and, 53
　independent, 54
　structure and, 70
　various stages of, 71–78, 81
　and being, 105
　collective, 117
　omnipotence and, 124–126
　subjectivity and, 126–127
　and reflection, 127
　as new, 127–28
　investment in, 130
　of God and possibility, 155
　and essence, 158
　bourgeoise, 171
　security of, 172
expectation
　of church, 4
　for productivity, 129
　and memory 133
　secular, 152–54, 172
　divine, 155
　and theology of hope, 157
　secular, 172

Facebook, 114, 117, 118, 120
factuality
　rules of, 16
　"alternative facts," 15

Index

end of, 144
of narrative, 174
of evidence, 164, 170, 177
Fæderlandet [The Fatherland], 101
faith
  and experiencing God, 6
  and existence, 32
  of Mike Pence, 34
  and Russian Christian Orthodoxy, 37
  and Putin, 38
  and Russian Jewish Orthodoxy, 43
  and Mynster, 50–51
  and Christendom, 52
  and Religiousness B, 78
  and nothing, 80
  and resting transparently in God, 81
  and Trump 84
  and Big Tech Companies, 117
  and theonomy, 122
Fake news
  and Trump, 4, 14–15
  my AAR paper, 8
  and Surkov, 18–19
  and Dugin, 19
Faris, David, 57, 61n17, 181
Farrell, Nicholas, 20–21n37
fascism, 26, 88, 90, 135, 141, 142, 144, 145
Fauset, Richard, 61n18
Fea, John, 181
fear
  Trump evokes, x, 124
  power and, 12
  and walking, 31
  as deep respect, 51
  and norms, 63
  and xenophobia, 66
  and rhetoric, 83
  and bugging, 89n33
  nostalgia and, 134
  and the future, 151–52
  and evil, 153
  politics of, 172
  and living, 178
Fehr, Tiff, 13n6
Feinberg, Scott, 96
Feldman, Noah, 181
feminism, 64, 65, 66
Fergus Fall, Minnesota, 175
Ficino, Marsilio, 137
Finland, 131
Flightgate, 170
Foer, Franklin, 181
foreign affairs
  Afghanistan, 167
  Canada, 95, 141
  China, 85, 151n6
  Germany, 66, 138, 140, 146
  Iran, 83, 140
  Israel, 42, 88
  Japan, 140
  Libya, 85
  South Korea, 85
  NATO, 85, 140
Fox News, 19, 20, 24, 76, 83
  and Trump, 15, 37, 56
  and CNN-MSNBC, 18
Fox, Emily Jane, 15n10, 34n3, 36, 84–85n10, 110, 111, 112, 181
Frank, Thomas, 97
Freed, Benjamin, 86n16
Frum, David, 36, 67, 68n48, 69, 181
FSB, 91
Furber, Matt, 174

Gall, Carlotta, 39–41
Gardell, Mattias, 138–39, 181
Gardels, Nathan, 161n6
Garff, Joakim, 35–37, 48n59, 49n62, 101–2, 182
Garland, Merrick, 61
Gearan, Anne, 67
geopolitics, 19, 136, 138–142, 181
Gibbens, Sarah, 84
Ginsburg, Tom, 2–3, 57, 61n18, 69, 161–62, 182
globalization
  global citizens, 6
  global conservatism, 19
  unipolar globalism, 20
  economic forces of, 58
  and populism, 63
  and alt-right, 64
  and Richard Spencer, 65
  and Trump, 67

Index

globalization *(continued)*
    and Russian mafia, 90
    renovating, 161n6, 182
Gnosticism, 138–39
God
    as construal of the Godhead, 9
    and AAR session, 8–9
    and Meister Eckhart, 9–10
    in Schelling, 9–10
    Trump and, 34
    and Putin, 43
    and Mynster, 51,
    and experience, 53
    and the self, 79–80, 155
    and faith, 81
    and the eternal, 105
    creates, 105, 132
    limiting, 123
    personal 124
    and omnipotence, 125
    and Martensen, 125
    and Mynster, 125–26
    and need, 129
    present, 131
    and glory, 131
    as actuality of possibility, 155–56
Godhead
    as divinity, 9, 74
    as substance in all things, 9
    in Meister Eckhart, 9–10
    in Schelling, 9–10
    and longing, 10
    trumps God, 10
    as Providence/Governance, 29
    and being, 74, 84
    creative transformation, 74
    and Religiousness A, 77
    and faith, 81
    as Fullness of Love, 179
Golden Age
    of Copenhagen, 3, 30, 120
    of Trump, 4
Goldman, Marshall, I., 90
Goldschmidt, Mëir Aron, 99–100
Goodwin, Doris Kearns, 164
Gorbachev, Mikhail, 96
Green, Joshua 137–38, 182
Greshko, Michael, 83–84n7

Griffin, Roger, 142, 182
Grimes, A. C., 87
Guénon, René, 137–38
guilt, 49, 76–77, 169

Hannay, Alastair, 23–24, 48–49, 101–2
Harding, Luke, 97–98
Haufniensis, Vigilius, 30, 105, 155
Hayden, Michael, 15, 68n47, 83n6, 183
heaven, 111, 130, 153–54, 172, 184
Hegel, Georg Wilhelm Friedrich, 122
    and the "world-historical," x, 127, 171
    and Kierkegaard, 122
    Martensen's assessment of, 122
Heiberg, Johann Ludwig, 122, 146
Heiser, James D., 137–40, 142n48, 182
Heyer, Hazel, 97n82
Higgins, Andrew, 138–40
Hitler, Adolf, 20, 37, 66, 140–41
Holmes, Stephen, 56, 63n28, 68n49, 183
hope
    and this book, x, 145
    signposts of, 1
    hopeful sense, 2
    to advance, 7–8
    and Regine, 26
    and Trump, 63, 134
    and Bannon, 66
    from 2018 election, 70
    and Javanka, 86
    and Møller, 101–2
    and the con artist, 110
    and Guénon, 138
    and Russia, 140
    and Kierkegaard's attack on Christendom, 151
    Kierkegaard links to possibility and the future, 152
    and fear, 152–53
    and elections, 154
    and love, 156, 158
    and democracy, 162
    theology of, 172
    and the good, 178
House Freedom Caucus, 82
Hughes, Carl, 29–30, 78, 182

Index

Hughes, Chris, 117
humanity
  fuller, 72
  abstract, 73
  structure of, 79
  deepest part of, 116, 159
  and free deciding, 128
  modernity as age of, 149
  as mutually correlated to Christianity, 149
  the responsibility of Christianity's gift to, 150–51
  of the other, 159
  respect for, 166
  and love's self-limitation, 170
  and autonomy 171
humor
  my attempt at, 6
  as resource, 54
  as boundary area, 71, 73–74
  and the attack on Christendom, 150
  value of, 166
  and the comic, 167
  and earnestness, 178
Huq, Aziz Z., 2–3, 57, 61n18, 69, 161–62, 182

imagination
  images in this book, xiii
  and storytellers, 16
  and Kierkegaard, 31, 49, 151–52
  and Trump's, 109, 151
  directed to the secular, 15
inauguration, 4, 36, 174
infinite
  and decision, 5
  longing for, 10, 29, 30, 74
  Kierkegaard's finding of, 23
  sense for, 73
  and humor, 73
  and the self, 79–80
  and money and mercifulness, 117
  Trump's need, 112
  and passion, 123, 127
  and choice, validation, and concretion, 128
  and hoping, 153, 156

and possibility, 158, 173
institutions
  of democracy, 1, 56, 57, 159
  of Denmark, 3
  denigration of, 6
  of Congress, 60
  and soft guardrails, 68
  and subversive partisanship, 70
  of the Senate, 116
  of media and publishing, 118
  and virtues, 145–46
  reclaiming democratic, 160–61, 167
  and money, 169
  and theology of hope, 172
Intourist (Goscomintourist), 95
inwardness, 52, 54, 74, 76, 104–105, 12
Irenaeus, 85
irony
  dissertation on, 27, 121
  boundary area, 71, 73–74
Isikoff, Michael, 13n4. 19n28, 20n23, 37–38, 94–95n67, 182
Islam, 12, 41,62, 64, 66, 137–38
Istanbul, 39, 41

Javanka, 86, 88
jest, 71, 73, 160, 171, 178
Johnston, David Cay, 37, 110, 114n22, 133–35, 182
Judaism, 37, 41–43, 99, 139
Judis, John, 62–63, 67, 182
Jung, Carl, 137

Kazin, Michael, 62, 182
Kangas, David J., 9n9, 121n44, 185
Keller, Catherine, 5, 182
KGB, 87–89, 91, 95
Kierkegaard, Michael Pedersen, xiii, 45–50
Kierkegaard, Peter Christian, 26, 27, 31, 48, 49
Kierkegaard's works
  Christian Discourses, 32, 52, 105–6, 125, 182
  The Concept of Anxiety, 44, 52, 105, 127–29, 155, 182
  The Concept of Irony, 27, 54, 121, 182

193

Index

Kierkegaard's works *(continued)*
  Concluding Unscientific Postscript, 30, 44–47, 52–54, 71, 73–78, 80, 101, 104, 105, 122–23, 126–27, 162, 182,
  The Corsair Affair, 52, 99–105, 183
  Three Discourses on Imagined Occasions, 53, 183
  Eighteen Upbuilding Discourses, 54, 129–32, 153, 183
  Either/Or, 44, 52, 71, 73, 101, 128, 130, 183
  Fear and Trembling, 44, 183
  For Self-Examination, 53–54, 183
  Journals and Papers, 5, 28, 53, 124, 151–52, 155, 160, 183
  Letters and Documents, 31, 183
  The Moment and Later Writings, 52, 79, 150–51, 183
  Philosophical Fragments, 44, 45, 105, 183
  The Point of View for My Work as an Author, 27–30, 104, 183
  Practice in Christianity, 52, 183
  Prefaces, 44, 79, 183
  The Sickness unto Death, 79–81, 105, 161, 155, 183
  Stages on Life's Way, 44, 54, 183
  Two Ages, 104, 183
  Without Authority, 157, 183
  Works of Love, 6, 63, 107–8, 152–53, 156, 158, 160, 183
Kingdom of God, 126
Kirmmse, Bruce H., 27n56, 44n50, 182, 184
kleptocracy, 69, 87–93, 181
Koffler, Keith, 138n27, 184
Kolderup-Rosenvinge, Janus Lauritz Andreas, 31
Kremlin, 18, 19, 21, 38, 38, 43, 95, 98, 136, 140
Ku Klux Klan, 67
Kulak, Avron, 8–9

Lakin, Sophie Lin, 61
Lasch, Christopher, 134n5
lawlessness, 69–70
leadership
  of Putin, 20, 43–44, 89, 91–93, 136
  of Trump, 5, 15, 20, 56, 96, 111, 113–14
  of Norman Vincent Peale, 34–35
  of Bartholomew I, 39–40
  of Metropolitan Epiphanius, 39–40
  of the Russian Orthodox Church, 41
  of Russian Jews, 42
  of Rabbi Berel Lazar, 42–43
  of Rabbi Menachem Mendel Schneerson, 43
  of Newt Gingrich, 60
  of Mitch McConnel, 60–61
  of Richard Spencer, 65–66
  of David Duke, 67
  of Mikhail Gorbachev, 96
  of Julius Evola, 138
  and elections, 154
Lenin, Vladimir, 87
Leningrad (St. Petersburg), 19, 87–91
Lepore, Jill, 17, 114n24, 164, 184
leveling
  and Golden Age Denmark, 3–4
  and Golden Age Trump, 4–5
  and irony, 74
  and humor, 73
  and the public, 103–4
  and speculative mediation, 122
Levitsky, Steven, 60n15, 68–70, 184
liberal constitutional democracy, 2, 57, 162
Liebensfels, Lanz von, 138–39
List, Guido von, 138–39
Llosa, Maria Vargas, 16n16, 184
Lown, Bernard, 96
Lynch, Michael Patrick, 114–17, 184

MacFarquhar, Neil, 39–41
Macron, Emmanuel, 67
Mafia, Russian
  and Trump's story, 13
  and religion, 37
  Jewish or Kosher Nostra, 41–42
  and Putin partnership, 89–90, 92–93, 95–97
Make America Great Again, 133
Maples, Marla, 84–85
Mar-a-Lago, 33

Index

Marantz, Andrew, 37, 184
Marble Collegiate Church, 34–35
Martensen, Hans Lassen, 120–22, 125, 146–50, 184–85
Marx, Karl, 153
Meacham, Jon, 135–36, 164, 167, 184
media
   and Trump, x, 13, 83
   and Putin, 91–92
   potency of social media, 4, 114–17, 117–120, 161n6
   and "alternative facts," 15
   proliferation of, 17–18, 114n24
   and the alt-right, 63–64
   and Scott Pruitt, 84
   and modernity, 138
Melman, Yossi, 42–43
memory, 16, 133, 139, 166
mercifulness, 108, 169
Middle Ages, 118
military, 19, 38, 85, 94, 136, 141
Mindock, Clark, 61–62n19
modernity
   and Kierkegaard, 31, 85, 147, 149
   and Rasputin, 38
   and Mynster, 51, 149
   and Trump, 57
   and Gingrich, 59
   and the alt-right, 64
   and information, 113
   and Dugin, 137
   and Guénon, 137–38
   and renovation, 161n6
money
   and Trump, 15, 82, 85–86, 94–98
   and Putin, 87–93
   and Bannon, 20
   and Michael Kierkegaard, 48
   and Javanka, 86–87
   and American government, 60
   and mercifulness, 108, 169
   and democracy, 169
Møller, Peder Ludwig, 99–102
Mueller, Robert and his Report, ix, 13, 21, 87, 99
Mussolini, Benito, 138
Mynster, Jakob Peter, 49–51, 125–26, 146, 148–49, 184

mysticism
   mystics, 9
   mystical, 9, 13, 138
   mysterious, 9, 179
   mystery, 163

Nance, Malcolm, 18–20, 42–43, 56n2, 65–66, 110, 184
nationalism, 5, 20, 37–38, 55, 63–67, 138, 140, 143, 181
Nelson, Derek, xiii–xiv, 34n4, 58n10
Neo-Eurasianism, 19, 137, 140
Netflix, 120n43
Netting, Karl, 111n8
New York Military Academy, 136
Newman, Omarosa Manigauot, 15–16n14, 36, 113, 184
Niebuhr, Reinhold, 167, 184
nihilism, 80, 84, 171, 178
norms, procedural or unwritten, 68, 167, 178
nostalgia, 133, 134
Nussbaum, Martha, 83, 184

objectivity vs. subjectivity, 108, 126, 134, 146–47, 170
O'Brien, Timothy L., 33–34n2, 56n1, 86, 94n62, 109, 184
Olsen, Regine, xiii, 23–27, 32, 48, 99
omnipotence, 123–26
originality and acquired originality, 157–58
other, the, xi, 5n4, 8, 24, 25, 60, 62, 78, 156, 170

passion, pathos
   and Trump, x
   and leveling, 4
   and thought, 23
   and God, 29
   and Christendom, 52, 79, 147
   and earnestness, 53
   and individuality, 54
   and measure, 74–75, 168
   expressions of existential pathos, 75–77
   and Religiousness B, 77–78
   and speculation 122

passion, pathos *(continued)*
   and the "how," 122–23
   and concretion, 26
   within dependency chain, 127
   and freedom, 128
   and injustice, 170
Pattison, George, 80, 184
Plato, 70, 156
pluralism, 17, 106, 168, 178
polarization, societal, ix, 18, 60, 115, 159
politics of fear (Trump), 12, 134, 173
politics of inevitability and eternity (Snyder), 144, 146, 148
populism, 12, 17, 20, 59, 60, 62–63, 161
possibilizing, 156, 172–73, 178
postmodernity, 30, 58,
potentiation, 80, 81, 130, 156
prototype, 53
pseudonyms
   Trump's, 13–14
   Kierkegaard's
   and Kierkegaard-world, 6
   and his narrative, 13
   as aesthetic writings, 27
   as "left hand," 28
   examples of, 30
   and conversations on walks, 31
   and complexity, 38
   and 1843–1845 writings, 44
   and imaginative walks, 49
   and immanent God, 51
   Johanne Climacus as humorist, 74
   and the *Corsair*, 101–2
   and a comprehensive authorship, 164
Providence (Governance), 28, 29, 47, 151

Rambo, Shelly, 163, 184
Rasputin, 19, 38
Rather, Paul, 136n9, 141
reason
   and professor, 4
   and Eckhart, 9
   and politics, 17
   and Mynster, 51
   and Kierkegaard, 75, 78

   and Hegel, 122
   and democracy,
reasons, reason-giving
   for Trump's beliefs, 34
   for Putin's ties, 43
   in democracy, 116–17
   for love's abiding, 107
   for claims made, 113, 116
   fascism offers none, 135
   receptive and reflective knowledge (Lynch), 116–17
reconciliation, 8, 130, 160
redoubling, 107–8
refraction of the eternal, 106–7, 168–69
relativization, 7, 73, 74, 130, 166
Religiousness A, 103, 105, 107, 109
Religiousness B, 103, 105, 109
Relotius, Claas, 174–75
Republicans, 36, 59–62, 111, 159
revenge, 83, 135
rhetoric
   Trump's, 83
   Kierkegaard's, 29, 78, 150, 182
Robinson, Marcia C., 8–9
Rorty, Richard, 187
Ross, Alexander Reid, 141–42, 184
Rubow, Paul, 99n1, 184
rule of law
   core institution of democracy, 2–3
   manifests democratic normativity, 68
   Trump's disrespect for, 70
   honoring, 167
   written and unwritten, 178
Runciman, David, 160–61, 184
Russophilia, 96

Sater, Felix, 95, 98
Schelling, Friedrich Wilhelm Joseph von, 9–10, 184
Schlegel, John Frederik, 25–27
Schweitzer, Peter, 70, 185
self
   and involvement, 29
   and absorption, 36
   and promotion, 40, 95
   and distrust, 53, 166
   and absolutizing, 53

Index

and understanding, 54, 85–86
and autonomy, 71, 128, 171
and theonomy, 128, 171
and reference, 56
and conscience, 165
actual, centered self, 71, 72
and humor, 73
and annihilation, 76
and guilt, 76–77
and thought-passion, 78
and criteria, 79–81
human self, 79
ideal self, 72–75
theological self, 79
infinite self, 80
Christic self, 80–81
and potentiation or intensification, 80–81
first vs. second, deeper, 129–30, 171–72, 179
and God, 155
and eternity, 105, 107
and redoubling of, 107–8
self-actualization, 73
and interest, 113
and choice, 126–127
and freedom, 128–29
and nostalgia, 134
and criticism, 150
imagination, 151
and possibilizing, 156
and becoming a lover, 158
and judging, 168
and limitation, 170
and examination, 175
selfishness, 70, 134–36, 166
Senior, Jennifer, 58n10, 59
Shevkunov, Tikhon, 37–38
shutdown, governmental, 82–83
Silentio, Johannes de, 30, 44
Silicon Valley, 117
Sims Cliff, 17, 185
"single individual," the, 26, 32, 102, 165
Smith, Mitch, 174
Snyder, Timothy, 143–45, 185
Socrates, 545, 124
see also Danish Socrates

Soviet Union, 19, 41, 42, 88, 95, 97, 98, 140
speculation, 45, 122
Spencer, Richard, 65–66
Sponheim, Paul R., xiii, 10n11, 125n47, 185
spirit
of awakening, 2
of criticism, 7
of success, 35
of Vladimir the Great, 38
of leadership, 39
and freedom, 40
as mean, 48, 99
of thuggery, 69
of desire, 78
and the church, 102
and Christian inwardness, 127
of newness, 132
and modernity, 138
of transformation, 138
of the world Tree, 139
of one underlying essence, 142
and self-criticism, 150
St. Petersburg (Leningrad), 19, 87–91
Stalin, Joseph, 41, 87
Stewart, Jon, 30, 185
storyteller, 16, 21, 32, 111
Strauss, David, 57, 185
Strauss, David Friedrich, 150
subjectivity vs. objectivity, 121, 146–47, 170
suffering
and young Michael Kierkegaard, 48
and the essential expression of existential pathos, 75–76
and the *Corsair*, 104
and the eternal, 105
and polarization, 159
and democratic setbacks, 160
and injustice, 167
and alcoholism, 173
Sweet 16, 164–75, 177–78

Taciturnus, Frater, 44, 101
temporality, time
this time, ix–x, 3, 90, 91

Index

temporality, time *(continued)*
  our critical, trying time, 1, 2, 5, 6, 54, 57, 117, 155, 169
  the past, 17
  and the aesthetic, 71–72
  one time, 106
  and the eternal, 77, 105–7, 152–54
  and love, 107–8
  development of Kierkegaard's attack, 148–50
  longer reach of, 164
  A Prayer for Any Time, 179
theology
  Kierkegaard as theologian, 3, 26, 27, 162
  of liberation, 7
  of "whispers and shadows," 29–30
  Michael Kierkegaard's interest in, 48–49
  Peter Kierkegaard's doctorate in, 49
  Søren's degree in, 49
  of Mynster, 50–51, 125, 1 49
  and Paul Tillich, 70
  form of the self, 79
  of Martensen, 120–22, 149
  and omnipotence, 123–26
  of Ficino, 137
  of Dugin, 141–43
  of Reinhold Niebuhr, 167
  of hope, 172
theonomy, 122, 128, 171
Thompson, Curtis L., 7, 8n8, 9n9, 121n44, 151, 185
Tillich, Paul, 70
Tomasello, William 94
Traditionalism, 137–38, 141–42
transparency
  and thought, 52
  and faith, 81
  and Jared Kushner, 86
  and the eternal, 106, 168
Treasury Department, 97
Trump campaign
  and William Barr, 13, 99
  and lies, 14
  and Fox News, 15
  and Norman Vincent Peale, 35
  and Trump's meanness, 67, 169
  and money, 87
  and the conman, 110
  and Trump's memory, 133
  and corruption, 169
  impact of, 174
Trump, Barren, 13
Trump, Donald, Jr., 97, 111–12
Trump, Eric, 97
Trump, Fred, 34, 94
Trump, Ivana, 34, 37, 95
Trump, Ivanka, 15, 43, 86,
Trump, Melania, 111
Trump Organization, 13, 97
Trump Tower, 35, 96, 98
Trump Village, 94
truth
  religious, 5n4, 138
  Trump's untruthful "truthful hyperbole," 14
  Trump's lies, 14
  idea of truth challenged, 17
  Trump playing fast and loose with, 18
  and Kierkegaard, 28
  doctrinal, 29
  confronted by, 32
  and the Gospel, 50
  inwardness and, 52
  and the absurd, 52
  visceral, 65
  and paradox, 77
  and love, 107
  protectors of, 120
  and subjectivity, 122–123
  and being capable of nothing, 130
  and the creating God, 132
  of generosity, 136
  witness to the, 148, 150
  Christendom belying, 150–51
  demands substantiation of claims, 164, 177
  speaking to power, 165, 177

Ukraine, 38–42, 92
Unger, Craig, 12n1, 5, 18–19, 41–42, 57n4, 87–98, 185
University of Pennsylvania, 109, 112
University of Southern California, 109

Index

Vladimir the Great, 38
virtue, virtues
  civic, 57
  of the common people, 62
  and the absurd, 78
  and institutions, 145
  of justice, 167
  align with goodness, 179

vision
  of Trump, 12, 16–17, 83, 133, 134, 135
  of Kierkegaard, 31–32, 131–32, 168–69, 171
  of Dugin, 142–43
  of humility (Whitehead), 163

Wastyl, Stefan, 92
Ward, Vicky, 86–87
Warner, Tom, 92
Watts, Duncan J., 113–14, 185
well-being, 16, 31, 130, 154

Wendling, Mike, 63–64, 185
Westphal, Merold, 55, 185
Wheeler, Andrew, 84
White House, ix, 13–1 5, 17, 36, 66, 69, 86, 110, 113, 135
  Reince Priebus, 11, 112
  Scott Pruitt, 84
  Rex Tillerson, 112–13
  Steven Bannon, 17, 29, 33, 65–66, 111
  Steven Miller, 17, 66
  Kellyanne Conway, 15
  Oval Office, 126
Whitehead, Alfred North, 163, 185
Wood, Graeme, 65n36
Woodward, Bob, 12, 14n7, 16n15, 33n1, 85, 111–13, 185

Zelničková, Ivana, 95
Ziblatt, Daniel, 60n15, 68–70, 184
Zuckerberg, Mark, 117

www.ingramcontent.com/pod-product-compliance
Lightning Source LLC
Chambersburg PA
CBHW060607230426
43670CB00011B/2009